DOMESTIC SERVICE

WESTERN UNION
TELEGRAM
W. P. MARSHALL, PRESIDENT

INTERNATIONAL SERVICE

8S484 Col. Tom Parker

February 6, 1964

Y LETTER PAID

HN LENNON, GEORGE HARRISON,
UL McCARTNEY, RINGO STARR
E BEATLES
MR. ED SULLIVAN
LMONICO HOTEL
2 PARK AVENUE
W YORK, N.Y.

NGRATULATIONS ON YOUR APPEARANCE ON THE ED SULLIVAN SHOW ND YOUR VISIT TO AMERICA. WE HOPE YOUR ENGAGEMENT WILL BE SUCCESSFUL ONE AND YOUR VISIT PLEASANT. GIVE OUR BEST TO R. SULLIVAN. SINCERELY.

ELVIS & THE COLONEL

As I See It

Sullivan Wasted Time with Beatles

By PAUL JONES

If Ed Sullivan can find no better use for the time allotted him on Sunday night than to devote it to such exhibitions as he presented last Sunday night I suggest that CBS-TV find something else to put in this hour of prime time.

Why Sullivan found it necessary to aid in the phony promotion of four rock 'n' roll exponents, all of whom resemble Moe of the Three Stooges, is beyond comprehension.

It was obvious to those who saw the Beatles, four young fellows from Great Britain, that they have not attained their present notoriety on the basis of their musical talents, for the sounds emanating from their mouths were anything but melodic.

Shorn of their mop-like hairdos they would look and sound like many other inferior rock 'n' roll groups which are still attempting to keep alive the fad which died when Elvis Presley entered the armed forces.

There is nothing attractive about the looks or the sounds of the Beatles.

"The British are coming!" — **Paul Revere in 1775**

"The Beatles are not merely awful; I would consider it sacrilegious to say anything less than that they are godawful." — **William F. Buckley Jr. in 1964**

"Something tells me I'm into something good." — **Carole King and Gerry Goffin (as sung by Peter Noone) in 1964**

BRITMANIA

The British Invasion of the Sixties in Pop Culture

COME ON

ORIGINS

THE INVASION

THE BANDS

SOLOS & DUOS

TELEVISION

MAGAZINES

HUMOR

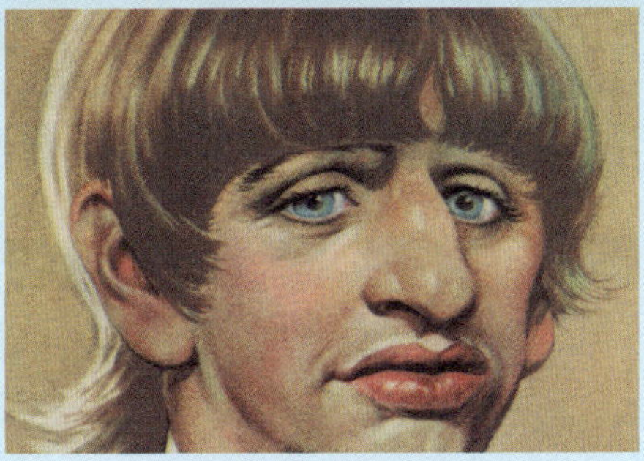

COMIC BOOKS

COLLECTIBLES

MOVIES

HERE, THERE

AFTERMATH

LET IT BE

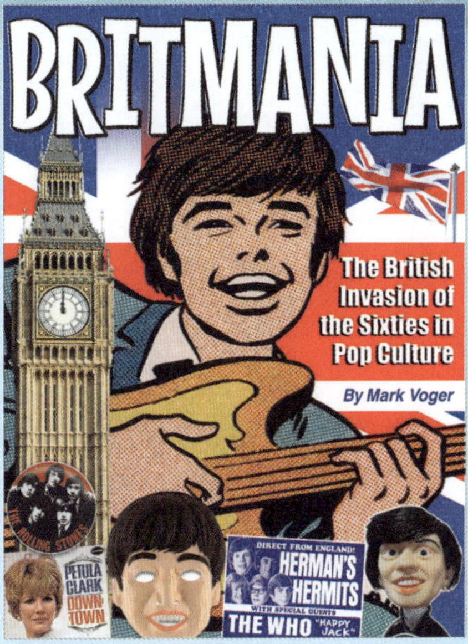

Written & designed by: Mark Voger
Publisher: John Morrow
Proofreader: Scott Peters

Front cover: *Modeling With Millie* #54 cover boy by Ogden Whitney and John Romita (1967) © Marvel Comics Inc.; Rolling Stones button and Herman's Hermits ad © current copyright holders; "Downtown" album cover (1965) © Warner Bros. Records; John Lennon mask © SELTAEB & © Ben Cooper, courtesy Heritage Auctions; Dave Clark doll © Remco, photo by Michael DiMaria

Frontispiece: "Both Sides of Herman's Hermits" (1966) cover by Frank Frazetta © MGM Records

Back cover: Model kit art by Bill Campbell (1965) © Revell; "Hold On!" poster detail (1965) © MGM; Ringo button © current copyright holder; "The Beatles" cartoon (1965) © King Features Syndicate; "Ferry Cross the Mersey" poster detail (1964) © United Artists; Paul McCartney doll (1964) © SELTAEB & © Remco; Hofner bass from 1963 publicity photo; *Summer Love* #46 cover detail (1965) © Charlton Comics Group

For Bobbi and Mary, fighting the good fight

ISBN-13: 978-1-60549-115-8
First printing, October 2022
Printed in China

Published by:
TwoMorrows Publishing
10407 Bedfordtown Drive
Raleigh, North Carolina 27614

Insets: Mad's "Blecch" Ringo © Warner Bros.; Millie the Model #41 cover detail © Marvel Comics; George Harrison doll © SELTAEB and © Remco; "A Hard Day's Night" © United Artists

Introduction

Not many 5-year-olds were aware of the Beatles in early 1964. I was no exception. "The Flintstones" were the only rockers I knew.

So the Beatles' historic first appearance on "The Ed Sullivan Show" on Feb. 9, 1964, would have been something I learned about later in life — and thought, "Gee, I wish I had seen that" — if not for a moment of real, live Beatlemania that magically transpired in my family's living room.

It was a cold Sunday evening in Woodcrest, a largely Jewish, largely middle-class neighborhood in Camden County in South Jersey. (We were the rare Irish-Catholic household.) I was in my pajamas, most likely watching "Walt Disney's Wonderful World of Color" on our black-and-white TV set, when my mother received a frantic call from our family babysitter, Debbie, who lived in the house directly behind ours.

Debbie pleaded with my mom to allow her and two friends to come over to watch "The Ed Sullivan Show." (The way I remembered it, Debbie's family's television had suddenly gone on the blink, just as she and her girlfriends were settled in to experience the Fab Four.) As Debbie's tone of voice made this sound like a matter of life and death, my mom immediately agreed.

So there I was in my pajamas in my living room watching three girls screaming — I mean *screaming* — at the television! I had no clue what was going on. But I am very grateful it happened that way, because I witnessed the dawn of Beatlemania with my own 5-year-old eyes in my own living room.

Forty years or so later, I attended the funeral service for Mr. McDermott, Debbie's father. I reminded Debbie of that night long ago when her family's TV set went on the fritz, but Debbie corrected me. The television was fine, she said, but her father — a dedicated and unapologetic sports fan — wasn't *about* to change the channel in the middle of a game he was watching.

If he had, I would have surely finished watching "Walt Disney's Wonderful World of Color" instead of witnessing a live broadcast of the Beatles' first-ever performance in America.

So to you, Mr. McDermott, I say: Thanks a million.

OVERNIGHT, THE BEATLES WERE ON EVERYONE'S lips. Broadcasters, newspaper columnists, comedians and sometimes even clergy all chimed in. The response was unanimously condescending — that is, unless a given commentator was 24 or younger. But in those days, print and broadcast media were (surprise!) very much an older White males' club.

I recollect that in the Feb. 10, 1964, edition of *The Philadelphia Bulletin* — this was the day after the "Sullivan" appearance — a staff columnist ended his piece with the following (and I paraphrase): "I will stick my neck out and predict that in 10 years or so, we'll be asking, 'Whatever became of the Beatles?'" I wish I still had that clipping so I could name (shame?) the offender.

The album that kept us kiddies up at night. © Capitol Records

I did, however, come across a clipping from the front page of the same edition of *The Bulletin,* as well as the "jump" page. In a United Press International (UPI) wire story titled "Beatles Send Teen-Agers Into Ecstasy," it is reported: "The four are John Lennon, 23, the so-called 'Sexy Beatle,' George Harrison, 21, the 'Quiet Beatle,' Paul McCartney, 21, the 'Bouncy Beatle,' and Ringo Starr, 23, the 'Beatle Beatle.'" (Whatever *that* means.)

Accompanying the UPI article was a staff report titled "British Quartet A Real Menace, Barbers Assert." The uncredited writer reported that John J. Monachelli, then president of the Pennsylvania League of Master Barbers, "wasn't even sure the Beatles — with their collar-length hair in the back and eyebrow-length bangs — should have been let into the country without being sprayed first. 'You know,' he said. 'Like they do to sheep.'"

This Beatle-bashing from the older generation was not limited to the media. It was happening everywhere, and my neck of the woods was no exception. Local adults in Woodcrest scoffed at the Beatles. But in telling ways, the grownups would acknowledge, albeit grudgingly, the group's appeal. Everyone admitted the Beatles were "cute." Some admitted they were funny. Some even admitted that their songs were (gasp!) catchy.

MY FOLKS USED TO THROW BOOZY parties on a Saturday night. My sister, brother and I have deeply ingrained memories of lying in bed at night trying to fall asleep, while downstairs, a noisy party raged. This drunken thrum was the soundtrack of our childhood. As the invited crowd grew louder and laughier, the turntable kept pace. (Two records I remember my father playing are "Java" by Al Hirt and "Lester Lanin Goes to College," just to clue you in on the level of hipness here.)

At some point around 1965 or so, when I was in the first grade, we kiddies heard something mighty strange coming up through the floorboards during one of my folks' boozy parties. Somebody had thrown on a *Beatles* album. What? How? It was an entire album side of Beatles, one song after another.

The reaction of the well-oiled crowd was, at first, uproarious laughter. (I'm guessing Mr. Jacobs jumped up on a table and played air guitar, in mockery of the Fab Four.) But with each passing song, a more sincere response coalesced. Against all logic, the adults were beginning to have straight-up fun with the music. They were dancing. We could tell. Few sounds are more distinct than stout ladies in overtaxed heels stomping on a linoleum tiled floor.

From that evening on, Beatles music became an entrenched part of the ritual during the boozy parties my parents threw. Late into a given night, when everyone was good and drunk, the needle was dropped on the Beatles album ... and the crowd went nuts.

Speaking of Mr. Jacobs, he mocked the Beatles in another memorable way. Back during the first flush of pervasive Beatlemania, fake hairpieces called "Beatle wigs" were marketed. (Ed Sullivan famously posed for photographers wearing one.) Mr. Jacobs purchased such a wig. He was kind of a squat guy, and kind of a joker. He put on a suit and the wig and, strumming a toy guitar, made like the Beatles as Mrs. Jacobs filmed him.

The Jacobses brought over their little 8mm masterpiece to show on our projector. Problem was, the movie was four minutes long, with no other gags or props or any sort of "finish" — just four minutes of Mr. Jacobs acting like the Beatles. It was hilarious for the first 30 seconds.

AP Wirephoto

RINGO STARR, one of the Beatles, takes pictures during a stroll in New York's Central Park yesterday.

Beatles Send Teen-Agers Into Ecstasy

New York, Feb. 10—(UPI)—Ed Sullivan's television show was turned into a screaming "beatleground" last night by an over-excited audience of teen-agers who went into ecstasy over England's rock 'n' roll quartet.

It was the first live television appearance in the United States for the mop-topped Beatles. Even Sullivan got into the act before his Columbia Broadcasting System show went on the air by wearing a Beatle wig.

The four British singers are in the United States on a ten-day visit which also will include two concerts in Carnegie Hall next

Continued on Page 10, Col. 2

British Quartet A Real Menace, Barbers Assert

The Beatles joined baldness yesterday at the top of barbers' hate list.

The Beatles are four shaggy-haired rock-and-roll singers from Liverpool, England, who have taken British teen-agers by storm and are now in the process of doing the same to American teen-agers.

The Beatles, hair aflutter, arrived in New York Friday.

The Pennsylvania League of Master Barbers held their annual convention yesterday at Palumbo's Restaurant. They denounced the Beatles as a threat to their business.

"Don't even mention that

Continued on Page 10, Col. 4

Breaking news from the front page of the Feb. 10, 1964, edition of The Philadelphia Bulletin.

I EVENTUALLY SPOTTED THAT BEATLES album in my parents' record collection. It was "Something New," a 1965 compilation, as opposed to a proper album of all new material. (When the question "What's your favorite Beatles album?" comes up, the answer is typically "Meet the Beatles!" or "Rubber Soul" or "Sgt. Pepper." No one ever says, "I can't get enough of 'Something New.' ")

"Something New" closes with *"Komm, Gib Mir Deine Hand,"* the German-language version of "I Wanna Hold Your Hand." (Give it a listen — it's positively joyful, not to mention culture-bridging.) To this day, when I hear it, I'm back in pajamas in the top bunk, wondering what the hell's going on.

A lifetime later, I asked my mother why, why, why there was a Beatles album in their collection. She explained that one Saturday night, my parents had invited to their party a younger couple who were new to the neighborhood. These two poor, unsuspecting young'uns materialized, bringing along their copy of "Something New" (presumably to spice things up for the oldsters), but forgot it upon exiting the party. This couple, it turns out, never again attended one of my folks' boozy parties — it wasn't their generation, after all — nor did they even return to reclaim the album.

The result: They may have lost a Beatles album, but they made Woodcrest a *lot* more hip.

Above: A 1960s Dublin postcard. Right: A 1960s London postcard. Top right: Label for the Rolling Stones' "Honky Tonk Women" (1969). "Honky Tonk Women" © ABKCO Records

PETER NOONE ONCE SAID HE AND HIS FELLOW Hermits were "Yankophiles" — that when they finally came to America, they couldn't wait to shake hands with their American heroes like Elvis Presley and Johnny Cash.

As the British Invasion movement built steam, Americans underwent a seemingly mass transformation into Anglophiles or "Britophiles." Our ears perked up whenever we heard a British accent, whether it was on TV, the radio or in person. If you were lucky enough to meet someone who spoke with a British accent, you could have listened to them read the *phone book* out loud, and thought it was Shakespeare. To this day, a British accent in America is currency — a door-opener, a golden ticket.

I was never in England, but did I make it to the British Isles once. This happened in the summer of 1969, when I was 11. It was a family trip to Gort, County Galway, Ireland, to visit Glenbrach, the farm my grandfather was born on. The most fun me and my siblings and cousins ever had was to climb up bales of hay, then swing from a rope tied to the rafters, and land on a hay pile. Over and over. It was more fun than Disneyland or anything.

London *was* on the trip itinerary. Can you imagine being in London in the Year of Our Lord Nineteen-Sixty-Nine? The epicenter of everything? But (sigh) it was never meant to be.

I was so psyched, because I was supposed to get my hair "styled" (as opposed to "cut") while in London. *Styled?* I can't say what, exactly, was going through my 11-year-old mind. Was I expecting to saunter into a London salon with my South-Jersey Catholic-school-boy haircut, and walk out looking like Roger Daltrey on the back cover of "Meaty Beaty Big and Bouncy"? Did I think they were going to *add* hair?

Alas, the London leg of the trip got scrapped after my grandfather, God rest his soul, came down with food poisoning.

That night, he was sharing a hotel room with me, my cousin Alfie, and my little brother Brian. Pop Pop told us he had a bad case of the "heebie jeebies." That's *one* way of putting it.

But during that trip, I did get a smattering of a hint of a wisp of an inkling of a notion of a feeling of a vague idea about maybe, *maybe,* what London kinda sorta *might* have been like in 1969, if you squinted your eyes — at least, to a Yankee hillbilly like me.

OUR TRAVELING PARTY MADE IT TO DUBLIN, THE capital of Ireland and its biggest city. Dublin in 1969 was bustling and modern and cosmopolitan, especially compared to the remote rural areas we'd previously been visiting. I'm not putting down pigs and chickens and hay — perish the thought. But after all those pigs and chickens and hay, I was suddenly seeing kinda hip young people (who probably wished *they* were in London, too) in kinda hip clothes strolling up and down O'Connell Street.

I remember once ducking into a fish-and-chips shop full of teens. Everyone in there looked like rejects from the Yardbirds sequence in Michelangelo Antonioni's "Blow-Up." Blaring from the jukebox was a rude new song I'd heard on American radio in in the days before boarding the plane for Ireland: the Rolling Stones' "Honky Tonk Women," a #1 hit in Ireland, England *and* America at the time. I remember thinking: No cigar, but close.

Our first cabbie upon arriving in Dublin was English — a young-ish fellow with long-ish hair. When he clocked our thrilled reaction to his accent, he laid on the charm. I remember him mock-punching my chin. He was so funny, so cool. Of course, he got a generous tip from us Yanks that day.

A lifetime later, I found myself wondering: Did *every* cabbie who drove American tourists around Dublin in 1969 speak with an English accent?

WE LITTLE SQUIRTS THOUGHT OF the Beatles as characters. Funny ones. To us, John, Paul, George and Ringo were like cultural descendants of Groucho, Chico, Harpo and Zeppo. Kid-targeted marketing reinforced this. There were Beatles dolls from Remco … Beatles Halloween costumes from Ben Cooper … Beatles bubble-bath toys from Colgate … Beatles lunchboxes from Aladdin ... Beatles bubble-gum cards from Topps.

What really confirmed this view in our fresh, pink brains was the Saturday-morning animated TV series titled, simply, "The Beatles." The Fab Four didn't voice their cartoon counterparts, of course, but the show utilized real-life Beatles songs. (Later kiddie shows like "The Banana Splits" had no such vast and storied repertoire from which to plunder.)

I remember hearing Beatles songs for the first time on the cartoon show. A case in point was "Baby's in Black." I was a child; I'd never heard that song on the radio or on a turntable, but there it was on the cartoon show. Without having seen the episode for many decades, I can still recall its premise, if vaguely: It had the Beatles rescuing the Mona Lisa. (I believe Leonardo da Vinci's iconic painting was stolen from a museum, and the do-gooding Beatles captured the thieves.) The lyrics fit like a drummer's glove; the "baby in black" in the song, you see, *was* the Mona Lisa.

So for me, "Baby's in Black" is not Side 1, Track 3 off the "Beatles for Sale" album. It's a song from a cartoon TV show. On this point, my mind cannot be changed.

Trade advertisement for Remco's Beatle dolls (1964). © SELTAEB, Inc.; © Remco

THIS BRINGS US TO A PARADOX, AND a source of confusion, that emerged during the British Invasion era.

The sunny, adorable faces of John, Paul, George and Ringo were everywhere — there were Beatles *ice cream bars,* fer cryin' out loud. (Thank you, Brian Epstein.) But the other Invasion bands were not commercially exploited to remotely the same degree, nor would that have seemed appropriate. Somehow, Beatles ice cream bars worked. Troggs ice cream bars might not have.

This humble effort titled "Britmania" is not solely about the Beatles; it's about the whole British Invasion movement, and the lasting imprint it still has on popular culture. *Britishness itself* became so fab, so gear, that a mania for All Things British took hold in America for a few fun, golden years.

As such, it seems only logical to expand the scope of the Invasion to include the movement's influence on non-musical media, like the movies (Eon Productions' James Bond series, Hammer Studios' Frankenstein and Dracula series); the fashion world (Twiggy, Jean Shrimpton); television imports ("The Avengers," "Secret Agent"); the sudden propensity for a British cast member to pop up as a series regular on American TV (David McCallum in "The Man From U.N.C.L.E.," Davy Jones in "The Monkees"); even comic books (DC's *Swing With Scooter,* Marvel's groovy Gears in *Millie the Model*).

So on those occasions when you detect a preponderance of Beatles coverage herein — and you will — please keep in mind that this only reflects the realities of the phenomenon. Back in the day, I'll bet there were 10 Beatles magazine covers to every one for all the other bands combined. (No, I haven't counted.)

I pursued behind-the-scenes players in the Beatles' origins for one reason, a truth I hold to be self-evident: The origin of the Beatles is the origin of the British Invasion movement itself.

Despite their immense charisma and talent, the Beatles *could* have ended up as just another obscure local band, in just another obscure locality. With any success story, luck is always critically involved. In the case of the Beatles, that chaos-theory butterfly was flappin' its little wings like *crazy.*

If the Fab Four had never become the Greatest Show on Earth, would the other British Invasion bands have crossed over into America, one after another after another? And if not, where would that leave us? I'll tell you. With a lot less cool music.

We'll just have to content ourselves to live in a world where there was no cartoon TV series featuring that zany Brian Jones or that madcap Charlie Watts. And no Halloween costumes of those cutups Ray and Dave Davies. And no lunchbox featuring those wisecracking Animals. And no Remco figure of that lovable Syd Barrett. And no bubble-bath toy of that kooky Keith Moon.

Probably a *good* thing.

Mark

BEATLES
Lady Madonna
The Inner Light
the MERSEYBEATS
fontana
"HAPPENINGS TEN YEARS TIME AGO"
The Yardbirds
Satisfaction
The Under Assistant
DECCA
THE ROLLING STONES
THE BEATLES
Nowhere Man
What Goes On
TELL HER NO b/w LEAVE ME BE
THE ZOMBIES
DISTRIBUTED BY LONDON RECORDS, INC.
BEATLES
I Am The Walrus
Hello Goodbye
The Pink Floyd
See Emily Play
LULU
"Best Of Both Worlds"
"Love Loves To Love Love"
EPIC
LONDON
45-9682
TELL ME
b/w I JUST WANNA MAKE LOVE TO YOU
THE ROLLING STONES
START A "ROLLING STONES" FAN CLUB
WRITE TO: MISS PATRICIA THOMAS
LONDON RECORDS
539 West 25 St.
New York 1, N.Y.
odeon
ANYONE WHO HAD A HEART
CILLA BLACK
JUST FOR YOU • LOVE OF THE LOVED • SHY OF LOVE
THE ANIMALS
DECCA
F12332
inside-looking out
outcast
Columbia
No Milk Today
MY RESERVATION'S BEEN CONFIRMED
Herman's Hermits
KINKS
YOU REALLY GOT ME
THE BEATLES
WHAT GOES ON
NOWHERE MAN
Capitol
THE ROLLING STONES
IT'S ALL OVER NOW
LONDON
The Dave Clark Five
OVER AND OVER
OVER AND OVER
EPIC
THE BEATLES
I'M DOWN/HELP!
Capitol

Who knew from sociopolitical implications?

As if following some insidious master plan, the smiling, "clean-cut" Beatles gained admittance to our shores with non-threatening looks and innocent lyrics about wanting to hold your hand.

But the cultural movement known as the British Invasion had its roots in something darker. The Beatles, the Stones, the Who, et al., weren't "posh" Brits, generally. They often came up in parts of England that you might have called "rough and tumble" back then, such as Liverpool, Manchester, Birmingham and Shepherd's Bush. Class was an integral component of these bands' relatability.

An early case in point: When the Beatles first landed in New York City in 1964, a press conference was held beneath prominent Pan Am signage. (Product placement out of the box — welcome to America.) Reporters were antagonistic, with questions fixated on the Beatles' hair: "Does all that hair help you sing?" "How many are bald, if you have to wear those wigs?" "Are you afraid of what the American Barbers Association is going to think of you?" "Are you going to get a haircut at all?"

This didn't throw the Beatles a whit. These boys, after all, grew up with beans on toast, not Earl Grey and crumpets. And not for nuthin', they were heckled by German sailors for two years. Those New York pencil pushers were no contest.

The Beatles merely grinned at their sarcastic questions, and volleyed back with *better* sarcasm. In these exchanges, the boys won over a lot of those cynical journalists.

OFTEN, THESE BRITS WERE "BLITZ BABIES" — that is, survivors of World War II as infants and toddlers who spent their childhoods living with rationing and playing in rubble. American rock 'n' roll turned them on, and gave them hope. They learned it, elaborated upon it, played it for us, and gave *us* hope.

Overwhelmingly, the Brits were attracted to music by Black American artists — you know, what programmers here once called "race music." (Look it up.) The young Brits were sponges, soaking up the work of the old blues masters (Muddy Waters, John Lee Hooker) and rock 'n' roll progenitors (Chuck Berry, Little Richard). So these boys were paying homage to American artists who, in many cases, were not given their due here, prestige-wise *or* monetarily. More than one British Invasion musician has wondered aloud if they sensed a kindred spirit in the work of these Americans because they, too, felt disaffected.

Then there were the screaming girls. Elvis Presley elicited screams when he swiveled his hips, but not at the same sustained, deafening levels that the Beatles and their cohorts inspired. Ed Sullivan's TV cameras captured girls crying snotty tears, as if they were in deep emotional turmoil. Come to think of it, they *were*.

Something mysterious and inexplicable was transpiring, a kind of mass catharsis brought on by approaching, or ongoing, pubescence. It looked painful and joyful at the same time. The British Invasion bands were, as the expression goes, merely the vessel.

STILL, THE BEATLES WERE CONSIDERED A FLASH in the pan — here today, gone tomorrow. The group not only lasted, they were followed by likewise British, likewise kinda-long-haired, likewise rock 'n' roll-playing bands such as the Stones, the Dave Clark Five, Gerry and the Pacemakers, the Kinks, the Who, the Yardbirds, the Spencer Davis Group, the Animals, the Zombies, the Hollies, Herman's Hermits, Chad and Jeremy ...

But *no one* guessed that these groups would make music that can be called important, with lyrics that can be called profound.

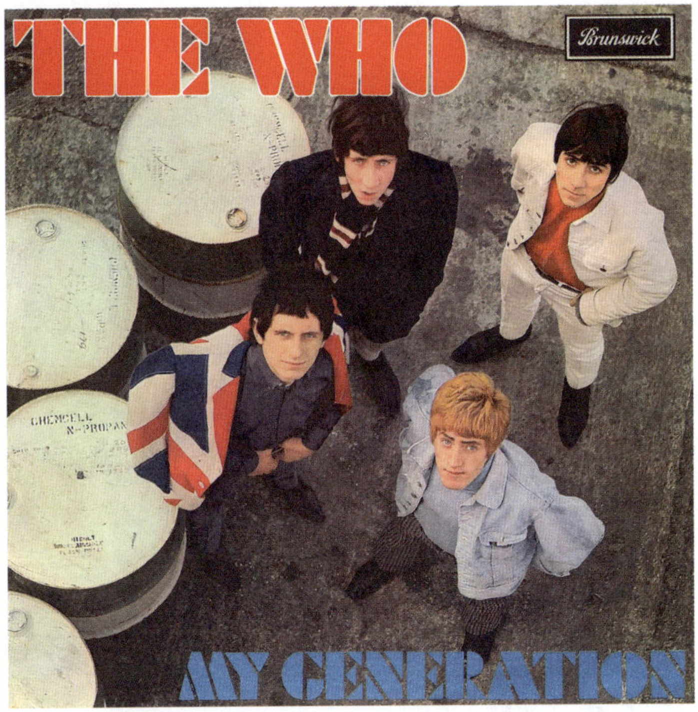

The Who and others brought fatalism to Top 100. Opposite: Picture sleeves with enlarged detail from "Lady Madonna."

The Stones risked biting the hand that fed them with their commentary on rampant American commercialism in "Satisfaction" (#1 in 1965): *"When I'm watchin' my TV / and a man comes on and tells me / how white my shirts can be / But he can't be a man 'coz he doesn't smoke / the same cigarettes as me ..."*

Their opening lyric to "Mother's Little Helper" (#8 in 1966) sounded like an indictment: *"What a drag it is / getting old ..."*

Roger Daltrey sang of fatalism in "My Generation" (#74 in 1965): *"People try to put us down / just because we get around / Things they do look awful cold / Hope I die before I get old..."*

Eric Burdon sang American composers' lyrics on two early hits by the Animals, and his haunted howl brought them to life. From Barry Mann and Cynthia Weil's "We've Gotta Get Out of This Place" (#13 in 1965): *"In this dirty old part of the city / where the sun refuse to shine / people tell me there ain't no use in tryin' / Now, my girl, you're so young and pretty / and one thing I know is true / you'll be dead before your time is due ..."*

More musings on poverty sung by Burdon, from Roger Atkins and Carl D'Errico's "It's My Life" (#23 in 1965): *"It's a hard world to get a break in / All the good things have been taken / But girl, there are ways / to make certain things pay / Though I'm dressed in these rags / I'll wear sable / some day ..."*

The most pointed lyrics of Mick Jagger's oeuvre are heard in "Sympathy for the Devil" (#55 in 1968), in which he pivoted from the Blitz of World War II to then-contemporary political assassinations in America: *"I rode a tank / held a general's rank / when the Blitzkrieg raged / and the bodies stank ... I shouted out, 'Who killed the Kennedys?' / when after all, it was you and me ..."*

The songs of the Stones, the Animals, the Who and others became timeless classics on their own merit, not because they were part of some bandwagon. Sometimes, these groups sang the truth.

Timeline

Wait, didn't our history textbooks tell us the British were the bad guys? Two-hundred years after King George did all his taxating without representating, we greeted the Beatles, the Rolling Stones, the Who, et al., with open wallets.

3/22/1765: Parliament increases taxes on the colonies with the Stamp Act, leading to the rallying cry "Taxation without representation is tyranny."

4/19/1775: The "shot heard 'round the world" at Lexington and Concord begins the Revolutionary War.

7/4/1776: The Second Continental Congress signs the Declaration of Independence.

Ogdensburg Journal

HITLER'S FORCES ATTACK POLAND BY LAND, SEA, SKY

POLAND ASKS BRITISH AID

9/1/1939: World War II begins. Many British Invasion musicians are children affected by the conflict.

3/1957: John Lennon forms the Black Jacks, later called the Quarrymen, in Liverpool.

9/17/1960: The Beatles make their Hamburg, Germany, debut at the Indra Club, with Best as their drummer.

8/12/1960: The Beatles audition drummer Pete Best.

8/1960: Lennon, McCartney, Harrison and Stuart Sutcliffe rename themselves the Beatles.

1959: Gerry and the Pacemakers form in Liverpool.

1958: The Dave Clark Five forms in Tottenham.

2/6/1958: McCartney introduces his school friend, George Harrison, to Lennon. Harrison joins the Quarrymen.

7/7/1957: Lennon and Paul McCartney meet at St. Peter's Church in Liverpool. McCartney joins the Quarrymen.

2/9/1961: The Beatles make their Cavern Club debut in Liverpool.

3/15/61: Sutcliffe quits the Beatles to pursue a career in painting.

10/1961: The single "My Bonnie" by Tony Sheridan backed by the Beatles debuts in Germany.

10/17/1961: Mick Jagger and Keith Richards meet at the Dartford train station.

11/9/1961: Brian Epstein attends a Beatles show at the Cavern, which leads to him becoming the band's manager.

1961: The Zombies form in Hertfordshire.

4/10/1962: Stuart Sutcliffe, 21, dies of a cerebral hemorrhage in Hamburg.

6/6/1962: The Beatles audition for George Martin at EMI. Martin eventually becomes the band's producer.

11/29/1963: "I Want to Hold Your Hand" debuts. It becomes the Beatles' first U.S. #1 hit.

11/22/1963: President John F. Kennedy is assassinated in Dallas.

2/1963: The nucleus of the Blues Breakers forms in London.

1962: The Rolling Stones form in London.

1962: The Hollies form in Salford.

1962: Chad and Jeremy form in London.

1962: The Animals form in Newcastle.

10/5/1962: The 007 movie "Dr. No" premieres as the Beatles' first single, "Love Me Do," debuts. Thus, two of England's most significant cultural exports of all time launch on the *same day.* Synchronicity!

8/16/1962: Epstein fires Best from the Beatles. Two days later, Ringo Starr joins.

1963: The Yardbirds form in London.

1963: The Kinks form in London.

1963: The Spencer Davis Group forms in Birmingham.

1963: Herman's Hermits form in Manchester.

1/20/1964: The album "Meet the Beatles!" debuts.

2/7/1964: The Beatles touch down at JFK International Airport in New York City.

2/9/1964: The Beatles appear on "The Ed Sullivan Show."

5/1964: "Wishin' and Hopin'" by Dusty Springfield debuts and climbs to #6.

7/15/1965: The movie "Having a Wild Weekend" starring the Dave Clark Five debuts.

6/5/1965: "Satisfaction" by the Rolling Stones debuts. It goes to #2 in America.

12/13/1964: The movie "Ferry Cross the Mersey" starring the Pacemakers debuts.

11/1964: "Downtown" by Petula Clark debuts. It becomes Clark's first #1 hit in America.

1964: The Troggs form in Hampshire.

1964: Pink Floyd forms in London.

1964: The Moody Blues form in Birmingham.

1964: The Who forms in London.

7/7/1964: The movie "A Hard Day's Night" starring the Beatles debuts.

5/30/1964: The Rolling Stones' self-titled debut album is released. The American version is subtitled "England's Newest Hitmakers."

7/29/1965: The movie "Help!" starring the Beatles debuts.

8/15/1965: The Beatles play Shea Stadium in New York.

9/25/1965: The animated TV series "The Beatles" debuts.

10/26/1965: Queen Elizabeth II bestows MBEs (Members of the Most Excellent Order of the British Empire) upon the Beatles.

11/1965: The Small Faces form in London.

12/3/1965: The Who's first album, "My Generation," debuts.

12/18/1966: The movie "Blow-Up" featuring the Yardbirds debuts.

1/30/1969: The Beatles give their final public performance on a London rooftop. The unannounced set was filmed for their movie "Let It Be."

7/17/1968: The Beatles' animated film "Yellow Submarine" debuts.

12/26/1967: The Beatles' TV special "Magical Mystery Tour" debuts in England.

12/12/1967: Jagger and Richards are arrested for drug possession at Redlands, Richards' Sussex home. Both are jailed and convicted.

9/1967: "To Sir With Love" by Lulu debuts. It goes to #1 in the U.S.

8/27/1967: Brian Epstein, 32, dies from an accidental overdose of pills and alcohol in London.

6/8/1969: Brian Jones announces he has quit the Rolling Stones.

Guitarist dies in pool

Brian Jones, 27-year-old ex-guitarist of the Rolling Stones, died early yesterday after a midnight bathe in the swimming pool at his fifteenth-century farmhouse, at Hartfield, Sussex.

With a Swedish friend, Anna Vohlin, aged 20, and a builder, Mr Frank Thorogood, who was modernising the house, Mr Jones went for a bathe after complaining of the heat. He was found later at the bottom of the pool.

7/3/1969: Jones, 27, dies while swimming at his home in Sussex.

7/5/1969: The Rolling Stones dedicate their Hyde Park concert to Jones. The show marks the debut of Jones' replacement, Mick Taylor, as a Stone.

12/8/1969: The Stones' infamous Altamont free concert, during which an audience member is stabbed to death in front of the stage, is held.

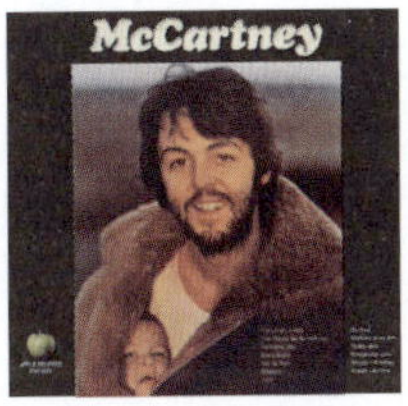

4/10/1970: McCartney announces the breakup of the Beatles (or *does* he?) in a press release for his album "McCartney." Anyway, they break up.

11/25/2021: Peter Jackson's docuseries "The Beatles: Get Back" debuts. And the beat goes on ...

8/24/2021: Charlie Watts, 80, dies of cancer in London.

1/13/2003: Pete Townshend is arrested on suspicion of possessing indecent images of children. He is cleared four months later.

6/27/2002: John Entwistle, 57, dies of a heart attack in Nevada.

11/29/2001: George Harrison, 58, dies of cancer in Los Angeles.

12/8/1980: John Lennon, 40, is shot dead in New York City.

9/7/1978: Keith Moon, 32, dies after a night of partying in London.

12/6/1970: "Gimme Shelter," which documents the Stones' 1969 tour (including Altamont), debuts.

5/13/1970: The movie "Let It Be" starring the Beatles debuts.

"I was so naive, I believed that in America, when everybody finished work, they went home, sat on the back porch and played the blues."

So said Spencer Davis, namesake of England's Spencer Davis Group. Once he arrived in America, of course, Davis was in for an awakening. It took the British Invasion artists, playing music born of their love of American blues, to reintroduce the genre here.

As Davis told me in 2006: "Americans were wondering, 'Well, where did (British rock) come from?' We always had to say, 'Well, it was *yours*. We got it from you.' Got it from people like Huddie Ledbetter, Big Bill Broonzy, Lightnin' Hopkins, John Lee Hooker. We were tipping our hats, essentially, to those old Black guys who made their own music, who had their own style, had their own meter and measures. Sometimes they never played a 12-bar blues; they might play an 11-bar blues or a 13-bar blues. In good faith, a lot of us copied those odd sort of measures."

"The first music I heard that got me excited was Jerry Lee Lewis, Little Richard, Elvis Presley, Chuck Berry," Rolling Stones guitarist Mick Taylor told me in 2003. "But then as I started to learn to play the guitar, I discovered that this music was really Black American music. So I did research. I just kind of learned more and more about American music.

"All of my contemporaries — people like Eric Clapton, Jeff Beck — we were all very much drawn towards American music. To us, American music was where it was at, especially blues music. All the English bands used to look to America for inspiration. But I guess we did something weird to it that made it more appealing (to Americans). Because really, all the so-called British Invasion was really just a bunch of English groups playing American music, or music inspired by American music."

John Lennon performs with his musical idol Chuck Berry on "The Mike Douglas Show" in 1972. © Westinghouse Broadcasting

YARDBIRDS GUITARIST BECK RECALLED HAVING his mind blown by hearing American musicians "bend" notes.

"I just wondered where the hell this place America was," Beck told me in 1999. "I just knew that none of the guys making those sounds were from England. I'd never heard scales or bending-of-notes (in England). It was all very squared-off English music.

"All of a sudden, someone's doing unbelievable things with notes. Welcome to the world of blues and rock 'n' roll, thank you very much. It was a bit like an air raid, like a musical air raid. There were bombs coming down the chimney every day. Having an older sister who was playing these records over and over was bliss, because I didn't have to wait forever to hear them on the radio. BBC was the only really clear station we could get, and they hardly ever played them. So we were tuning into American Forces Network (AFN) to get hear American rock records.

"The people of my era, they'll all tell you the same thing: You either had a friendly guy in the record shop who wouldn't mind you bugging him to play these things, or you got lucky and got pocket money and bought them yourself.

"On the radio, there was 'Be-Bop-A-Lula,' which I loved. It did something to my head. Everybody has their single. Mine was 'Be-Bop-A-Lula.' And 'Hound Dog' and 'Lucille.'"

Rock 'n' roll aside, Beck was also affected by straight-up blues.

"I remember hearing blues for the first time; I never got over that," the guitarist said. "I don't know who it was — maybe Ray Charles. It sounded a bit gospelly. You know, 1952, '54. You don't forget that sound. You just become converted from the minute you hear a really bluesy voice. I never really let go of it. Periodically, if I stumble across a Johnny Burnette record, that's gonna get played. Those licks never leave your soul."

Justin Hayward of the Moody Blues got his fix from Radio Luxembourg. "After 6 at night, they played all kinds of American rock 'n' roll," he told me in 2004. "I was addicted to Buddy Holly, the Everlys and Eddie Cochran, like a lot of English boys were."

Zombies keyboardist Rod Argent interpolated jazz into his style. "I grew up, really, until I was 11 years old thinking I only liked classical music," Argent told me in 2008. "Then I heard 'Hound Dog' and all those early Elvis things. Completely turned my head around. Very soon after that, I discovered Miles Davis and John Coltrane and Cannonball Adderley and Bill Evans. That knocked me completely sideways as well."

Peter Noone of Herman's Hermits couldn't wait to visit the United States.

"I was pure 'Yankophile,'" Noone told me in 2011. "I knew all of Johnny Cash's songs. I knew Woody Guthrie. I read all the John Steinbeck.

"I was the American fan in England. I came to America and I wanted to meet Johnny Cash and Elvis Presley and Conway Twitty, because we thought they were all rock stars. They were all just rock stars to us. They weren't country-and-western; we didn't know about that. Where's Jackie Wilson? How can I meet Elvis Presley? So I just came here to meet all my American heroes."

THE BRITISH MUSICIANS SOMETIMES GOT TO RUB elbows with their American idols in Europe. For instance, the Beatles worked with Little Richard and Gene Vincent in Hamburg.

"The American folk-blues festivals had been going on in Europe for some years prior to the British blues scene, so that was also a factor," John Mayall of the Blues Breakers told me in 2005.

"Those concerts were the first time we saw these legendary figures. But as soon as the British blues scene was established, they started to come over and work with the bands.

"I think I was the first one to do a backing tour for John Lee Hooker. He was the first to come over and do something like that. I worked with John Lee for a whole month. That was great. And then T-Bone Walker and Sonny Boy Williamson and Eddie Boyd. I worked with all those guys. It's just a great memory to have."

Blues masters Big Bill Broonzy, Howlin' Wolf and John Lee Hooker, and "skiffle" king Lonnie Donegan. Publicity photos

Ian McLagan recalled working with several blues legends prior to joining the Small Faces. "My first band, the Muleskinners, we did pretty good," McLagan told me in 2013. "We backed up Howlin' Wolf, Sonny Boy Williamson, Hubert Sumlin and Little Walter, all within a short time. That was quite an education. I mean, it was one thing to open for the Stones, but to actually be backing *Little Walter* was just unbelievable."

THE AMERICAN INFLUENCE CAN BE TRACED BACK farther, to World War II, believed singer Tony Sheridan, who sang lead on the Beatles' first record release, "My Bonnie."

"If you were born in Britain in 1940, of course, then you had bombs dropping on your heads," Sheridan told me in 2003.

"A lot of American servicemen came over to Britain to sort of help and do their thing. We kids between the ages of nothing and 5 absorbed all of this in one way or another. We were well aware that something was going on. Little kids are. That goes for John Lennon; it goes for anybody born in the early '40s in Britain.

"So we heard all sorts of American music. In fact, there was no British music to speak of. It was all American imported, anyway. So we heard these sounds. We saw these different uniforms. We saw that they looked better, more 'flash.' Kids noticed that."

Sheridan first heard American rock 'n' roll when he was 15.

"I was in my puberty stage," he said. "I thought, 'That's what I remember from when I was 2 or 3.' Having admired all that very early on, I thought, 'Well, I'd rather do that than play the violin.' I decided to get myself a guitar, learn a few chords, comb my hair, and get on a stage. But where was the stage? The stage was down at the local pub in the provincial town I was born in (Norwich).

"So I was Elvis for a while. I didn't tell anybody. In those days, I was copying. We copied like mad — Eric Clapton and the Beatles and the Stones. We all copied. So we were all very much influenced at this crucial time by you guys. And we brought it back there. It was like bringing coal back to Newcastle."

THE POST-WAR PERIOD YIELDED AN AMERICAN-influenced British music genre that attracted many Invasion artists.

"After World War II, there wasn't much for teen-age boys with raging hormones to do except look for girls and kick a ball around the street," Hollies singer Graham Nash told me in 2002.

"There wasn't much to do before we started in the work force. That changed drastically one day when 'skiffle' came along."

Skiffle — a folk-blues hybrid often played on homemade instruments —was England's precursor to rock 'n' roll.

"Skiffle was a very primitive form of almost jug-band folk music," Nash continued. "The man that brought it to England was called Lonnie Donegan. He was very famous.

"It was so simple. One acoustic guitar. A 'tea chest' bass, where you take a tea chest and put a broom with a piece of string connecting the two, that you could use as a bass. And a washboard which, you know, ladies used to wash the family clothes with. You'd put thimbles on your hand and use it as a percussion instrument. That was incredibly simple and available for most people."

"I imagine the Quarrymen — you know, Lennon's band before he joined the *other* lot — probably started out listening to Lonnie Donegan, as did (singer-guitarist) Alexis Korner," Spencer Davis chimed in.

"But skiffle was essentially do-it-yourself. And that's essentially what we did and, I suppose, what the Beatles did and the Stones did, under the leadership of the guy that founded the band, of course, which was Brian Jones, as we all know."

"So there were a lot of skiffle bands born," said Nash. "Later came the advent of rock 'n' roll, and the early R&B stuff from Rufus Thomas and Danny Spellman and the Coasters and people like that, and then Buddy Holly and the Everly Brothers and Elvis and Jerry Lee Lewis and Chuck Berry and Gene Vincent and Eddie Cochran and the Platters. All of this was affecting kids who already were into skiffle music, so that transition was very easy. That's what we spent our early years listening to."

Liverpool to Hamburg

Does it need to be said? The Beatles were born at the moment John Lennon and Paul McCartney first laid eyes on one another.

This occurred on July 6, 1957, a Saturday, at an event put on by St. Peter's Church in Liverpool. From this humble first encounter, the Beatles saga would take many twists and turns: personnel shifts, band name changes, poverty, petty theft, encounters with strippers, "uppers"-fueled marathons, jail time, deportations, death, a lot of laughs and, of course, a lot of great music. It all had to happen before the world would be conquered by, all together now, "four lads from Liverpool."

Lennon (born 1940 in Liverpool) was the leader of the Quarrymen, a skiffle group that performed at St. Peter's social that fateful day. Formed the previous year as the Black Jacks — even in this embryonic stage, name changes happened — the Quarrymen were made up of school chums from Lennon's alma mater, Quarry Bank High School for Boys.

McCartney (born 1942 in Liverpool) grew up in a musical family. His father was a trumpeter; there was a piano in the house. On the recommendation of a mutual friend, McCartney saw the Quarrymen. He had musical ambitions of his own.

Lennon recalled that the Quarrymen did Gene Vincent's "Be-Bop-a-Lula" on that day. McCartney recalled them doing the Del-Vikings' doo-wop hit "Come Go With Me" (and goofing up the lyrics). The boys struck up a conversation about (what else?) rock 'n' roll. Lennon was impressed that McCartney could sing and play Eddie Cochran's "Twenty Flight Rock." Not long after that initial meeting, he invited McCartney to join the Quarrymen.

John Lennon, then 16, fronting the Quarrymen in Liverpool on July 6, 1957.

The next February, McCartney recommended a school chum of *his,* George Harrison (born 1943 in Liverpool). McCartney pointed to Harrison's ability to play Bill Justis' instrumental "Raunchy" note-for-note. Harrison demonstrated same, and Lennon invited him to join also. Just like that, three-quarters of the Beatles were in place.

THE FIRST-EVER JOB THAT THE BEATLES' first-ever manager hired them for wasn't exactly a path to superstardom. Lancashire native Allan Williams (1930-2016) was a promoter and cafe proprietor in Liverpool who was instrumental in bringing the Beatles to Hamburg: He booked them, drove them there in his van, and fed them along the way. This became the make-or-break period that made the Beatles.

"At first I didn't know they *had* a group," Williams told me in 2003. "I had a coffee bar, the Jacaranda, which was situated, oh, about 100 yards from the unemployment exchange. And all the groups didn't like working, because it interfered with their rehearsing. The groups would come to the Jacaranda after they received their 'dole' money (unemployment benefit). It was known as 'rockin' dole' in those days," Williams laughed. "I used to let them rehearse in the basement, because the basement wasn't used until night."

This is where the Beatles, which then included Lennon's friend Stuart Sutcliffe (born 1940 in Edinburgh) came in. Recalled Williams: "Unknown to me, the Beatles — who I just knew from the art school, which was also about five minutes away — they used to miss their lectures and hang around the Jacaranda, listening to the groups like Gerry and the Pacemakers, the Big Three and like that, all big names in Liverpool in those days. Well, I had a problem with the graffiti, you know, in the ladies' toilet (restroom) upstairs.

Lennon, George Harrison, Paul McCartney and Pete Best in an iconic 1962 promo card for the Cavern Club in Liverpool. The boys were still wearing the black leather that marked their Hamburg days, but not for much longer. Publicity photo

"I had to share the toilets in the daytime with a little sweet shop. These old ladies were complaining about the obscene graffiti which the girls used to write. You can *guess* what they wrote.

"Stuart Sutcliffe — you know, the first Beatle — and John Lennon were from the art school. I just had them down as what we called 'coffee bar layabouts.' They were always bumming free coffees and toast from the girls. And then knowing these lads were from the art school, I said, 'Do you fancy redecorating the ladies' toilet for a weekend? Because I've got complaints about the graffiti.' And so the first contact, the first money I ever paid them, was painting the ladies toilet! I preferred the graffiti to the mess they made of it. They must've thought they were budding Picassos."

WILLIAMS, STILL UNAWARE THAT LENNON AND Sutcliffe were in a group, put on a concert of Liverpool bands at a boxing stadium in May 1960. The multi-act show was attended by Larry Parnes, an influential London-based promoter. "After the show," Williams said, "we all went back to the Jacaranda for coffee and that. And Larry Parnes was so impressed with the Liverpool groups. The Beatles were in the audience. And they were listening to the conversation between Larry Parnes and me. And Larry Parnes wanted me to send my Liverpool groups to Scotland to back some of his rock 'n' roll stable, like Johnny Gentle and a fellow called Duffy Power.

"When I went in next day, John Lennon approached me and said, 'Hey, Al, when are you gonna do something for us, like?' I said, 'Well, there's no more painting to be done here.' And he said, 'No. We've got a group.' I said, 'Well, I didn't know that. Where do you play in the area?' He said, 'Oh, we play in the art college every Saturday night. Would you manage us?' "

Lennon told Williams that his band was called the Beatles. (Sutcliffe invented the name, which was inspired by the Crickets. As for the B-E-A-T spelling: Well, the boys were a "beat group.")

Continued Williams: "I said, 'A very strange name, that, isn't it?' Because it was always: Cliff Richard and the Shadows; Cliff Bennett and the Rebel Rousers; Tommy Steele and the Shadows. The groups were just backing groups to a singer, as it were.

"I didn't even audition (the Beatles). I just thought: These are pleasant lads. It'll cost me nothing to give 'em a helping hand."

But the Beatles needed a drummer. Williams asked Brian Casser of the Big Three if he knew anyone, and Casser met with the group. Recalled Williams: "Cass said, 'What's the name of the group, lads?' And John said, 'The Beatles.' 'Oh,' he said, 'that's f***ing stupid. You'll never get anywhere with a name like that. Who's the leader of the group?' And John said, 'I am.' And Cass said, 'Well, how about Long John Silver and the Beatles?'

"They didn't like the name. But because he (Casser) was more influential on the Liverpool scene then, they went out and called themselves the Silver Beetles. But they soon got rid of the name. I think they only did, maybe, 25 gigs as the Silver Beetles."

It was a brass ring waiting to be grabbed: A chance to back up pop star Billy Fury, among others. But the competition was fierce.

As Williams organized an audition of about 10 groups to play behind "Larry's Boys," a roster of well-known singers in Parnes' stable, he hesitated for a moment when the Beatles came to mind. Recalled Williams: "By then I thought, 'Well, the Beatles are good enough to go in for the audition. I'll throw them in at the deep end.' To my amazement, at the end of the audition with all the other Liverpool bands, Billy Fury said, 'I like those Silver Beetles.' So I said, 'John, you've got the job.'

"But Larry Parnes had spotted that Stuart Sutcliffe, who was John Lennon's best mate, wasn't a very good guitarist. In fact, Stuart was that nervous — he played with his back to the audience." (According to McCartney, Sutcliffe didn't face the audience at the band's request, to mask his lack of playing ability.)

"So Larry Parnes said, 'Yes, but we can't afford a five-piece. You'll have to get rid of the bass player.' John said, 'No. We're a group. We're not splittin' up.' I was absolutely amazed, because most groups would have given their right arms to be the backing group for the famous Billy Fury. But even then, I thought, they (the Beatles) must have planned what they were gonna do, that they weren't gonna split up just to become a backing group."

A gig came of it anyway. Parnes booked the Silver Beetles to back Johnny Gentle on his week-plus tour of Scotland — not that Harrison, for one, recalled the experience fondly. "It was a pretty pathetic tour," Harrison said in the 1995 TV documentary "The Beatles Anthology." "We were like orphans or something. Our shoes were all full of holes. Our trousers were a mess. We didn't have uniforms. And this guy, Larry Parnes' fella, Johnny Gentle, he did have this posh suit. *We* were crummy.

"The band was horrible. We were really an embarrassment. We didn't have amplifiers or anything. By the end of it, we were broke. We were all cold and freezing and just miserable. That was it. We all came back to Liverpool, and nothing happened, really."

A CARIBBEAN STEEL BAND REGULARLY PLAYED evenings in the basement of the Jacaranda. " I went down there one night," Williams recalled, "and the steel band had disappeared! And I said to the girl, 'Where's the group?' 'Didn't you know? They'd gone to Hamburg.' Well, it could have been on the *moon*. I said, 'Hamburg?' Without telling me, they disappeared."

Knowing that the Beatles were currently inactive, Williams hired them as fill-ins to play the Jacaranda basement.

"I can always remember the first time they played," he said. "This is to show you how hard up they were in those days. George came up and said, 'Have you got a brush?' I said, 'Yes, I've got a brush.' 'Have you got a mop?' I thought they must have spilled something. They want to mop up. I said, 'Well, the basement's clean.' He said, 'I know. It's all right. Just give us them.'

"Well, they hadn't got any mic (microphone) stands! They used to tie the mics — which belonged to the art school, which they'd stolen or 'borrowed,' but the art school never got 'em back — and have their girlfriends hold the mics up while they played. They used to tie the mic up at the end of the broomstick, as it were. Can you imagine? Well, Cynthia Lennon — John's first wife — was one of the girls. They had to sit in what we called the 'black hole of Calcutta,' because it got so packed, and these poor girls were holding these mics up all night for them. They played 'til 2 or 3 o'clock in the morning."

MEANWHILE, WILLIAMS RECEIVED A letter from the steel band, a group fronted by Lord Woodbine, a Trinidadian singer. Recalled Williams: "They said, 'Why don't you come to Hamburg, Allan? There's plenty of work in Hamburg, and it's so alive.' I thought, 'That's not a bad idea.' So I went with Lord Woodbine, who was a character. In fact, he finished up in Liverpool having a strip club."

A digression: According to Williams, Woodbine once hired the still-fledgling Beatles to accompany an exotic dancer who balked at doing her act with a mere juke box. "They did the show," Williams said, "so one of their first professional jobs was backing a striptease girl.

"George Harrison was, I think, only about 16 at the time. And of course, the girl did the strip, and then after she finished stripping, she had to walk through the group in her nudity to get to the dressing room, which was — well, it wasn't a dressing room. It was where they used to dump the coal, like a coal cellar, which we *converted* into a dressing room."

Billy Fury wanted the Silver Beetles. Johnny Gentle (inset) got them. Publicity photos

From left: Allan Williams, his wife Beryl, Lord Woodbine, Stuart Sutcliffe, Paul McCartney, George Harrison and Pete Best in Arnhem, Holland. The group posed at this monument after getting lost on their first trip to Hamburg. Courtesy of Roan Best

FOR SAILORS AND TOURISTS IN SEARCH OF alcohol, prostitutes, loud music, or even a good fistfight, Hamburg was *the* place. To sniff out work for his stable of bands, Williams traveled to the German port city infamous for debauched pursuits.

He recalled: "In Hamburg, I heard this rock 'n' roll music coming out of this basement club called the Kaiserkeller in the Große Freiheit, which is off the Reeperbahn. So I thought, 'Wow, this could be the place.'

"I went down to the basement, and there was this atrocious German band just singing like parrots (in German accent), *'Tutti-frutti, oh rootie, tutti-frutti, oh rootie ...'* Oh, it was awful!

"The place was packed, but none of the kids would get up and dance to it. And then when they said *'Der pauser,'* which is 'the intermission,' and they put the jukebox on, the place was jumping.

"I thought, 'Wow. I've cracked it. This is the place I'm gonna send the groups to.' So I made myself known to the owner of the club (Bruno Koschmider). I said, 'Would you ever consider having a live Liverpool group?' He said no. So I'd written Hamburg off, I'd thought, altogether."

Allan Williams in 2003.
Photo by Kathy Voglesong

A while later in London, Williams was showcasing another Liverpool band, Denny and the Seniors, at a club called the Two Hours Coffee Bar, when he spotted Koschmider. Recalled Williams: "I thought, 'Christ, that's the fellow from the Hamburg club, the Kaiserkeller. What's *he* doing here?' So I said, 'Hey, Koschmider!' He said, 'Yah, Herr Williams.' His English wasn't very good, but I found an Austrian waiter who spoke German, and he translated for us.

"Koschmider was so intent on having an English group, that instead of coming over to Liverpool, he went to London and was asking everybody, 'Where can I find the Beatles?' And of course, London is the capital; Liverpool was 300 miles up in the country, like. So he was directed to the Two Hours Coffee Bar. They said, 'Well, all the groups hang out at the Two Hours Coffee Bar,' which was very famous. He went there, but of course, nobody had ever heard of the Beatles — never even heard of *Liverpool* in those days."

WILLIAMS AND KOSCHMIDER STRUCK a deal. "I said to the Beatles: 'You want to go to Hamburg?' They said, 'Yeah! Oh, Christ, we'd love to!' But they needed a drummer again."

In rapid succession, the Beatles lost their last two drummers: Tommy Moore and Norman Chapman.

Said Williams: "Tommy Moore didn't get along very well with John Lennon. John, you see, had a very sarcastic wit about him, and he tore this poor lad to ribbons, you know, taking the p*** out of him, as we say. And so Tommy Moore packed up. He said, 'I can't stand that John Lennon.' "

Not much time passed before Moore's replacement, Chapman, was drafted into military service.

"They remembered they used to play sometimes, when they were the Quarrymen, at a coffee bar on the outskirts of town called the Casbah," Williams said of the club operated by Mona Best, whose son, Pete, happened to be a drummer.

"They remembered Pete Best. They'd also heard through the grapevine that Pete Best had just got a new set of drums."

"See if you can get Pete Best to come to the Jacaranda, and let's see if he's any good," Allan Williams advised the Beatles.

According to Best (born 1941 in India), he and the Beatles "blasted through" about six songs. "They were just standards which everyone played," the drummer told me in 2001. "I wasn't worried about it. They went away to a corner — Stu Sutcliffe was with them then — and had a little bit of a *mutza, mutza, mutza* amongst themselves. About a minute later, they came back and said, 'Pete, you're in. You're on your way to Hamburg.'"

As Harrison put it in "Anthology": "We did a quick audition with him, jumped in the van, and went to Hamburg."

BUT IT TOOK MONEY TO GET TO HAMBURG. "IN those days, they were still that poor," Williams said. "We used to sell toast (at the Jacaranda). But if you had jam on your toast, it was a penny extra. And I can still see Paul McCartney shouting at John Lennon, 'You must be f***in' mad! It's a penny extra to have jam on your toast!' Paul McCartney's got jam on his toast *now,* I'd say.

"So they had no money to go to Hamburg. All the lads all went by boat and train, but the Beatles hadn't got a carrot. I had a minibus which seated about 14 people. I said, 'OK, then. I'll drive you to Hamburg in the minibus on the understanding that I'll pay all the expenses and you'll pay me out your wages.' So they all agreed that they would pay me 10 pound out of their earnings to go to Hamburg, and then I paid the boat fees and fed them."

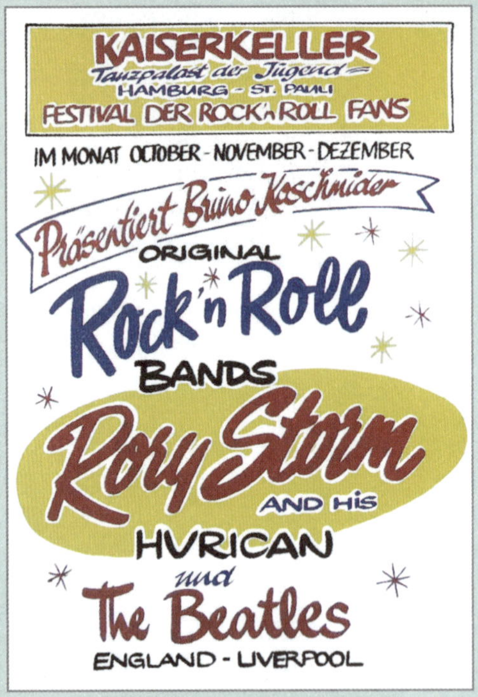

En route, the group — which included Lord Woodbine and Williams' wife, Beryl — got lost. "We finished up at a famous battleground in Holland called Arnhem," Williams said. "It was a big battleground where the English paratroopers all got massacred. As far as the eye could see was white crosses. There must be thousands buried there, young lads 18 and that. We had our photograph taken. And on the back of the cenotaph, it had 'Their Name Liveth for Evermore.' How poetical could you get? The Beatles in this famous photograph in their first-ever job outside of England, and it's got on the back, 'Their Name Liveth for Evermore.'"

While strolling in Arnhem, the group ducked into a music shop.

"When we came out," Williams said, "they all went into fits of hysteria, laughing and joking. I said, 'What's the joke?' John Lennon pulled out a mouth organ, a harmonica. He'd stolen a bloody harmonica from the shop! I said to Woody, 'We're not gonna make Hamburg. We're gonna finish up in jail with this lot.'"

UPON ARRIVING IN HAMBURG, THE BEATLES reported to the Kaiserkeller, where they were informed that they were booked to play *another* venue, the Indra Club, down the street. "We went there, and it was a strip club," Williams said.

"The Beatles went, 'Oh, Christ! We haven't come all the way to Hamburg to play in a strip joint again!' So I said (to the German promoter), 'Look, this is a rock 'n' roll group.'

"He said, 'Last night for stripper. Tomorrow, rock 'n' roll club.'"

BILLED AS THE BEATLES FOR THE FIRST TIME, the five young men played their first Hambug shows at the Indra.

"But the noise was too much," Williams said. "There used to be an old lady who lived above in a flat, and she complained to the police, so they closed it down. The owner had the idea that he would have *two* bands working in the Kaiserkeller, alternating — one would play for an hour. But the playing times were atrocious. The Beatles went there for three months, which was extended for another two months, and the playing times were six or eight hours a night. It was eight hours at the weekends, Friday and Saturday. But even during the week, it was 'til 2 or 3 in the morning."

Between Sept. 1960 and Dec. 1962, the boys played around 281 shows at the Indra, the Kaiserkeller, the Top Ten Club and Star-Club in Hamburg. *"Mach schau,"* German for "Make a show," was a repeated directive from club bosses.

"IT WAS TIRING," BEST SAID of the Hamburg days. "We'd never experienced anything like that. Normally, when you were playin' in Liverpool, it was possibly two, three hours a night, maximum. If *that* much. But when we got out to Hamburg, we suddenly realized we were playin' six, seven nights a week, eight hours a night. And weekends would go on even longer than that. But it was a case of, 'OK, roll your sleeves up and here we go.' You know, 'We're gonna conquer the German audience, whichever way it might be.' You very quickly adjusted to it."

At certain Hamburg clubs, waiters regularly carried "uppers" (speed pills) to slip to musicians who were drooping. Liquid encouragement was also involved. "There was a lot of beer," Best said. "Lots of drinkin' onstage and off. And all the other temptations which came with that, in as much as the women and the fights and the gallivanting and the pranks we used to play on the audience."

THE BEATLES' BLACK-LEATHER STAGE COSTUMES were born of several factors — but mostly necessity.

"With the long hours we were playing, the stage suits we'd gone out in had rotted and dropped apart, with the sweat and all the rest of it," Best said. "They'd be stitched together, but they kept splitting. Then one day, they just fell apart, and that was it. So we were faced with the problem: What are we gonna wear onstage?

"Leather was very expensive in Liverpool, and there wasn't a lot of it 'round. But in Hamburg, it was an everyday commodity. So we turned 'round and said, 'Oh, it would be great to wear leather onstage.' Because we can wear it offstage; we can wear it onstage; we can live in it; it's hard-wearing. And so we did that.

"Of course, when we came back to Liverpool, it was very much a case of: 'My God, look at these guys. They wear leather!' And the sound that we were producing — which was very raw and energetic and powerhouse — complemented the leather image."

Sights of Hamburg include the bright lights of the Reeperbahn and the five original Beatles at the Indra Club. Photo illustration

ONSTAGE JOKING BECAME AN EXPECTED PART OF the Beatles' shows. Recalled Best: "We did mock fights on stage, where the audience would think, 'My goodness me, the band's fightin' with one another!' But it was all just to let off steam. John would jump off the piano, doin' his Nureyev splits in the air. He used to split his jeans nearly every night when he did it. The old toilet attender would be ready with a sewing needle and a thread to strap John's jeans back together again, ready to get him to go back onstage for another jump off the piano.

"We would go *into* the audience. We used to do some slow numbers, which would get the audience onto the floor doin' the 'smoochies,' as we used to say — you know, the romantic side of it. Of course, the minute they'd get onto the floor, we'd kick into a hard-edged, very rock 'n' roll number, a raucous number. While they'd be smoochin' away, we'd suddenly change the tempo.

"The audience started to expect it. So when a slow number came up, they'd all take to the floor and they'd be smoochin' away, knowin' full well that the second half of the number, we were goin' to be the lads who would jump offstage and get amongst the audience. We'd be in amongst the audience, laughin' and jokin' and dancin' with 'em. Just good-natured entertainment.

"All of that transpired while we were over there. But when you look back, it was the development, it was the learning curve which we were going through. All of those factors helped to make the Beatles what they were, actually, in Germany."

DEPORTATIONS OF THREE BEATLES OCCURRED within a 10-day period in late 1960. Harrison, then 17, was deported for violating curfew. "They had an order banning anyone under 18 (from working) after midnight," Williams said. "They couldn't work in the red-light district, which the Kaiserkeller was in. You know, it was full of brothels and all sorts in the Reeperbahn."

Speaking of juvenile things, McCartney and Best were deported after setting a condom aflame in the Kaiserkeller, in a farewell gesture before the Beatles moved to the Top Ten Club. They were jailed for three hours. According to McCartney, someone from the Top Ten covered their bail, in a sense, with a bottle of Scotch.

"To get their deportment orders lifted, I had to go to the German embassy and explain that it wasn't their fault; that Herr Koschmider was supposed to get them the permits; and that George Harrison was now 18," Williams said.

"And so the German consulate was very good. He said, 'OK, I'll make inquiries.' And then they said to me, 'Now, look. They can come back (to Hamburg) now, but you will have to sign an agreement guaranteeing their good behavior. If they get into trouble, you will have to pay their fines.' Like a fidelity bond.

"So they went over. They were getting about 150 pounds between the lot of 'em. But 150 pounds in 1960 was good money. There was no inflation in those days."

THE BOYS MET FELLOW LIVERPUDLIAN RINGO Starr, who was then drumming for Rory Storm and the Hurricanes, in Hamburg. Starr (born 1940) sat in with the Beatles when Best was indisposed, resulting in undeniable chemistry. *Hmmm ...*

Sutcliffe met and became engaged to German photographer Astrid Kirchherr, who is credited for encouraging the so-called "Beatle haircut," and who chronicled the boys' Hamburg period with her thoughtful, and now iconic, black-and-white photography.

Sutcliffe — who, at heart, was always more of an artist than a musician — quit the Beatles in March 1961. He died of a cerebral hemorrhage on April 10, 1962, at the tragically young age of 21. Best said that the Beatles were expecting Sutcliffe to meet them at the airport when they flew in for their fourth Hamburg stint.

"Of course, when we got there, Astrid was at the airport," Best recalled. "When we asked where Stu was, Astrid basically turned 'round and told us that Stu died a couple of days beforehand of a brain hemorrhage. That's how we got to know about it.

"We were absolutely shell-shocked. It was the first time that I'd actually seen John Lennon, you know, break down and cry in public. That's how affected he was over Stu's death."

While in Hamburg, the Beatles sometimes played backup for a fellow Brit. This would lead to their first professional recording.

In 1961, during the group's second Hamburg stint, they occasionally supported singer Tony Sheridan (1940-2013) at the Top Ten Club. Norfolk native Sheridan — then a rising star in Germany — returned the favor by jumping onstage at Beatles gigs. Sheridan and the boys were scouted by Bert Kaempfert, an A&R (artists and repertoire) man for Germany's Polydor label.

"He approached us and said that he would like to record us," recalled Best. "And of course, we were like children with sweets, weren't we? It's like, 'My goodness, me!' Here we are in Germany, and we've got a recording contract. It was incredible.

"The only problem was, we didn't realize what we were signing. I mean, it was still total enjoyment, still total ecstasy to actually record. We thought that we were actually going to record in a studio — you know, you see these pictures on the television and the films where it's a recording studio, even though this was way back in 1961.

"In fact, when we actually arrived at the destination, it was a school hall. It was recorded in a school hall with a mobile stage unit and a recording unit. This was how Bert Kaempfert used to record his orchestra. He felt that the acoustics in it were good for a rock 'n' roll sound, a live sound. He basically got us to set up on stage as we would be playing at the Top Ten Club.

"So we rattled off about eight numbers. Some of them were with Tony Sheridan, and some of them were just us."

The session resulted in a single. A rock 'n' roll cover of the traditional Scottish ballad "My Bonnie" became the first-ever release from the Beatles, though they were billed as the Beat Brothers.

BACK HOME IN LIVERPOOL, ALLAN WILLIAMS was having a bad luck streak. A new club he opened burnt to the ground in what he deemed a suspicious fire. He was low on funds.

"Then I got a message from Stuart Sutcliffe to say that John Lennon was refusing to pay my commission, because they were claiming they got the work themselves," Williams lamented.

"With all the problems, it was harder for me to get them over the second time than it was the first time. And by then, I thought, 'Aw, f*** it. I don't need this aggro (aggravation) from a group.' So I said — I even wrote them a letter saying it — 'Right. I've finished with you. And I'll fix it. But you'll never, ever work in Liverpool again.' And it was *me* that never worked again!"

For Williams, Hamburg is what made the Beatles.

"A lot of people say to me, like jokingly, 'How do you become a Beatle, Allan?' I say, 'Well, you go to Hamburg, you work there for five months, seven nights a week, playing eight hours a night. That ought to break you or make you.' And it made the Beatles. It wasn't Liverpool who made the Beatles. It was Hamburg.

"So much so, when they came back from Hamburg, everybody thought they were a *German* band. Because they used to say to Paul McCartney, 'Oh, you speak very good English, don't you?' Of course, he could speak German, and he used to play them on a bit. Because they'd be called: 'Direct from Germany, the Beatles!'

"That was the start of Beatlemania, but it was a parting of the ways for me. Anyway, it was a lot of fun. I didn't do it for the money. Well, they never *had* any."

In the "Anthology" TV documentary of 1995, McCartney remembered Williams good-naturedly, calling him "a great bloke, a real good motivator. He was very good for us at the time."

"I've still got an IOU from Paul McCartney," Williams revealed. "He must be the only millionaire who owes me 15 pounds. How can he sleep at night? Fifteen bloody pounds and he's a millionaire! And he used to argue for payin' extra puttin' jelly on his toast."

The band's first professional recording: "My Bonnie."

Sleeve © Polydor (U.K. release); record © Decca (U.S. release)

Tony Sheridan

"My Bonnie" began as a joke.

That was Tony Sheridan's recollection of his historic recording session with the Beatles — plus the fact that it was done on very little sleep.

"Getting up at 7 in the morning when you go to bed at 5 is not easy, as you would appreciate," the singer told me in 2003. "And being sort of picked up and taken off. (In mock German accent) *'OK! Get up!'* In Germany, things are German. You must appreciate that, too. *'Get up, boyz! We're going to the studio!'* And so we went to the studio.

"And then, very quickly, we had to decide, with (producer) Bert Kaempfert's assistance, what songs we were going to record. Of course, we had a big repertoire by this time. Bert was saying to us, 'Well, you've got to please the Germans. You've got to do a bit of this, a bit of that.' We thought, 'We'll come up with something approaching an LP, but first, we'll do a single.'

"He asked us, 'What do you know that the Germans know?' We said, half-jokingly, 'What about "My Bonnie?"' And he said, 'Yes! Yes! What does it sound like?' What we did was a very different sort of version. We did it in two takes.

"So it was a joke. But some jokes have a life of their own sometimes, so it became a living thing. It became a single. It sort of got the Beatles off the ground in a roundabout way, as well."

How was it that Sheridan and the Beatles nailed "My Bonnie" (a song they hadn't planned to record) in two takes?

He explained: "These sessions were more or less a case of jumping off the stage, getting into the so-called studio, which was in a school hall, and doing the same thing again that you'd done onstage. We were very well versed in what we were doing in those days. We didn't make mistakes. We improvised solos, but there are still hardly any mistakes in an improvised solo.

"The version that came out was the second take. It was good enough for Bert Kaempfert, so it was good enough for us. We thought, 'Well, if we please him, on the next one we can please ourselves.' But we never had a chance to do a next one. If we *had* done 10 versions of 'My Bonnie,' they would have all sounded very different."

Sheridan was asked how he and the Beatles responded to one another when they first met up in Hamburg.

"It confused them completely," he said. "Because up 'til that time, they thought they were the only ones who were doing it (playing music) this way. We were like-minded at the time.

"I never would have got together with the Beatles if they'd have been a s*** band. They wouldn't have got together with me, had they not admired something about what I was doing."

The singer admitted that the Beatles had one thing over him: "They had a little bit more ambition. They went back (to England) and they made it, and I stayed in Germany and sort of made it in *my* way. But I was satisfied. I've always been a low-key person. I've had the best of both worlds."

"We did it in two takes," said singer Tony Sheridan, shown in 2003. Photo by Kathy Voglesong

So who was this 'direct from Germany' band? It was the Beatles, alright, but not the same Beatles that left for Hamburg in 1960.

The band returned to Liverpool intermittently between five Hamburg stints. Pete Best recalled a particularly memorable gig the Beatles played as returnees at his mother's club, the Casbah — one of those occasions when they were introduced as "direct from Germany."

Said the drummer: "The atmosphere in the club was, 'Who are these guys from Hamburg?' 'Is it a German band?' Of course, when we got down there and they realized who it was, there was a bit of: 'Hang on a minute! They've all played here under different guises with different bands.' "

The Beatles

Then again, it *was* a new band. Hamburg had left its imprint on the Beatles.

"When we came back from Germany, with all of this going on, we didn't change our habits," said Best.

"We basically did what we'd done in Germany when we came back to Liverpool. We smoked onstage, we drank onstage, we swore onstage, and it captivated the audience in Liverpool. So it worked for us, you know, the grind of those Hamburg days."

From top: A 1962 promotional card of the Beatles; manager Brian Epstein; producer George Martin

LIVERPOOL-BASED RECORD-SHOP proprietor Brian Epstein (1934-1967) prided himself on his ability to fill special requests. One day, he got a head-scratcher from a walk-in customer. Epstein recounted that moment in some detail, in a prologue to his 1964 memoir, "A Cellarful of Noise."

Wrote Epstein: "At about three o'clock on Saturday, Oct. 28, 1961, an 18-year-old boy called Raymond Jones, wearing jeans and a black-leather jacket, walked into a record store in Whitechapel, Liverpool, and said: 'There's a record I want. It's "My Bonnie" and it was made in Germany. Have you got it?' "

Epstein wrote that when he asked who the record was by, Jones replied, "You won't have heard of them. It's by a group called the Beatles."

As it happened, Epstein's shop, NEMS (for North End Music Stores), was around the corner from the Cavern Club. After attending several Beatles shows there, he met with the group, eventually offering his services as a manager with the promise of better gigs *and* money. It was an offer the boys couldn't refuse.

The arrangement marked a new direction for both Epstein and the Beatles. Epstein (who once contemplated an acting career) jumped into the role of talent manager with gusto. Epstein would also represent Gerry and the Pacemakers, Cilla Black and Billy J. Kramer, among others.

But in assuming management of the Beatles, Epstein inherited something that annoyed him: the recording contract the Beatles signed with Germany's Polydor label at the time they recorded "My Bonnie" with Tony Sheridan.

"When we were taken over by Brian Epstein, he wanted us to have an English recording contract," recalled Best. "You know, the German contract wasn't what he really wanted. So he got in touch with Decca, right? And then, of course, you have the famous Decca auditions — January the 1st, 1962 — when we played about 15 songs. Mike Smith was the A&R man for that. And we all thought that, yeah, the deal was in the bag. But as history portrays now, Decca turned us down.

"So what confronted Brian then was: He'd been turned down by the biggest record company in England, which Decca was at that time. So then, he started going through, in sort of merit order, the other companies. And he found that he wasn't gettin' very far, 'til he approached EMI."

EMI WAS INITIALLY COOL. THEN CAME yet another fluke of luck for the Beatles. When Epstein had the band's bulky demo tape converted into the more convenient disc format, the gentleman who did the transfer liked the music, and gave Epstein a tip that eventually led to a meeting with George Martin, a producer who specialized in comedy albums for the EMI imprint Parlophone. Martin wasn't exactly enamored of the Beatles' sound at first, but Epstein's pushing led to an audition. On June 6, 1962, the boys recorded four songs with Martin, including "Love Me Do."

Recalled Best: "We were signed up by EMI — OK, it was the Parlophone division of EMI, but it was still EMI, which is a big corporation. And I suppose that was the opening we'd been waitin' for, as we went after an English recording contract to establish us and put us on the map."

The Beatles were growing on Martin, but there was a problem: He was unhappy with Best's drumming. The other three Beatles, too, had a growing feeling that the chemistry was better with Ringo Starr, who had filled in for Best on several occasions in Hamburg. It all led to Epstein calling Best into his office for a meeting that wasn't easy for either man.

"Historically, it may look like we did something nasty to Pete," said Harrison (who pushed for Best's dismissal) in "Anthology." "It may have been that we could have done it better."

Pete Best

“Life's not over,” said Pete Best, shown in 2001.

Photo by Kathy Voglesong

It's a heartbreaking moment in the history of rock 'n' roll.

Pete Best played drums during the Beatles' formative first two years, through the legendary Hamburg gigs, right up to their first recording session with producer George Martin, only to get sacked just before John Lennon, Paul McCartney, George Harrison and their new drummer, Ringo Starr, rocketed to superstardom.

In a 2001 interview, Best gamely fielded the question he'd contemplated for most of his life: What led to that fateful day when Beatles manager Brian Epstein fired him?

“It came without any forewarning,” the drummer said.

“I was called in on that particular day — I think it was August 15th or 16th of '62 — totally unaware of what was going to happen. You know, we'd recorded. We were going to go back to put the finishing touches to ‘Love Me Do.’ We had the contract with EMI. Everything was lookin' rosy, 'til 15 minutes with Brian Epstein, and Brian basically said, ‘Pete, you're no longer in. The boys want you out, and *Ringo's* in.’

“I suppose, puttin' it in a cliché, it was like a bombshell. Or, as we say in Liverpool, ‘gob-smacked.’ Right?

“And it did upset me, to be quite honest. And it did cause me a lot of heartache, a lot of financial embarrassment. Because very soon after that, as the world knows now, ‘Love Me Do’ went into the charts, and — *pshffft!* — the phenomenon was started.

“But what you've got to do is knuckle down and turn 'round and say, ‘OK, life's not over.’ You still believe in yourself. You still believe in your own abilities and your own talents. I joined another band. It was a case of trying to prove to people that the reason which *they* gave wasn't the real reason.

“But it became very, very evident that no matter how fast I chased 'em with a good band — right? — they were streets ahead of me,” Best added with a laugh.

“I mean, they were moving so fast. It was like they were on a Japanese ‘bullet' train, and I was on the No. 10 tram in Liverpool.”

Four decades later came a gesture from the Beatles that went a long way toward mending their relationship with Best. The drummer was awarded royalties for older tracks he'd played on (including that first take of “Love Me Do”) on the Beatles' “Anthology I” album of 1995.

“It was something I'd never expected,” Best said of the royalty payments. “OK, who would expect something after 40 years? And of course, you've established your own lifestyle, you've achieved your own pinnacles, and you're quite happy with what you've achieved in life and the way you've built your family up and the security you've got for them, and striving to keep yourself in that position where you can hold your head up high.

“But, yes, it has basically set up a nice, secure base for my family for years to come.”

Across the universe

A new drummer, a new manager, a new record contract, a new look. But a rocky start preceded the Beatles' ascent to pop stardom.

Producer George Martin, who would shepherd the Beatles through 22 singles and 13 albums, recalled that his first meeting with their newly minted manager, Brian Epstein, was something of a last-ditch effort for the band.

"In January of 1962, Brian Epstein was, by then, quite wary of interviewing record company executives; he'd been to all of them," said Martin (during a 1999 lecture in Red Bank, NJ, which I attended). "By then, the Beatles were a joke in the business. Even our own company (EMI) had given the thumbs down to this group. No one would touch them. I didn't know that. When my name was given to Brian Epstein, he knew he had hit rock bottom.

"I immediately liked the four boys — not for their music, but for their wacky sense of humor. They were four young men desperate for someone to recognize their talent. George was 19.

"The Beatles actually confirmed what I already knew about going out on a limb. They never disappointed me with a song. Each song that came off the line was a gem. They never rehashed; they never gave me 'Star Wars II.' They were never content with what they could see; they were always looking beyond the horizon. It was damned exhausting. But it was invigorating, too."

Epstein, who was fastidious about his own appearance, oversaw the band's new look. (Goodbye, leather; hello, matching suits.) Their Hamburg days behind them, the Beatles continued to hone their craft at Liverpool's Cavern Club as they embarked on their recording career. The rockiness came in during their earliest Cavern gig with newly installed drummer Ringo Starr. "The first gig in the Cavern after I'd joined was pretty violent," Starr said in the 1995 "Anthology" TV documentary. "There was a lot of fighting and shouting. Half of them hated me, half of them loved me. George got a black eye."

SINGER-GUITARIST TERRY SYLVESTER was playing the Cavern during this period with his band, the Escorts. "It was very tightly packed," Sylvester said of the venue when we spoke in 2005.

"Hard to explain. Very small place. Very frightening place. There was only one entrance and exit: the front door. There was no back door. You'd go to the dressing room — you had to carry your amps through the crowd.

"It wasn't a licensed venue; in other words, you couldn't get alcohol. Your best chance was a Coca-Cola and a hot dog. It was more like a youth club, a very small youth club. You'd see the same people all the time. They dressed a little bit differently down there than they did elsewhere in the country."

Sylvester confirmed the prevailing wisdom that the bustling music scene in Liverpool stemmed from its status as a port city.

"Liverpool was kind of unique," he said. "There's many reasons why. The Cunard ships used to leave Liverpool and go to New York. In Liverpool — and the Cavern Club in particular — a DJ called Bob Wooler was playin' records that weren't gettin' played anywhere else in the U.K. There were records by, for instance, the Shirelles. They weren't gettin' played on the BBC at the time, but were gettin' played in Liverpool at the Cavern Club.

"All the Liverpool groups used to hear these songs, and we'd just go, 'I want that song!' We'd borrow records off of Bob Wooler to take home and rehearse. I mean, I love Cliff Richard, but he would do one type of thing. But the Beatles were doin' Larry Williams' 'Dizzy Miss Lizzy,' Chan Romero's 'Hippy Hippy Shake.' There was a definite scene happenin' there that was happenin' nowhere else."

THE BEATLES WERE CLIMBING THE charts in England in 1962 and '63 with "Love Me Do" (#17), "Please Please Me" (#2) and "From Me to You" (#1). New York-based promoter Sid Bernstein, a self-described Anglophile, took notice.

"As a soldier in World War II, I spent a lot of time in England before we went into Germany and other lousy places," Bernstein told me in 2001.

"I got so involved with English people, the English countryside and the English press and newspapers, that I carried that habit on long after I left the Army. I loved reading about what was going on in England, so I'd pick up one or two English newspapers almost every week, OK?

A Liverpool institution: The Cavern Club.

Paul, smoking? Naughty, naughty. On Brian Epstein's orders, the boys traded their leathers for matching suits. Publicity photo

"And I became what obviously was the first guy in America to read about what was happening in England in 1962 and '63.

"I'd not heard the Beatles' music, but I was so taken with their rapid climb in England. It seemed almost overnight that the records caught on. They went far beyond that little club, the Cavern. All of a sudden, people all over England were starting to clamor for dates — Brian Epstein later told me this — for dates on the Beatles. That's what turned me on. I said, 'I've got to bring them to America. The language is the same.'"

Objective No. 1 was to locate Epstein's phone number.

Said Bernstein: "I shall never forget this number. It was: Childwall-6518. That did it. Took me three weeks to find that number. He hadn't yet settled in London. The operation was still out of his home or certainly out of Liverpool. His mother answered the phone. Brian told me, 'You're the first American to call me.'"

Bernstein struck a deal with Epstein to have the Beatles make their American debut at Carnegie Hall, no less, in New York City. Bernstein also arranged travel and lodging for the group. Yep, it was Bernstein who booked the Pan-Am jetliner from which Lennon, McCartney and Starr took their first steps on U.S. soil. (Harrison had earlier visited his older sister Louise in Illinois.)

THEN CAME A TWIST OF FATE: ALTHOUGH Bernstein was technically the first American to book the Beatles, it so happened that Ed Sullivan became the first to present the group to American audiences, albeit via the medium of television.

"Before they came, Sullivan had heard about them," Bernstein said. "He chose a date. I booked them with Brian for Wednesday, Feb. 12, 1964, which was Lincoln's birthday. I figured the kids would be out of school. Got that? Since they were coming to America, Ed Sullivan booked them for his Sunday show on Feb. 9. You got it? So they were already being promoted on 'The Ed Sullivan Show.' They were no longer a secret."

Especially considering that in January, "I Want to Hold Your Hand" became the group's first #1 hit in the U.S., and Capitol Records did a rush release of the album "Meet the Beatles!"

"That brought the ticket price up, when word got out," said Bernstein. "The going rate for a star attraction at Carnegie Hall in those days, mind you, was $3.50 for the upper balcony, $4.50 for the mezzanine or the middle balcony. And my tickets were being sold by speculators — I hadn't even heard of the words 'speculator' or 'scalper' until that day — those tickets were going for $75, $100 and $150 for orchestra! I saw scalpers selling them."

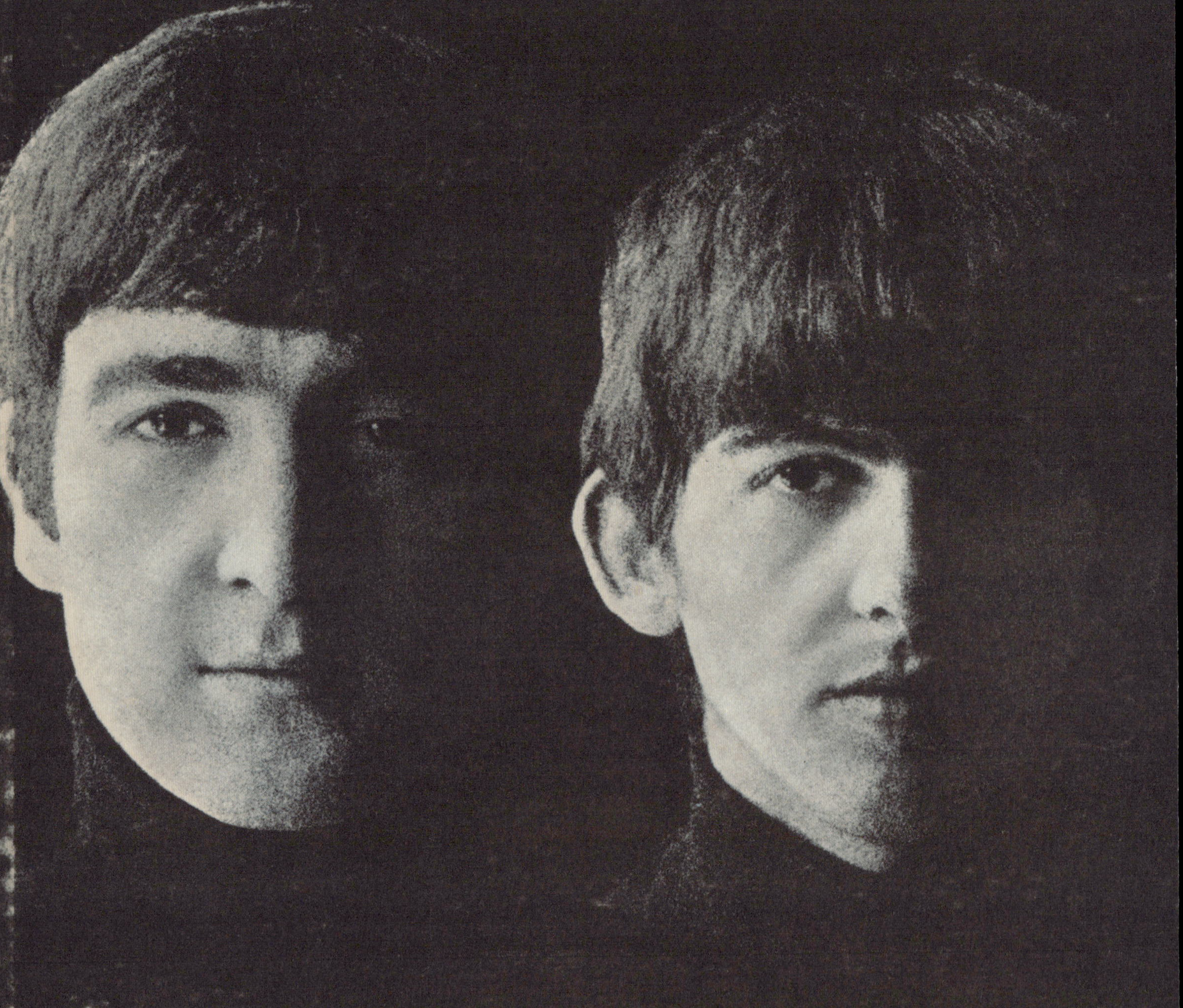

'Meeting' the Beatles

"The First Album by England's Phenomenal Pop Combo" went the tagline for Capitol Records' "Meet the Beatles!" It wasn't. Technically, that distinction went to Vee-Jay Records, a Black-owned label founded in 1953. Vee-Jay's album "Introducing the Beatles" came out on Jan. 10, 1964, beating Capitol by 10 days. But Vee-Jay didn't have nearly the reach to properly handle this emerging supergroup. Capitol — who infamously passed on the Beatles in the first place — sued Vee-Jay. (It's complicated.) "Meet the Beatles!" preceded "The Ed Sullivan Show" by 20 days, as Beatlemania spread.

The cover of "Meet the Beatles!" is surprisingly moody, considering the sunny image then projected by the group. At Brian Epstein's invitation, photographer Robert Freeman shot the band in the dining room of a Bournemouth hotel with the curtains closed. Swathed in darkness, only the boys' heads are shown — in half-shadow, to boot. The risky choice paid off. "Meet the Beatles!" presents one of the most iconic images of the band. The album sold over 5 million copies. Freeman shot four more Beatles album covers, including "Rubber Soul."

"Meet the Beatles!" © Capitol Records

Capitol
RECORDS
HIGH FIDELITY
GOLD RECORD AWARD
AUDITED AND CERTIFIED BY
RIAA
QU LITHO IN U.S.A.

The Beatles landed at an airport renamed for U.S. president John F. Kennedy, who had been assassinated the previous Nov. 22.

Disc jockey "Cousin Brucie" Morrow was on hand on Feb. 7, 1964, when the Beatles' stepped onto the tarmac at the former Idlewild Airport in New York, and were greeted by an estimated 3,000 fans (a number Morrow intimated was inflated).

"I was at Idlewild with our news director," recalled Morrow when we spoke in 2003. "I was broadcasting live over a telephone. We didn't have any fancy digital wireless equipment in those days. No mobile phones, no cell phones. So I was on a telephone broadcasting what was happening.

"It was very well-orchestrated. It was not like a lot of people think — wild, helter-skelter. First of all, there were not tens of thousands of people at the airport. Because the police and the security at the airport herded in a few hundred people on the top of the buildings to watch them. There were a couple hundred people at the tarmac to greet the Beatles. Idlewild was exciting, to see them come in — on Flight 101, by the way."

"Cousin" Brucie Morrow.
WABC-AM

Immediately following the flight, the Beatles faced, or faced *off* with, assembled journalists.

"They were herded into a makeshift press area in the Pan Am building," Morrow recalled. "This was put together. There were hundreds of us from the media there. A lot of television.

"But 99 percent of those people were hostile. The hostility came from, I think, ignorance. They were representing, in those days — the newspapers and television and a lot of radio — parents. When a new generation is about to take the baton and the power from the preceding generation, there's a war. There's a fight. They hold on as long as they can. So there's a lot of anger. They don't want to give up the power.

"Well, here are these four 'mop tops' who are creating all this havoc in Europe, and it's very obvious — because we started playing the music on radio — that this was going to be the next trend for at least six months. None of us, not one of us geniuses, realized that the Beatles were going to become part and parcel of the fabric, which equals the culture, of our lives. Once that happens, there's no stopping it. Once it surpasses just a record or music, you have a tremendous cultural experience, an explosion.

"So they were put into this press conference. This really illustrates the early, original time when they came here. The press was very sarcastic and rude. The boys, by the way, were quite nervous. Even with all their success over in Europe, they now came to see where the streets were paved with gold. They knew if they were gonna make it big, they had to make it in the United States. The press was not very polite to them at first.

"I spoke to John Lennon. I told him not to worry about it. I said, 'These people do not represent the audience, and it's all going to change around.' Which, of course, it did very quickly.

"There are certain things in life, as part of our culture, which eventually get written up by the poets, because the poets follow culture, of course," Morrow added. "There are certain things you never forget as long as you live. I still have that day within me."

FOLLOWING THE PRESS CONFERENCE, the Beatles were whisked to the ritzy Plaza Hotel at Central Park, a New York City landmark.

"There must have been 1,500 people waiting in front of the Plaza Hotel as the Beatles arrived that morning," said Bernstein. "I was one of those 1,500. Nobody knew who I was at that time. I thought, 'Doesn't anybody recognize me? Doesn't anybody know that I may be partially responsible for all this?'

"There was a little reception for them given by Capitol Records. Brian invited me up to their suite, and I met them. They had an adjoining suite to Brian's. He brought me in. They were looking out at the crowd below singing Beatles songs and waving up at their window. They were so excited.

"I heard Ringo say to Brian and, bless his heart, George and John, 'Hey, we've never had anything like this in England before!' He later said to me, 'This is a bigger reception than we've had in all of England,' where they had scored so big so quickly. They were really taken by it and getting a laugh out of it — the kids screaming and yelling, as they were from the street below."

Goofing on the press.
Photo illustration

In newsreel footage, from left: The jetliner arrives; a rooftop-eye-view; McCartney and Starr respond. Photo illustration

The Beatles had *their* eyes on the phenomenon as well, watching themselves on TV and listening to themselves on radio, even as they were being interviewed live by New York disc jockeys such as Murray the K (who later called himself the "fifth Beatle").

"They had a good sense of humor, you follow?" Bernstein said. "They took it all very lightly. They were like my kids at that age or anybody's kids at that age. They were late teenagers. For them, it was fun. I don't think they realized the dimension of influence they had — of importance, of a sense of history, yet, that they *still* have."

ANOTHER BROADCASTER CAME TO recognize the Beatles' talent, and understand their appeal. Newsman Larry Kane, then based in Florida, traveled with the band through 1964 and '65.

Newsman Larry Kane.
WCAU-TV

"They had come to Miami for a brief visit in February of 1964," Kane told me in 2003.

"I was the hard news guy there, the crime-and-corruption guy. The program directors came to me and said, 'The Beatles are coming on this big American tour. Can you try to get an interview with them in their closest location to Miami?'

"So I wrote a letter to Epstein. I put in my business card, which had a list of the other six stations that the company I worked for owned. The other six were R&B stations aimed primarily at an African-American audience. He didn't know that; he didn't know much about American broadcasting to begin with. He saw seven stations and said, 'Wow, this guy must be a radio mogul.' He invited me (to travel with the Beatles). They charged us about $2,500, which covered the charter plane, hotels, travel arrangements. There I was, my heart racing, ready to go on this amazing trip."

Amazing, yes, but it wasn't *all* fun and games.

"I got a bloody nose in San Francisco," Kane recalled. "I was pushed down all over the place. I was banged up quite a bit.

"The thing that was so amazing was the intensity of the emotion. You see it in photos or video, but it's something else to actually *be* there and see these ordinary people — anywhere from 10 to 16 years old, and they got older as the tours progressed — breaking down police barricades just to get close to the Beatles. It wasn't done out of vengeance or protest or anger. It was all joy.

"The other amazing thing, being around it, was what people would do to get close to the Beatles. The good things and the bad things — the little girls with candy kisses, bagels with Ringo's name on them, baked cookies. I got a few report cards slipped to me," Kane added with a laugh. "And then, of course, some of the young women were offering more than just company. It was pretty incredible to see people acting like that. It was amazing to see the intensity of it."

Kane was initially ambivalent about the Beatles — "Paul McCartney never met a mirror he didn't like," he told me at one point — but he was eventually won over by their music.

Kane was asked if, after the two years during which he covered the Beatles, he could have guessed the impact the band would have on the culture.

"Absolutely not, and anybody who tells you otherwise is full of it," he said without hesitation.

"Even in 1965, when they were well established, if you had told me we'd be talking about them (decades later), I would have thought you were smoking something. I just couldn't imagine it. I had a feeling the Beatles were going to be around for a while, but I never thought they would leave the musical legacy they have. Who would have guessed?

"I think if you'd asked them at the time — 'What do you think? Where are you guys going to go?' — they would probably say they'd never break up, which they always said. I don't think they ever, ever expected the incredible, enormous impact that they had culturally throughout the world."

Ringo Starr

"I was in the greatest show on Earth — for what it was worth," goes a lyric written by John Lennon and sung by Ringo Starr.

The song is "I am the Greatest" (from the 1973 album "Ringo"), in which Starr reprises his Billy Shears character from the Beatles' 1967 masterpiece, "Sgt. Pepper's Lonely Hearts Club Band." Starr was one quarter of the Beatles, arguably the most influential band in rock, if not music itself. I interviewed the drummer by telephone in 2001 and 2008. He also answered my questions during press conferences held in New York City in 1999, 2000 and 2003.

Q: In the book "The Beatles Anthology" (2000), you said the Beatles were "just a group of scruffs" when you first saw them.

STARR: Even though I said that in the book, they were the band that I would go and watch. You know, I still loved them as a band, but *we* were the big shots, Rory Storm and the Hurricanes. It was in Liverpool, and they were rehearsin' in the back of a coffee bar (the Jacaranda), and we were off to go to Butlin's (a resort played by the Hurricanes) to be professionals.

Q: John asked you to shave your beard and get a haircut when you joined. Were you insulted?

STARR: No. Because they all had this — now, it's called the "Beatle cut," of course, which a guy in Germany (Jürgen Vollmer) did for them. That was just one of John's lines, you know. I mean, nothing would have happened if I'd have kept the beard. I would still be in the band (laughs).

Q: What do you remember about first touching down in America on Feb. 7, 1964?

STARR: It's probably one of the many exciting moments I've had in my life. To come to America as a musician from England and get that reception was incredible. And that our records were sellin' in America by then — because, we had two that *didn't* sell (laughs). It's just still one of the incredible memories for me. I even felt New York while I was on the plane flyin' into it. I felt it even from the plane — the *engines*.

Q: What did the four of you think might happen once you landed?

STARR: Well, we were hopeful, that's all. You know, George had gone to America on holiday, and kept goin' into the record stores askin' for our record, and nobody had heard of us. So we didn't know what to expect. But as soon as we got off the plane, everything was OK (laughs). And then to get that reception (at the Plaza Hotel) that we knew nothin' about, it was just brilliant.

And then, besides the kids outside waitin', just the thrill of bein' in the hotel and havin' all these TVs on and radios — you know, the media madness that was goin' on. We could actually talk to the radio stations and hear ourselves on radio. We were just from England; it's a bit different over there. So it was exciting.

Q: When you filmed "A Hard Day's Night," it's amazing how four amateur actors communicated so well on the screen. Were you surprised at your own success, the four of you?

STARR: No. We were four clowns, really, who play instruments.

Q: "A Little Help From My Friends" became like a theme song for you. What do you recall of recording the vocal track (in 1967)?

STARR: The only difference of opinion we had: The original line said, *"What would you do if I sang out of tune / would you throw a tomato at me?"* I said, "I'm not gonna sing that." Because we'd just been bombarded with all those jelly beans on tour, so I was not going to sing that.

Q: For (the 1970 film) "Let It Be," how did the four of you agree to play on the roof?

STARR: Well, it was an idea we had around that time. You know, first of all, we were gonna play in a volcano in Hawaii and places like that. In the end, the Beatles always took the easy route. So we said, "Oh, let's go on the roof!"

Q: In the "Anthology" docuseries, it almost seemed like you, Paul and George were burying the hatchet before our eyes.

STARR: Well, what hatchet was that, you know what I'm sayin'? I mean, you know, we're all together; we're doin' that; we're gettin' on; and we finished filming; and we all went home.

Q: Have you and Paul grown closer since George's (2001) death?

STARR: We're just still old pals, you know? We're not hangin' out with each other any more than we did. We're not phonin' each other any more often. If we're in the same city, we'll hook up.

Q: You've toured all your life. Do you still get a buzz from it?

STARR: The gig, playin' the show, is the best part for musicians. *Gettin'* there is boring. You gotta get on the bus, the plane, the train, whatever it is. If they had a transporter — if it *was* actually "Star Trek" — it would make life a lot easier.

"We were four clowns, really, who play instruments," said Ringo Starr, shown in 2003.

Photo by Kathy Voglesong

With his shifty eyes, corpse-like posture and Nixonian warmth, Ed Sullivan looked more like an HUAC witness than a TV personality.

So it's understandable why people that didn't grow up with Sullivan — who seemed uncomfortable in his own leathery skin — wonder how such an unlikely looking person became a variety show host. Sullivan's ascension to the role came from other media, not that this is a satisfactory explanation.

In the 1930s, Sullivan (1901-1974) wrote a newspaper column of show-biz news and gossip which led to radio broadcasts of same. When his TV show debuted in 1948, it was titled "The Toast of the Town." So he kind of snuck up on us, you see. "The Ed Sullivan Show" aired until 1971.

TV host Ed Sullivan.

In his television heyday, Sullivan was known as a kingmaker, an arbiter of taste in America, the host with the most. Getting on Sullivan's Sunday night variety show, which was broadcast live from New York City, was, as James Cagney declared in "White Heat," top of the world.

But today, really, Sullivan is best remembered for one thing: having presented the Beatles' debut before the American public to the high-pitched screams of teenage girls, thus kicking off the musical movement known as the British Invasion.

Previously, there had been nothing remotely like the Beatles on the program. A typical Sullivan broadcast presented a mix of old-guard and contemporary musicians and comedians; musical numbers by Broadway casts; circus performers; and novelty acts. These included plate spinners, puppeteers and, in the case of Señor Wences, a plate-spinning puppeteer.

Sullivan was relentless in his pursuit of the Next Big Sensation — ratings were his god — which is why he scrambled to book the Beatles. Said Bruce Morrow: "Sullivan put 'em on television, and parents, I think, realized at that time that these people were not the devil. They were not part of the devil's scheme. They were all right. They were clean-cut kids. They were going to be OK."

A record 73 million viewers tuned in to the Feb. 9, 1964, show.

America first saw Pete Best on TV's "I've Got a Secret" (1964). Best implied to host Garry Moore, left, that he chose to leave the Beatles.

TWO DAYS AFTER THE SULLIVAN SHOW, JAY AND the Americans opened for the Beatles at the group's first proper concert in America, which was held at the Washington Coliseum.

"When I saw the crowd and listened to them screaming, I knew there was something to this stuff," lead singer Jay Black told me in 2005. "When you think about the influence the Beatles had — I don't know where music would have gone around 1963, 1964. Everybody's waiting for that next thing. Elvis (Presley) was already eight years into the business. So the Beatles started a whole new thing. People say, 'How did it feel to meet the Beatles?' Hey, they were very nice. What am I gonna say?"

For their first American album — the one on Vee-Jay Records — the Beatles covered not one, but two songs by the American girl group, the Shirelles: "Boys" and "Baby It's You."

"I never met the Beatles," Shirelles singer Shirley Alston Reeves told me in 2015.

"We were (playing) in England. I remember the Beatles were just becoming popular. When we were there, (reporters) asked us, 'What do you think of the Beatles?' We didn't know who they were talking about! So we faked it. 'Oh, we think they're great.'

"Later on, we laughed about that many a time."

MORROW BELIEVED THE BEATLES ARRIVED AT a time when Americans were in dire need of some cheering up.

"We were going through a terrible time in our nation," the DJ said. "We needed some relief. We had just lost a president. We were going through economic problems. We were going through very heavy political problems and international problems. We had racial strife coming, really, to a head. But the Beatles helped with that quite a bit. They brought a lot of people together. They affected the way we dressed and the way we spoke, too, by the way.

"I'll give you an illustration of that. Two weeks before the Beatles came in, little Joey from the Bronx would call me up (on the air) and say something like: 'Hey, uh, Cousin. Whaddaya say you play a record for me an' my goil? Play somethin' by Dion — he's a good Bronx kid. Willya? Love yer show, mann.'

"All right. The Beatles come in; capture our hearts; we watch 'em on TV; listen to 'em on radio. And this is the same kid calling me two weeks later: (in British accent) 'Ello? This is Joseph of Longshire. I say, Sir Brucie, would you mind terribly playing a record for me 'n' me bird?' Suddenly, everybody was speaking the King's English! We dressed differently, spoke differently, looked differently. Everybody was an Anglophile."

The Beatles had an effect on *artists,* too. The band played a decisive role in shifting control from record labels to recording artists. Traditionally, management told talent what to do next. The early Beatles' dream was to compose, perform and publish their own songs. (McCartney always expressed admiration for Buddy Holly for this reason.) With strong enablers like Epstein and Martin, the Beatles changed that power dynamic.

AS THEY'D HOPED, THE BEATLES "CONQUERED" America, which paved the way for further penetration by their fellow Brit-rockers the Rolling Stones, the Dave Clark Five, the Kinks, the Animals, et. al. Promoter Sid Bernstein carved a niche by continuing to hire British bands to play our side of the Atlantic.

"I found it was the music, the mystique of the music, the British thing, that flavor, that finally caught on," Bernstein told me in 2001.

"So I went after the next big group that was coming up. Still reading — not hearing them — but reading in the English newspapers about what was happening in England.

"So I did a progression of the first 10 or 12 British groups. I don't remember the exact order, but of course the Beatles were first; the Rolling Stones were second; the Dave Clark Five were third; the Animals were fourth; and maybe the fifth was the Moody Blues. The Kinks were in there and a few others. So I caught on to that. I caught on that this was what's happening. Of course, it turned my life around."

Were the Stones a bit gruffer or rougher than the Beatles (as publicists would have us think)?

"Yeah, a little bit gruffer," Bernstein allowed. "So gruff that the lady who booked the attractions (at Carnegie Hall) told me, 'Mr. Bernstein, never come back here again,' after the Stones concert. It was a little gruffer and tougher and rougher of a crowd."

So, to be clear, the Beatles were OK with the powers-that-be at Carnegie Hall, but *not* the Rolling Stones?

"Well, they were upset with the Beatles and the noise thing," said Bernstein. "They said the walls were shaking and the pictures on the walls were going to fall off. It was that kind of an ovation and reaction. They'd never seen that before. But the Stones even outdid *that*. It was an entirely different crowd, OK?"

Still, Bernstein enjoyed the Stones' company.

"We got very friendly," he said, "because I brought them over the first four or five times in a row. I hit it off beautifully with Andrew Loog Oldham, who was the manager and the producer of the Stones. We had a nice relationship. They were a 'can't miss' proposition, you follow? Then again, we weren't looking at 55,000 seats. We were looking at — since I was barred from Carnegie Hall at the time — I brought them to the Academy of Music, which was on 14th Street, which had 3,400 seats. And again, they did two shows each time I brought them."

Promoter Sid Bernstein.
Courtesy of Bernstein

MEANWHILE, BACK IN LIVERPOOL, THE international phenomenon was having a local effect.

"It's almost defies description, really," said singer-guitarist Terry Sylvester, a loyal Liverpudlian.

"I mean, I was a Cliff Richard fan, an Everly Brothers fan, a Buddy Holly fan, an Elvis (Presley) fan. That seemed a long way from Liverpool at that point. And then all of a sudden — mainly because of the Beatles — everyone was looking at Liverpool, England. It was strange to see.

"I remember being very proud when I first saw the Beatles actually get into the charts. I lived in the next row to Paul McCartney. Obviously, I knew them. We used to do the same shows. I was so proud that someone from Liverpool was in the charts. It was kind of a weird feeling, because normally, it's people from London or certainly the United States.

"And the next minute, everyone's looking at Liverpool! All the A&R men from the record companies are comin' up on the train, signing up anybody who looks half decent. 'Can you sing? It doesn't matter. You *look* good.' All that kind of stuff goin' on. And then it just roller-coastered."

The Rolling Stones

The wisdom then and now is that the Beatles wore the white hats, and the Stones wore the black hats. This has served the Stones well.

In 1963, when David Bowie was 16, he went to see a Little Richard show in England. Opening were the Rolling Stones.

"They weren't very well known," Bowie told TV host Michael Parkinson in 2002. "There's about six kids rushed to the front. You know, *that* was their fan base at the time. Everybody was there for Little Richard. And it was priceless; I'd never seen anything so rebellious in my life. Some guy yells out, 'Get yer hair cut!' And Mick (Jagger) says — and I'll never forget these words — 'Wot, an' look like *yew?'*

"I thought, 'Oh my god, this is the future of music!' "

THE STONES FORMED IN LONDON IN 1962. The founding lineup is rock history itself: singer Jagger and guitarist Keith Richards (both born 1943 in Darford); guitarist Brian Jones (1942-1969, born in Cheltenham); bassist Bill Wyman (born 1936 in Lewisham); and drummer Charlie Watts (1941-2021, born in London).

From 1964 through '69, the group scored 18 Top 40 hits, including the #1s "Satisfaction," "Get Off of My Cloud," "Paint It Black," "Ruby Tuesday" and "Honky Tonk Women." The Rolling Stones continued placing singles in the Top 40 through 1989.

But chart success was not the point. Considering their well-reported misadventures (drug busts, affairs, in-fighting) and the sharp lyrical themes of their music (*"I was raised by a toothless, bearded hag"* somehow springs to mind), the Stones were as much a lifestyle as a band.

Most significant is the group's track record as a live act. For more than a half-century, the Rolling Stones filled stadiums.

Rolling Stones singer Mick Jagger in 1966 with a spiffy jacket and an up-to-the-minute microphone.

MICHAEL PHILIP JAGGER, ACCOUNTANT: THAT seemed to be the path of the London School of Economics student. But Jagger loved to sing, and voraciously collected and listened to American blues and pop.

"Eventually, as you do, I gravitated towards a number of singers who were really quite good, like Buddy Holly, Eddie Cochran, Elvis Presley and Chuck Berry," Jagger recalled in the Stones' 2002 book, "According to the Rolling Stones." He remembered seeing Berry in the 1959 concert film "Jazz on a Summer's Day." The first album he ever bought was "Muddy Waters at Newport."

Richards recalled that Jagger had that album under his arm during the historic meet-up that led to their musical partnership, at the Dartford train station on Oct. 17, 1961. The two began listening to records together, and decided to try playing some music at the home of a mutual friend, Dick Taylor (later of Pretty Things). They started seeing bands in clubs, and first saw Jones (who then called himself "Elmo Lewis") playing at the Ealing Jazz Club. Two more players in the pre-Stones era were Ian Stewart, a pianist with a flair for boogie-woogie, and drummer Tony Chapman.

AS JONES, JAGGER AND RICHARDS got serious about music, they pooled their worldly possessions in a Chelsea apartment, affectionately remembered by Richards as "living skint and nasty in the peeling refuse bin of Edith Grove."

Two players (who were themselves destined for rock stardom) caught the early Stones at a place called the Crawdaddy Club. "We used to go and watch the Rolling Stones play near where we lived in Richmond," Yardbirds drummer Jim McCarty told me in 2003.

"We saw the Stones, and then all of a sudden we heard this R&B music that we'd never really heard before. You know, we'd only heard it, really, through the Beatles or the Stones.

Fresh-faced kids, from left: Charlie Watts, Bill Wyman, Mick Jagger, Brian Jones and Keith Richards. Colorized publicity photo

"Then we formed a band through friends from school and from art school. We all combined. We actually took over from the Rolling Stones when they left their residency at the Crawdaddy. When they started having hits, they went on tour around the country, and we got their residency. So we took up where they left off."

Small Faces keyboardist Ian McLagan told me in 2013: "Someone was talking about this blues band playing a few miles from where I lived. It turned out to be the Rolling Stones. At that time, they were a blues cover band. They were great! I went to see them every Sunday. I followed them around. I helped with their gear. I talked to their agent and booked them for an art school, with my band to open. Their agent and I became good friends.

"When the Stones came back from their first American tour, they put my band on the bill. Opening for the Stones! By then, they were on the rise. They weren't a blues cover band anymore."

No, they weren't, largely thanks to Andrew Loog Oldham who, as Brian Epstein's employee, once promoted the Beatles. Oldham became the Stones' manager, crafting the band's "bad boy" image.

"Andrew wanted to make the Rolling Stones the anti-Beatles," explained Jagger in the 2012 documentary "Crossfire Hurricane."

"So if you've got heroes, you've got an anti-hero, like in a movie. You've got good guys and bad guys. It wasn't just an accident. He thought the Rolling Stones would suit that image. It's good to have an actor who'll play the part."

ROCK 'N' ROLL MUSIC, THE VERY FOUNDATION OF the Rolling Stones, began in America. A foundation of *another* kind was introduced to the band in the United States: face powder.

As Jay and the Americans singer Kenny Vance told me in 2008: "We wound up going out to California to be on 'Shindig!' and 'Hullabaloo.' They would put makeup on you. And what happened was, we kind of got used to wearing the makeup. Every time we had a show, we would put the makeup on."

Then came a 1964 gig which proved to be historic.

"(DJ) Murray the K hires us to be the opening act for the first time the Rolling Stones play at Carnegie Hall," Vance said. "So we're all up in the dressing room. It's one big room — us and the Stones. We're like these 'squares,' you know, from Brooklyn.

"I'm putting on makeup. So Mick Jagger and Brian Jones come over to me and say, you know, with an English accent, 'What is *that,* mate?' And I said, 'Oh, it's makeup.' So they took the makeup sponge and they start to put makeup on themselves!

"It was out of context, you know what I'm saying? These guys were wearing sweatshirts, and *we* were all dressed with alpaca sweaters and tight pants and doing, you know, choreography," Vance added with a laugh. "It cracks me up to think: That was the first time the Rolling Stones ever saw a guy putting on makeup."

It wasn't the *last* time Jagger wore makeup, Vance was assured.

"That's for sure," came the singer's reply.

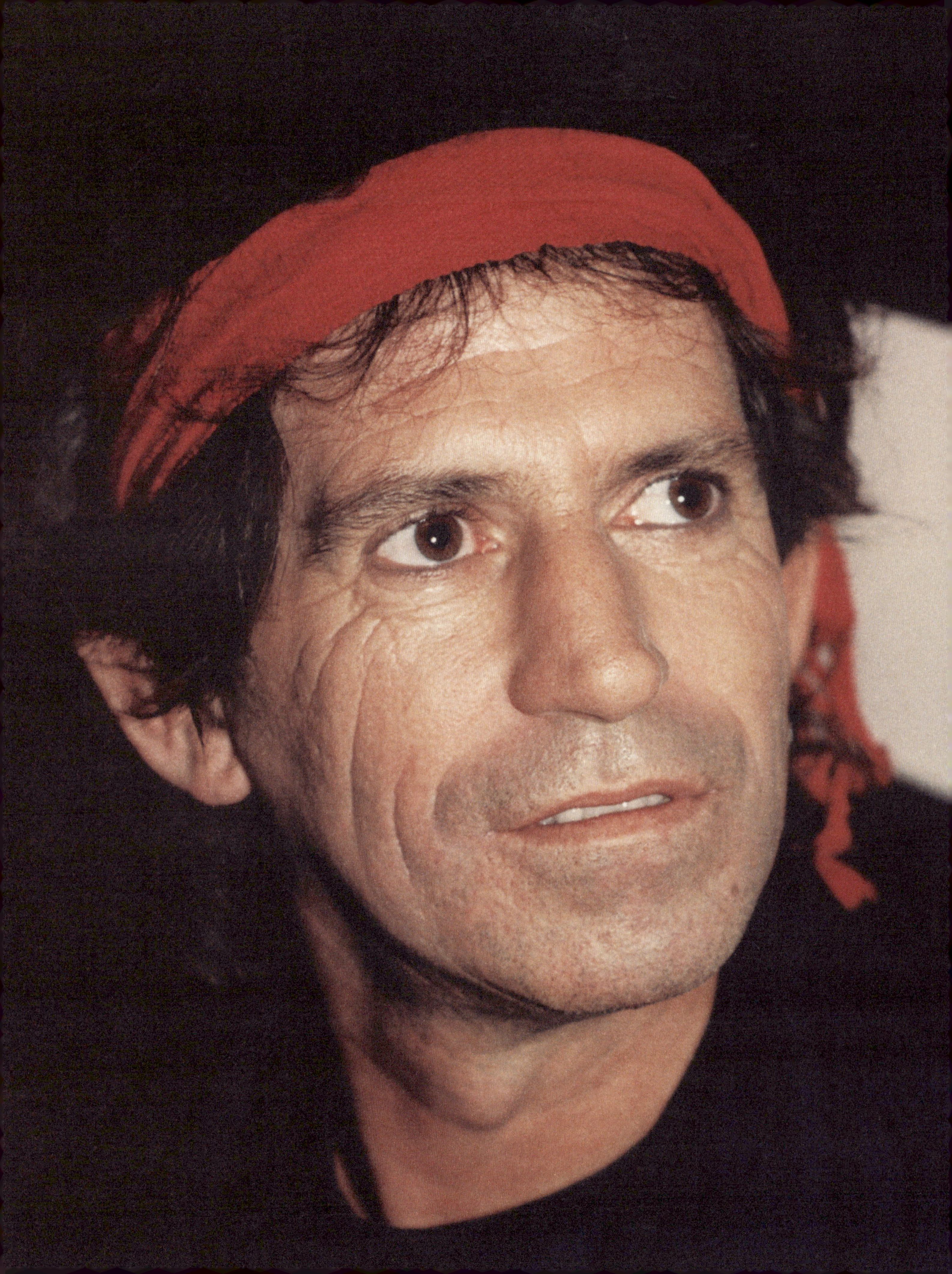

"The first time I got applause was singing 'Bewitched, Bothered and Bewildered' at the age of 4 at Christmas," said Keith Richards.

The Rolling Stones guitarist added, during an interview for the 2002 book "According to the Rolling Stones," that he grew up listening to Sarah Vaughn, Billy Eckstine, Ella Fitzgerald and Louis Armstrong. "I have no doubt that I first heard Chuck Berry, Elvis (Presley) and Little Richard on my transistor radio courtesy of Radio Luxembourg or the BBC," he said.

"The first record I bought, or nicked, was 'Good Golly Miss Molly,' but I didn't have anything to play it on."

Richards' early life was heavily affected by the events of World War II, which was common among Brits of his generation. In his 2010 memoir "Life," Richards wrote of Dartford: "It contained the biggest arm of Vickers-Armstrongs (an armament manufacturer), which was pretty much a bull's-eye, and the Burroughs Wellcome chemical firm. And on top of that, it was around Dartford where German bombers would get cold feet and just drop their bombs and turn around. … It's a miracle we didn't get it. The sound of a siren still makes the hair on the back of my neck curl."

Richards adored his maternal grandfather, Gus, whom he credited with sparking his interest in the guitar. The origin story of Keith Richards, Guitarist — and his grandfather Gus' role in it — had been told and retold by Richards over the years.

"I'll never forget the guitar on top of his upright piano every time I'd go and visit, maybe from the age of 5," Richards wrote in "Life." "I thought it was always there. And I kept looking at it. 'Hey, when you get tall enough, you can have a go at it,' he said. I didn't find out until after he was dead that he only brought that out and put it up there when he knew I was coming to visit."

Richards' mother, Doris, recalled that her father taught Richards "a few chords." She once told *Everybody's Magazine:* "Keith was always worrying for a guitar of his own. When he was 15, I bought him one for 10 pounds. From that day, it has been the most important thing in his life."

WITH CHUCK BERRY AS HIS guitar god, Richards forged a career as one of rock's greatest guitarists, songwriters, performers and, not insignificantly, personalities. Richards embodied the rebellious attitude of rock 'n' roll.

Jagger and Richards became a songwriting team at Oldham's insistence. Richards' recollection is that Oldham locked them in a kitchen with a guitar and said, "Don't come out without a song." Jagger cited "Tell Me" as their first composition; Richards intimated it was "As Tears Go By."

A 1967 incident sealed Richards' growing reputation as rock's No. 1 outlaw. A party hosted by the guitarist at Redlands — his moat-protected 15th-century house in Sussex — was raided on Dec. 12 of that year. "Nude girl at drug orgy," screamed one tabloid headline. Richards and Jagger were arrested for drug possession; jailed (albeit briefly); convicted; and ultimately released.

When, during the trial, a prosecutor asked Richards if he thought it was "quite normal" for a woman to wear only a rug at a party, the guitarist's reply was classic Keith: "We are not old men. We are not worried about petty morals."

"Keith was brilliant," Dave Davies of the Kinks told me in 1998. "He always maintained that rough-and-ready rock 'n' roll attitude that he had when he started, which is really cool.

"All great rock 'n' roll musicians have very distinctive styles. Brian Jones was a really good guitar player; his style was so totally different from Keith, but complemented it. Brian was more into the sort of mystical side of it, which is needed as well."

WHEN RICHARDS TOOK UP THE WEIGHTY TASK OF writing about his life, he knew he would have to own up concerning the Richards/Jones/Anita Pallenberg love triangle. Realizing that this was a legacy-establishing moment, Richards chose not to pull any punches in recounting Jones' bad behavior — the drugs, the professional unreliability, the violence.

In 1967, Richards had been staying with Jones and Pallenberg for a while. He wrote: "I would hear the thumping some nights, and Brian would come out with a black eye. Brian was a woman beater. But the one woman in the world you did not want to try and beat up on was Anita Pallenberg." When Jones was suddenly hospitalized for pneumonia during a road trip, Richards wrote, Pallenberg "made the first move" in his Bentley "somewhere between Barcelona and Valencia." When Jones reunited with Pallenberg and Richards in Marrakesh, they initially pretended nothing was going on. Violence broke out again between Jones and Pallenberg, with Jones suffering broken ribs. Under cloak of darkness, Richards and Pallenberg fled.

"It's said that I stole her," Richards wrote, sounding somewhat defensive. "My take on it is that I rescued her. Actually, in a way, I rescued him. Both of them. They were both on a very destructive course."

Keith Richards riffs on "The Ed Sullivan Show" in 1964. Opposite: Richards in New York City in 1988.

"Ed Sullivan Show" © CBS Television Network; 1988 photo by Kathy Voglesong

Bill Wyman

If only sidelong glances and smirks could talk

MICK JAGGER SHOOK HIS BUM. KEITH RICHARDS sucked on his cigarette. Bill Wyman smirked — as he traded sidelong glances with Charlie Watts. It was a smirk that seemed to say: *"There they go again."*

This occurred with comforting frequency during three decades of Rolling Stones concerts. In 1992, Wyman became the first original Stone to willingly walk away from the band. (This triggered verbal floggings from Jagger and Richards in the media). I spoke with the Stones' founding bassist during telephone interviews conducted in 1999, 2001 and 2005.

Q: It seemed like yours and Charlie's lives were a bit more, shall we say, "on track" than the other guys when you two joined up.

WYMAN: Oh, totally. When I joined the band in early December 1962 — the 8th, I think it was — my son was 8 months old. I'd been married since 1959. I had responsibilities at home. I had a steady job. I couldn't piddle about in some band that wasn't going to make any money, really. When I joined those guys, Charlie was still at work. He was still quite smart. (Pianist) Ian Stewart was still at work. We were the three. And the *other* three weren't. Brian and Keith were practically a couple of what we would term "beatniks" in those days. They didn't do any work. They stayed in bed all day. They *smelled.* It was disgusting, actually.

Q: Sounds precarious. Why did you, a family man, take the risk?

WYMAN: You know, I really liked the music when I first played it. And they received me quite warmly — after the first evening, anyway, when Brian and Keith hardly spoke to me. But Mick did, and Ian Stewart. They made me feel at home. They liked my equipment. And then it just all fell into place after a week, and I was playin' the way they wanted. They fired their drummer and got Charlie. That was it. As soon as Charlie came in the band, we had a solid foundation to build with. We never looked back.

Q: You had an especially close relationship with Brian Jones.

WYMAN: I used to hang out with Brian for most of the '60s, you know, after Mick and Keith and (manager) Andrew Oldham kind of didn't. It was mostly me and Brian that hung out. We shared rooms in the hotels right through the mid and late '60s. I probably saw more of him, then, than any of the others.

Q: What do you say to fans who think Brian Jones was "just" an original member, that he was a druggie, a disposable commodity?

WYMAN: I want to put the record straight, because amongst many, many Stones fans, they don't even know what Brian Jones *did.* They know his name and they know he'd been in the band once. As far as Brian was concerned, he was the most intelligent person that was ever in the Stones. He was the most articulate speaking. He had the most variety of musical instruments he could get something out of or perform on. He was very creative. He was a wonderful person and a real s*** at the same time.

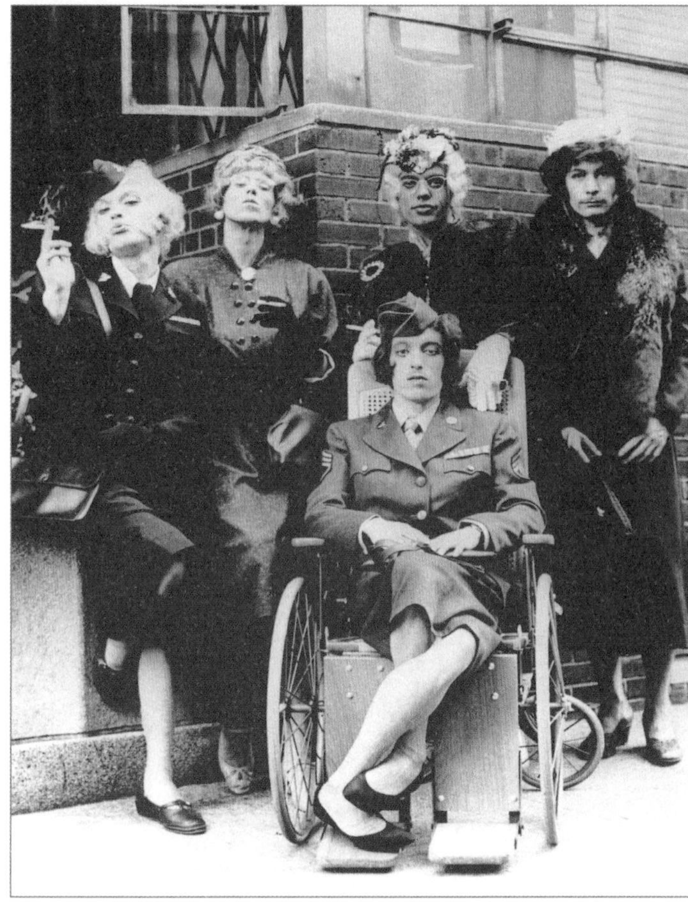

Wyman (in wheelchair) and his fellow Stones wore drag to sell records. At least, that was their claim. © Decca Records

He could switch from one to the other. So you couldn't love him forever, but you always forgave him, because he had such a sweet nature on one side. And then he'd do the *dirty* on you. He'd say, "I'm sorry, man, I didn't mean it." You'd say, "Aw, OK, Brian, just don't do it again." And you'd forget all about it.

Q: And, not for nothin', the Stones was originally Brian's band.

WYMAN: Brian invented the name. It was Brian's idea that we play that kind of music. It was all Brian! When the band started out, for the first two years, Brian was the most popular member. Brian got all the fan mail. All the girls went after Brian. They didn't *look* at Mick. It's only when you get into late '64, '65 — the time when we started to go to America and all that — when Mick started to become more prominent.

Andrew Oldham took Brian out of the running, to be honest. Prevented him from doing interviews and that. So he killed Brian off, really, in the media. And then, of course, Mick became more and more and more prominent. Turned out to be, probably, the greatest live entertainer who's ever been, which is fantastic. And Keith, probably one of the best rhythm guitarists who's ever been.

Q: "Out of Our Heads" (1965) was a pivotal album, with originals that marked a maturing sound — "Satisfaction," "Play With Fire," "I'm Free," "The Last Time." What do you recall of making it?

WYMAN: It was in RCA Studios, Hollywood, wasn't it? Keith and Mick had started to write a few reasonable songs. I mean, they'd been trying to write for a few years under Andrew Oldham's commands, I should say (laughs). They started to come up with some pretty good songs by then, so we started to do them, like "Heart of Stone" and things. We were also discovering some more soulful singers, as opposed to blues artists — Otis Redding, people like that. We did it at RCA in four-track. Of course, Brian at that time was experimenting with all kinds of instruments. I was doing a little bit as well, in that way. I tried out a six-string bass on a few numbers, I remember. But we were trying different things with all kinds of sounds. It was a lot of fun.

Q: Did you do some gallivanting while in Los Angeles? This was 1965 — still very much "early days" for you boys.

WYMAN: It was almost like going on holiday, you know, from England. You went out into the sunshine! There were lots of pretty girls around. There were great places to go. You'd meet people like the Everly Brothers and Phil Spector and Jack Nitzsche, those kind of people. You got to go to sessions for them — Gold Star Studios (in Los Angeles), it was called — and meet the people that were singin' for Spector, the girls and all that.

You'd go into RCA with the sun shinin', and then come out, and the sun was *still* shinin' sometimes, because it was morning (laughs). But it was really pleasurable to do it that way. When we worked in England, you know, it was always "in between." It was usually in the afternoon that we would record, between doin' a photo shoot in the morning and gettin' in a van to go and do some gigs in the evening. We used to do three-hour sessions in the afternoon. And just to have, like, two or three *weeks* over there, just enjoyin' it in a really nice hotel — I think it came out in the music like that. They were fun times.

Q: Does your costume on the "Have You Seen Your Mother" sleeve— a military lady in a wheelchair — have a backstory? It's like "Monty Python" before there *was* a "Monty Python."

WYMAN: Exactly (laughs). A few of my aunts — my dad's sisters, actually — were members of the Women's Auxiliary Air Force. I used to stay with the family there, so I did see them backwards and forwards in their uniforms. I thought I'd do that (twisting) with me legs, just for a laugh.

Bill Wyman and smoke in 2000.

Why the jazzy, swing feel to Charlie Watts' drumming? He grew up listening to Billy Eckstine and Frank Sinatra — his dad's favorites.

Eckstine was, in fact, the first performer Watts saw play live.

"We bought him his first drum set for Christmas when he was 14," Watts' mother, Lillian, once told *Everybody's Magazine*.

"It cost 12 pounds. He took to it straight away, and often used to play jazz records and join in on his drums. The neighbors were very good. They never complained."

Watts started off in bands that played skiffle, Dixieland and, of course, jazz. He had been drumming for Alexis Korner's Blues Incorporated prior to joining the Rolling Stones in 1963.

Watts was aloof regarding pop stardom. In interviews, he batted away most Stones questions, but loved to talk about drumming and especially his heroes in jazz such as Thelonious Monk, Jelly Roll Morton, Art Blakey, Miles Davis and Charlie Parker.

While he was an art student, Watts wrote and illustrated a 36-page book as a portfolio piece, "Ode to a High Flying Bird," inscribed as "My tribute to Charlie 'Yardbird' Parker." (The book was published by Beat Publications in 1965.) Watts once said that when the Stones arrived in New York City in 1964, his first thought was to make a pilgrimage to the jazz mecca Birdland.

Watts' allegiance to the old masters informed his drumming on Stones songs. He just might have been the best snare man in rock.

He was also a snappy dresser. "Charlie Watts would spend day after day in Savile Row with his tailors, just feeling the quality, deciding which buttons to use," Keith Richards wrote of the drummer in his memoir, "Life." Watts cut his hair short in the middle 1970s, a fashion choice then unheard of for a rock drummer.

Richards' memoir also contains an anecdote that encapsulates Watts' quiet demeanor. In 1984 in Amsterdam, Jagger (who'd had a few beverages) phoned Watts' hotel room at 5 a.m., woke Watts from his sleep, and bellowed, *"Where's my drummer?"*

Watts hung up ... got dressed ... knocked on Jagger's hotel room door ... entered ... told Jagger, "Never call me your drummer again" ... punched Jagger ... and departed without another word. Richards noted that Watts had taken the trouble to apply cologne.

Charlie Watts at the kit on "The Ed Sullivan Show."

SITAR ON "PAINT IT BLACK" ... THEREMIN ON "2000 Light Years From Home" ... dulcimer on "Lady Jane" ... accordion on "Ruby Tuesday" ... slide on "No Expectations" ...

Brian Jones is called a founding guitarist of the Stones, but the fact is that he was a multi-instrumentalist who played harmonica, dulcimer, Mellotron, flute, cello, maracas, organ and tanpura.

"Brian Jones, actually, was the kind of guy you could give any instrument to, and leave him alone for about a half an hour, and he'd have something, he'd be playing something on it," Dave Mason told me in 2004. "Brian was an extremely talented guy."

He was also a musicologist on a constant hunt for new sounds.

"I went out with Brian Jones," Spencer Davis told me in 2006. "I did like his record collection. Whenever the Stones came back, he'd always have something new. He came back with an Otis Redding LP, 'Otis Blue' (1966), which I was just in love with. In fact, I may *have* that record. He might have given it to me."

"Brian had something special," Wyman told me. "I think it was sorely missed for a few years after he'd gone, even though he kind of deteriorated in a bad way, musically. Up 'til the end of '66, early '67, he was playing some wonderful stuff."

But from 1967 on, Jones' life became a series of drug busts, hospitalizations and absenteeism from his Rolling Stones duties.

Artist Brion Gysin wrote: "He was the kind of man who would take anything you gave him. Offer him a handful of pills, uppers and downers, acid, whatever, and he'd just swallow them all."

Jones' former girlfriend Anita Pallenberg told author David Dalton: "He was a total burnout before the busts. He took acid."

Pallenberg added that Jones also took STP, amphetamines, Desbutals and Dexedrine, though never heroin.

"Acid made Brian feel like one of the elite," wrote Richards. "He really loved taking too many downers, Seconals, Tuinals, Desbutals, the whole range." (Richards also cited Quaalude use.)

"Keith and I did drugs, but Brian took too many drugs of the wrong kind, and he wasn't functioning as a musician," Jagger said in the documentary "Crossfire Hurricane" (2012). "I don't think he was that interested in contributing to the Rolling Stones any more. He wasn't turning up to the sessions, and he wasn't very well. In fact, *we* didn't want him to turn up, I don't think."

Said Watts in the same film: "Brian's role, when we first started the band — or when *he* first started the band — had been very much as the leader. But he didn't have the capacity to go further than that, or the band went in a direction he couldn't cope with."

"My ultimate aim in life was never to be a pop star," Jones once told a TV interviewer. "I enjoy it with reservations. But I'm not really sort of satisfied either artistically or personally.

"Let's face it," he added with a sad smile, "the future as a Rolling Stone is very uncertain."

Brian Jones started a band called the Rolling Stones.

It began as a modest blues band playing local clubs, and rose to the top of the entertainment world. Seven years later, his fellow Stones (and good friends) Mick Jagger, Keith Richards and Charlie Watts drove to Jones' Sussex home, Cotchford Farm — which was once owned by "Winnie the Pooh" author A.A. Milne — to fire their bandmate.

All agreed that Jones seemed to know it was coming, and quietly acquiesced. Watts recalled that Jones spoke of starting a band with drummer Mitch Mitchell.

Within three weeks, Jones was gone.

His date of death at 27 is generally given as July 3, 1969, but — in Jonesian fashion — that's not a certainty. Prior to midnight on July 2, Jones was swimming in his pool; shortly *after* midnight on July 3, he was pulled from the bottom of the pool by his girlfriend, Anna Wohlin, who applied artificial respiration as Frank Thorogood, a builder who was making repairs to Jones' home, and Jenny Lawson, a nurse, called an ambulance.

By the time help arrived, Jones had died in what was ruled "death by misadventure." And, boy, was that the case.

The guitarist's funeral was held in his hometown of Cheltenham on July 10. Watts and Stones bassist Bill Wyman attended the service, but not Jagger or Richards. "It was going to be too much of a circus," Richards said in "Crossfire Hurricane." "Hyde Park (a 1969 concert dedicated to Jones) was the funeral. And the bit about the burying and shovels and all of that, it's not that important to me."

The tragedy was summarized in a famous quote by Who guitarist Pete Townshend: "Oh, it's a normal day for Brian. Like, he died every day."

The theory that Jones' death was caused by Thorogood was put forth by Wohlin, and by the authors of two books about the tragedy published in 1994.

"I knew all along he did not die a natural death," Wohlin told *The Mirror* in 2013. "I'm still sure of it."

Brian Jones looks smart in an early TV appearance. Overleaf: The five original Stones backstage in Asbury Park, NJ, in 1966. Author's personal collection

The Dave Clark Five

THERE ARE ANY NUMBER OF POP STARS WHO used their work in music to break into the movies. You *could* say the namesake of the Dave Clark Five did it the other way around.

Prior to pop fame, Clark worked as an extra and stuntman in 40-plus films, such as "The V.I.P.s" (1963), "I Could Go On Singing" (1963), "A Shot in the Dark" (1964) and "Beckett" (1964). "If you sneezed, you'd miss me," he once joked of the period.

"(It's) the equivalent of being a tea boy in a television studio," Clark told a TV interviewer about being an extra. "I was interested in film, and it gave me a chance to see great directors at work."

He eventually landed a job crashing a car in a movie. ("It wasn't heroic. You're strapped in with roll-bars and things. It was very choreographed.") With the 300 pounds he was paid, he funded the Dave Clark Five's first recording, which he sold to EMI.

The earliest incarnation of the group formed in Tottenham in 1958. The DC5 placed 17 Top 40 hits between 1964 and '67, including "Glad All Over" (#6), "Bits and Pieces" (#4), "Because" (#3), "I Like It Like That" (#7) and "Catch Us If You Can" (#4).

Listeners sometimes mistook DC5 songs for those of the Beatles. To combat this, the DC5's music was promoted as the "Tottenham sound," so as not to be confused with the "Merseyside sound." Pop magazines sometimes fanned the flames of a (totally fictitious) rivalry between the two bands. A place called Tottenham Royal was the DC5's equivalent of the Cavern Club.

BEST-KNOWN LINEUP: Singer-keyboardist Mike Smith (1943-2008, born in Edmonton); guitarist Lenny Davidson (born 1942 in Enfield); saxophonist Denis Payton (1943-2006, born in Walthamstow); bassist Rick Huxley (1940-2013, born in Dartford); drummer Clark (born 1939 in Tottenham)

The DC5 performed on "The Ed Sullivan Show" 18 times, more than any other Invasion act. Likely as a nod to Clark's movie past, the boys played themselves as stuntmen in the film "Having a Wild Weekend" (1965). In Lucille Ball's 1966 special "Lucy in London," the DC5 wore top hats and white gloves as they sang "London Bridge" while strolling along ... *guess where?*

"I firmly believe that without American music, there would not have *been* a 1960s British Invasion," said Clark during the band's Rock and Roll Hall of Fame induction in 2008, when they were introduced by actor (and DC5 fan) Tom Hanks. "We were inspired and influenced by Elvis Presley, Little Richard, Jerry Lee Lewis, Fats Domino, Sam Cooke, Ray Charles, to name but a few. What an amazing array of talent to get one's creative juices flowing."

From left: Mike Smith, Lenny Davidson, Denis Payton, Rick Huxley and Dave Clark.

From left: Gerry Marsden, Freddie Marsden, Les Chadwick and Les Maguire.
© Columbia Records

Gerry and the Pacemakers

SOME SMILES ARE CONVINCING BUT INSINCERE. How can we tell? We *can't,* really, but there was always something about Gerry Marsden's goofy grin that warmed the cockles.

Two instances from his extracurricular life may indicate that Marsden's smile was genuine. He won awards for advocating on behalf of his beloved Liverpool, including being made an MBE for raising funds and awareness (enlisting fellow Liverpool guy Paul McCartney) in the aftermath of the 1989 Hillsborough disaster which claimed 97 lives. And, to make children laugh, Marsden took many pies in the face on British TV's "The Sooty Show."

Marsden's group, Gerry and the Pacemakers, had much in common with the Beatles. Both bands hailed from Liverpool; both were Cavern Club fixtures; both were recorded by George Martin; and both were managed by Brian Epstein. In fact, the Pacemakers were the second band Epstein signed after ... do I *need* to say who?

The Pacemakers formed in 1959, and put out seven Top 40 hits in America between 1964 and '66, including the dreamy "Don't Let the Sun Catch You Crying" (#4), the bouncy "How Do You Do It?" (#9), and the achingly beautiful, Marsden-penned Liverpudlian anthem "Ferry Cross the Mersey" (#6).

In the wake of "A Hard Day's Night," the Pacemakers were starred in a movie, also titled "Ferry Cross the Mersey" (1964). When Epstein told Marsden he was planning a Pacemakers movie, Marsden replied: "Don't be daft." The singer was out on a dinner date when the melody for the title song popped into his head. He called his mother and asked her to hold his tape recorder up to the phone while he sang the tune. (The dinner date was cut short.)

BEST-KNOWN LINEUP: Singer-guitarist Gerry Marsden (1942-2021); pianist Les Maguire (born 1941); bassist Les Chadwick (1943-2019); drummer Freddie Marsden (1940-2006). All were born in Liverpool except Maguire, who was born in Wallasey.

The movie lays out the band's backstory. In flashback, scruffy children in hand-me-downs play happily in dreary streets, while in voiceover, Marsden calls Liverpool "one of the toughest places in England. When we were kids, we had to make our own entertainment. We'd play anywhere — any open space or wasteland." Marsden recounts the humble early days of the band: "Fred used to play an old biscuit tin with the top cut out."

SOMETHING VERY COOL HAPPENED FOR MARSDEN in the years following his Pacemakers fame. In 1983, Frankie Goes to Hollywood covered "Ferry Cross the Mersey" — singer Holly Johnson was a Liverpool boy, too — as the B-side of the group's racy song "Relax." Despite being banned by the BBC, "Relax" was a hit, and charted for 10 weeks in the U.S., rising to #10.

In 1986 in *Rolling Stone,* David Fricke reported that "Relax" was "to date, the biggest-selling single in British pop history."

Marsden told Fricke he first learned of FGTH's cover of "Ferry Cross the Mersey" after his daughter Yvette, then 19, heard it in a dance club. Fricke wrote that, though Marsden was unsure of how much moolah he pocketed from FGTH's cover, he was then collecting about $250,000 a year in royalties. "I won't let anyone say a bad word about Frankie," Marsden told Fricke.

The Who

From a working-class area called Shepherd's Bush emerged a band that became one of rock's most enduring and influential.

As musicians, each member of the Who was unique and inimitable: singer Roger Daltrey (born 1944), guitarist Pete Townshend (born 1945), bassist John Entwistle (1944-2002) and drummer Keith Moon (1946-1978), all London boys. When performing live, Townshend, Entwistle and Moon would go off on individual flights of fancy, but they were always playing the same song.

In the late 1950s, Daltrey, Townshend and Entwistle were each attending Acton County Grammar School, a boys' school.

"I suppose our town was not very dissimilar to, like, the Bronx," Daltrey said of Shepherd's Bush when we spoke in 1998. "We were not financially wealthy, but we were incredibly rich."

Like many British musicians of his generation, Townshend came from a musical family. His dad, Clifford, recorded as "Cliff Townsend (alternate spelling intended) and His Singing Saxophone."

Daltrey formed a skiffle group, the Detours, with a guitar he made in a sheet metal factory at which he worked.

"I started making my own guitar when I was 11 to 12 years old," Daltrey said. "By the time I was 12, 13 years old, we were playing what was the equivalent of your early American folk songs, which were brought to us by a guy called Lonnie Donegan."

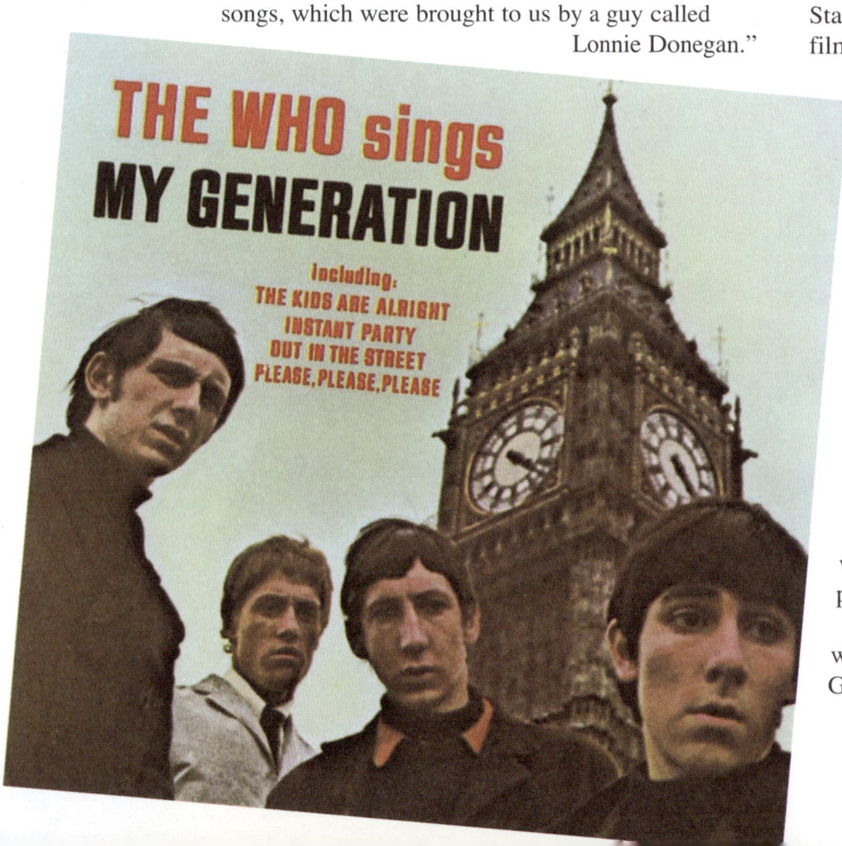

BY 1962, TOWNSHEND AND ENTWISTLE WERE ALSO in the Detours. Daltrey recalled that the band was playing the Oldfield Hotel in Greenford when they were approached by Moon, who was wearing orange hair due to a peroxide mishap. (He was a huge Beach Boys fan.) Moon told Daltrey: "I hear you're looking for a drummer, and I'm much better than the one you've got."

"The first time I met Keith," Entwistle told me in 1999, "he was like a little gingerbread man. He had ginger hair on a brown suit, a brown shirt with brown shoes and one of those fake orange tans."

Moon joined the Detours in April 1964. The clownish "Moonie" completed the equation. His thrashing, unpredictable drumming was the perfect complement to Entwistle's virtuosity, Townshend's power chords, and Daltrey's macho front-man style.

"He *did* kind of blow us away," Entwistle said.

"Actually, the first gig that we did (with Moon) was someone's wedding, believe it or not. That was the first time he blew us away. Because he actually tied his drums to this pillar on the side of the stage, so he wouldn't fall over when he played the solo! And the drums were, like, *heaving* out, sort of, at about 45 degrees, held together by this big reel of rope."

MEANWHILE, TWO ASPIRING FILMMAKERS, CHRIS Stamp and Kit Lambert, were on the lookout for a band to make a film about. By then, the Detours had renamed themselves the High Numbers, and were identifying as a "mod" band. In those days, English youths often identified as being either a "mod" (fashion conscious) or a "rocker" (street tough).

Stamp and Lambert caught a High Numbers show and decided to manage the group. The band underwent another name change — "the Who" beat out "the Hair," thankfully — just as England's music scene was blowing up in 1963.

The Who stumbled onto a publicity hook in 1964, when Townshend smashed his guitar during a gig at the Railway Hotel Harrow & Wealdstone, in Harrow. (As an art student, Townshend saw a presentation by artist Gustav Metzger, founder of the "auto-destructive" art movement. Townshend interpolated Metzger's concept into his guitar-smashing bit.) This became a calling card for the Who. Another Townshend trademark: his "windmill"-style guitar strumming technique.

"We were one of a million bands," Daltrey said. "How do we get noticed? It was just one of those lucky things that happened. A lucky break, to coin a phrase, which got us noticed."

The band's debut single, "I Can't Explain" (#8 in the U.K.), was helped immensely by the English TV show "Ready Steady Go!" but failed to crack the Top 40 in the United States.

There was only one Who. From left: Keith Moon, Pete Townshend, Roger Daltrey and John Entwistle. Colorized publicity photo

TOWNSHEND ADMITTED THAT "I CAN'T EXPLAIN" was inspired by the Kinks' "You Really Got Me" in its use of power chords. This was no surprise to Kinks guitarist Dave Davies.

"The Who played with us," Davies told me in 1998.

"They opened for us a few times. That was back when they were known as the High Numbers. Because they sort of hit it big a bit later — a year or two later — than we did. So they came on our heels, as it were. They were big Kinks fans. You could tell they were watching everything that we did."

Later in 1965, the Who recorded its debut album, "My Generation" (released in America the following year as "The Who Sings My Generation"). The band's mastery of their instruments was evident from the first, in this collection of 12 pop-rock gems. Look no further than Entwistle's iconic bass solo on the title track.

"We did the album in two afternoons, I think it was," Daltrey recalled. "It would have been about eight hours of recording.

"It was all virtually live, really. But in my opinion, for what it's worth, any album that goes on longer than six weeks is probably going to end up a disaster," Daltrey added with a laugh. "Where *we* were concerned, that's certainly been the truth."

Still, it took until 1967 for the Who to finally pierce the Top 40 in America — even *if* "hits" were not what this band was about. Between 1967 and '69, the boys charted with "Happy Jack" (#24), "I Can See for Miles" (#9), "Call Me Lightning" (#40), "Magic Bus" (#25), "Pinball Wizard" (#19) and "I'm Free" (#37).

1967 proved to be a time warp-y year for the Who.

In June, the band played a blistering set at the Monterey Pop Festival, which ended with Townshend sacrificing a Stratocaster, naturally. (Next up was Jimi Hendrix, who set *his* Strat on fire in what the Who perceived as an act of artistic infringement.) The following month, the Who embarked on an America tour as the opening act for ... *Herman's Hermits?*

"I just try and give out what I would like to be given back," said Roger Daltrey, shown in 2000.

Photo by Kathy Voglesong

Roger Daltrey

Primal screamer

Daltrey rocks "Shindig!" in 1965. © American Broadcasting Company

HE GAVE VOICE TO THE FRUSTRATIONS OF A generation as the singer of, well, "My Generation." As frontman of the Who, Roger Daltrey remained a moving target, twirling his microphone with athletic accuracy amid the mayhem that was a Who show. We spoke during two interviews conducted in 1998.

Q: On a typical day when you were a teenager prior to the bands, what did you do for kicks? What was Shepherd's Bush like?

DALTREY: We had very close family and social ties. It was a very good sense of community in those days. It was before they stuck everybody in high-rises, and split the communities up. From then on — from the age of 13 on — I was a member of a thing we have in England called the Boys Brigade, which is similar to your (Boy) Scouts. But it wasn't so much on the camping thing. It was more to do with, like, the gymnasium and things like that. Just activities where you get together in groups of people. I was into music then. That's where I used to take my guitar with other kids who had guitars. That's where we started playing.

Q: When the Who formed, you were being promoted as "the" mod band. Were you guys really mods, or did (then-managers Chris Stamp and Kit Lambert) push you into it?

DALTREY: We were pushed into it. Our eyes had to be opened to the potential, but once we got into it — I mean, we were more rockers than mods. We were, you know, rockers in mods' clothing. But we *became* mods, yeah. We certainly did.

Q: "Ready Steady Go!" helped to break the Who. We Yanks don't realize how much influence the show had on the music scene in England. Do you agree that "Ready Steady Go!" was a cultural force on behalf of musicians as well as fans?

DALTREY: That's right. First of all, you were playing *live*. It wasn't just miming and people dancing. It wasn't just bands in the charts; it was bands coming up from all over England. It was just a totally free format. That was the difference of "Ready Steady Go!" Obviously, you had a certain amount of regimentation, but compared with the American shows, it was incredibly free.

Q: The Who pioneered the rock-opera form with "Tommy." Did you feel you were playing a role instead of just singing songs? Were you acting in the studio when you recorded "Tommy"?

DALTREY: I was always the part in my head. I think that's where great actors exist. You can either do it or you can't. I think acting is something we all can do. It's whether we've got the ability to just let go of what we are and become someone else. Truly let go. And the problem with rock 'n' roll is that it demands such strong images. It demands a strong image of the performer.

Acting is exactly the opposite. It demands an image that you can completely let go of, so people can believe you are somebody else. It wasn't so much what I was seeing as what I was *feeling*. I felt the pain of Tommy. I felt the isolation. That's what I tried to express in the songs. I tried to put myself, in my mind, in exactly that situation. It was traumatic. Those years were traumatic for me. Because some of the part always rubs off while you're doing it.

Q: "Live at Leeds," which documents a 1970 concert, is one of the great Who albums. What can you tell me about Leeds, the venue? It sounds like, I dunno, Woodstock. What did it look like?

DALTREY: (Laughs) I hate to disappoint you. It was, like, a high school gymnasium — or, should I say, one *down* from a high school gymnasium. It was like an English campus facility or an assembly hall. Difficult to describe. You couldn't call it a theater. But if you notice, in a lot of those songs, I'm singing with my eyes shut. I'm just in another world. It's the kind of performer I was.

Q: Have you ever whacked yourself with a microphone while you were twirling it? When you throw the mic in the air, what are the odds you'll catch it — say, nine times out of 10?

DALTREY: Um, I've only ever hit anybody once, and that was intentionally. That was somebody who threw something at me, so I threw something back.

Q: You were said to be handy with your fists as a lad. You've admitted this yourself. Have you mellowed since those days?

DALTREY: Well, I dunno. I think so. I mean, sometimes I don't like myself very much. I just try and give out what I would like to be given back. Really, it's as simple as that.

John Entwistle

Best. Bassist. Ever.

JUDGING BY SONGS LIKE "BORIS THE SPIDER," "Cousin Kevin," "Fiddle About" and "Ted End," one might get the impression that their composer is a rather dark character.

"Ah, he's a miserable bastard, John Entwistle," came the reply of, yep, John Entwistle, founding bassist of the Who. Entwistle was not only the Best Bassist Ever — everyone's entitled to their opinion, except on this question — he wrote some *bleak* songs.

"It was kind of a direction to go in," Entwistle told me.

(His musings are from interviews conducted by my brother, Brian Voger, in 1996, and by me in 1998, 1999 and 2002.)

"I always wore black clothes, and I was supposed to be, like, the strong, silent bass player. When I was writing songs, I started off writing for a children's album — like, sort of horror stories, horror songs for children. Things like 'Boris the Spider,' 'Silas Stingy' and all that kind of stuff was directed at little kids."

As for his close association with his song "Boris the Spider": "I've encouraged the spider thing. I've got a pet tarantula at home."

"MY ORIGINAL INSTRUMENT WAS PIANO WHEN I was 6," Entwistle recalled. "Then trumpet and French horn when I was 11. I taught myself to play the bass when I was 14."

His background in brass figured in much Who music, especially the band's 1969 rock opera "Tommy," which Entwistle called an "extremely heavy albatross" (and to which he contributed two compositions). Not only did he arrange and play all of the horns on "Tommy," Entwistle stressed, but he did "all the arranging and all the playing on everything the Who released" on brass.

"Pete and myself, we did synthesizer and brass at the same time," he said. "People don't realize I played most of the horns on 'Tommy' with a tooth missing. I'd just come from the dentist, and the manager said we've gotta do this. So I played most of the horn parts with my tongue stuck in the cavity, to stop the air escaping."

But bass guitar was where his bread was buttered. Entwistle was well aware he made many media outlets' "best bassist" lists.

"It used to be (Paul) McCartney, Jack Bruce and me," he said.

"When you read the magazine polls, it's always Jaco Pastorius (who died at age 35 in 1987). The problem for the musicians who survive is that the ones who *died* are always the best ever."

Were there any bassists who influenced Entwistle? "Nobody really did," he said, while adding, "I admire McCartney for his ability to put a bass part together that you can sing with.

"The closest influence I have is (early rock 'n' roll guitarist) Duane Eddy — without the tremolo, of course. I actually got to meet Duane Eddy, and he came down to my house in the country for the weekend. I loved his first album ('Have Twangy Guitar, Will Travel,' 1958). I think his first album really influenced me.

"It was strange; I guess I'd mentioned Duane Eddy in interviews. He'd been following my career for years, all those years before we met. We got on really well, and everyone kept saying, 'Is this your big brother?' Same color hair."

John Entwistle on "The Smothers Brothers Comedy Hour" in 1967. Opposite: Entwistle and instrument in 1999.

Playing bass on the 1968 song "Magic Bus" was no challenge. "It's kind of boring," he said of the song written by Townshend. "Um, the key of A, basically. The riff is in A through 'til the end, and it gets a bit monotonous for the bass player. Pete swears that during the live recording of it, I actually fell asleep at one point."

THE WHO HAVE A REPUTATION AS A VOLATILE outfit, which is not surprising, considering the volatility of the group's sound. In 1996, Entwistle was asked if the old stories are true, that the Who sometimes physically fought with one another.

"Yeah," the bassist said. "We didn't throw *that* many punches. There were definitely arguments and room-trashings, because people got frustrated with each other." He then added that a Who reunion was "120 percent" out of the question. (Of course, the bassist participated in many Who reunions after that statement.)

Entwistle once told me of his relationship with Townshend: "Basically, Roger Daltrey is the only man in the world who can tell me to turn my bass down. So we (Entwistle and Townshend) have, like, a guarded sort of respect for each other." I later saw Entwistle tell radio co-hosts Keith Roth and Aimee Kristi on the air: "You don't talk to Pete Townshend. You *listen* to him."

If it's any consolation, I can offer a snapshot of Entwistle's view of inter-Who relations in his final days. The following — from an interview conducted six days prior to Entwistle's June 27, 2002 death at 57 — may fall short of "Kumbaya," but it ain't bad.

"Oh, we get along fine. Well, we get on *better* when we're playing in front of an audience," he said with a laugh. "You know, we've been friends for a long time now. Forty years. It's terrifying. So we kind of know each other pretty well. We know each others' sore points and how to make each other happy, I guess."

Pete Townshend does his trademark "windmill" guitar strum on television in 1968, and onstage with the Who in 2000.

"The Rolling Stones Rock and Roll Circus" © ABKCO Films; 2000 photo by Kathy Voglesong

THE CAREER OF THE WHO WOULD TAKE ANOTHER surprising turn. Like the Beatles, the Who made the transition from mere pop stars to creators of significant music. Witness the rock operas "Tommy" (1969) and "Quadrophenia" (1973), and the group's anthem-heavy masterpiece "Who's Next" (1971).

Townshend channeled his tortured childhood into the Who's double-album "Tommy," which relates the tale of a "deaf, dumb and blind boy" with "crazy flipper fingers" who becomes a "pinball wizard." Having "played" the title role while recording "Tommy," Daltrey starred in Ken Russell's 1975 film version.

Prior to writing "Tommy," Townshend gave a lengthy interview about his early concept to *Rolling Stone,* which the magazine published virtually unexpurgated. Townshend and his interviewer, Jann Wenner, later agreed that the guitarist was largely talking off the top of his head, which helped solidify many of his ideas.

STORIES ABOUT "MOON THE LOON" ARE LEGION.

"Just before the (Herman's Hermits) tour, we told Keith off because he was playing slow," Entwistle said. "He adopted the assumption that we were gonna throw him out of the band. He was on the end of a pier — Ann Arbor or someplace like that. He was leaning. There was a thick rail around the outside of the pier with a drop of about 30 feet into raging waves.

"He said, 'OK, I'm leaving the group!' and just rolled over and plunged 30 feet into the water. None of us were real strong swimmers, so this big, strapping roadie dove in and struggled after Keith.

"Keith just rode in on the tide. When the roadie finally crawled onto the shore, Keith was sitting cross-legged on the shore."

Peter Noone told me in 2002: "In Asbury Park (New Jersey), me and Keith Moon swam back from the end of the pier. We ended up walking around Asbury Park in our underwear, which was pretty cool. We nearly lost Moon that night. I mean, he tried to kill himself millions of times. *That* night, he got trapped under the pier with the tide comin' in. You know, it was kind of fun."

So Noone and Moon walked around Asbury in their drawers?

"We went to the hotel," Noone explained. "We were all staying at the hotel, which was near the pier. It was one of those things where you go up to the desk, and they ask to see your I.D., and, you know, you're standing there in your underwear. 'Yeah, yeah, right.' 'We're musicians. We're *English.'* 'Oh, all right, then.'"

But Noone said the legendary story of Moon driving a car into a swimming pool during his raucous birthday party in 1967 — resulting in Moon losing a front tooth and the Who being banned from the Holiday Inn hotel chain for life — is just that: legendary.

"Like everything, the story's much better than the reality," Noone said with a laugh. "The older I get, the better it is.

"What happened was, about 20 minutes into the party, Moon fell down, and my 'minder' grabbed him by his underpants. Moon hit his teeth on the table, and was taken in a helicopter to get his teeth fixed overnight, so he could do the show the next day. 'Who can fix it?' So we rented a helicopter. I mean, the Who were great, because they had no money, but they always paid their share."

"We lost our clown," said Roger Daltrey of the death of Keith Moon.

On Sept. 2, 1978 — hours after partying heavily at an event thrown by Paul McCartney — Moon died at 32 of an overdose of medication meant to curb symptoms of alcohol withdrawal.

As it happened, the Who had just released their first studio album in three years — the band's longest period between studio albums up to that point. "Who Are You" came out on Aug. 18, just 15 days prior to Moon's death. (On the album's cover photo, the drummer is shown sitting in a director's-style chair on which is stenciled: "NOT TO BE TAKEN AWAY.")

Though the drummer was heavier and sometimes struggled while recording the album — his bandmates have been candid about this — the old Moon fire can be heard in such songs as "Had Enough," "Sister Disco," "Trick of the Light" and the title track. Moon's passing changed the Who forever.

"Of *course* it was never the same," Daltrey told me.

"We knew that. Mainly because of the way John and Pete play. They're individual players. What people didn't realize was, the style of Moon's drumming — his drumsticks were, for want of a better analogy, like 'knitting needles.' The percussive things he used to play knitted John's very busy bass parts and Pete's very rhythmic kind of guitar playing together.

"We lost our clown. We lost that part of it. And we lost the danger that Moon brought to it."

There has been nothing, before or since, like the rhythm section that was John Entwistle and Keith Moon.

"Well, it was completely off the wall," Entwistle told Brian Voger. "I mean, neither of us knew what the hell we were doing half the time, but sometimes it worked. I guess part of it was trying to outdo each other. Over the years, we kind of learned — we had an idea of what we were going to do next, and we just flowed with it. And it worked."

The many moods of Keith Moon, from the Who's appearance on TV's "Shindig!" in 1965.

The Kinks

You really got them! The Kinks, from left: Ray Davies, Dave Davies, Mick Avory and Pete Quaife. Colorized publicity photo

Long before the Gallagher brothers of Oasis fought over their first toy, there were the Davies brothers: singer Ray and guitarist Dave.

As founders of the Kinks, Ray and Dave forged one of the most tempestuous relationships in rock. The Kinks formed in 1963, in the Davies' home turf of Muswell Hill in North London.

Between 1964 and '66, the Kinks scored eight Top 40 hits, including "You Really Got Me" (#7), "All Day and All of the Night" (#7) and "Tired of Waiting For You" (#6). The band's sound was then raw, and the lyrics (from main songwriter Ray) were clever. Dave was an early exponent of guitar distortion.

TWO EVENTS LEFT THEIR MARK ON THE EARLY Kinks. Prior to charting in 1964, the band was summoned to open for the Beatles in Bournemouth. In Ray Davies' telling, when he shook John Lennon's hand backstage, Lennon tersely reminded him that the Kinks were only there as a "warm-up." This slight made the Kinks work all the harder on stage. "You Really Got Me" — which was yet to be recorded — drew a rousing response from an audience that was there to see the Beatles.

The following year, the Kinks had embarked on their debut American tour. But a snowballing series of incidents — including an onstage tussle among band members, and the band threatening to cancel a show over payment — caused the Kinks to be banned from performing in America (by the powerful American Federation of Musicians) for four crucial years, through 1969.

BEST-KNOWN LINEUP: Singer Ray Davies (born 1944); guitarist Dave Davies (born 1947); bassist Pete Quaife (1943-2010); drummer Mick Avory (born 1944). All were born in London except Quaife, who was born in Devon.

Ray has intimated that retribution against the Kinks was a factor. Asked what caused the ban in a 2015 TV interview, he cryptically cited "bad management, bad luck, and bad behavior."

But the Kinks did not crawl home to die. The band eventually resumed touring and recording through distinct phases: concept albums ("Preservation Act I"); a return to roots ("Sleepwalker"); and as stadium rockers ("Low Budget"). Considering the ambitious arrangements of later Kinks material, I asked Dave Davies if he felt songs like "You Really Got Me" and "All Day and All of the Night," with their rawness and directness, are more evocative.

"Actually, I think you can say a lot more through passion, sometimes, than you can through sophistication," he allowed.

"Passion can be more sophisticated than trying to explain and analyze things. That's what communicates: a *feeling*. That's kind of been my job in a way, to express ideas in feelings and emotions. That's what rock 'n' roll is. Listening to those early Buddy Holly and Howlin' Wolf records, and all those influences, singing about pain and their girlfriends and all of this — but there's something else happening. There's this energy. This expression."

Ray Davies

A life examined (with three chords and a backbeat)

AS A SONGWRITER, RAY DAVIES has always been something of a memoirist. Davies didn't expressly deny the charge when I spoke with the Kinks leader in 1998.

Q: "You Really Got Me," which started it all, is at heart a very simple, direct song.

DAVIES: It was the fifth song I ever wrote. I was about 16. My intention was to write a blues song, or something a bit jazzy. It wasn't until the band started playing it that it was transformed into something kind of raw. We put it in our shows, and it got a big reaction. We had to record it twice to get it right (laughs).

Q: Your music has often reflected your own life. I'm thinking of "Schoolboys in Disgrace" (1975), "Come Dancing" (1983), "The Storyteller" (1998). Is life one big autobiography for you?

DAVIES: I thought that would be the case when I started "Storyteller." But what happened was, I kind of detached myself from it. I'm telling this story over the course of an evening, but it's not *me*. It could happen to any kid today. It's just like a kid growing up in a suburb, wanting to make a mark on the world. So I kind of rationalized it like that.

Q: How have your extracurricular activities differed from working within the Kinks?

DAVIES: Normally, with the Kinks, you go from one album to the next, and you really only promote one album for as long as its life span, which is normally about a year to 18 months. "Storyteller" (the live production) was permitted to grow along the way. I developed it like a stage show, rather than do an album first. The "Storyteller" album came as a result of two years' touring, so it was fairly well worked out. It's the opposite way one normally goes about making an album.

Q: Many point to the Kinks' early-'70s period as a time of profound growth: "Muswell Hillbillies" (1971), "Everybody's in Show-Biz" (1972), "Preservation Act I" (1973), "Preservation Act 2" (1974). Did the material on those albums surprise you, when you revisited them years later for the reissues?

DAVIES: I listened to it, yeah. I found a couple of really good tracks that weren't on the albums, which were sort of demos at the end of sessions. It's nice to put it all into perspective.

Q: But when you listened to it again, did you kind of go back to the artist that you were then?

DAVIES: Obviously, you have to, because the music — like with (Davies' 1994 memoir) "X-Ray" — the music tells your life story. It's this autobiographical thing. You're going through different things in your life. And, of course, it will reflect itself on the music, so it's inevitable that there will be a certain amount of reflection.

Q: You've done this before. For "Soap Opera" (1975), you developed a stage show with backup singers and added musical accompaniment. Do you believe it was misunderstood?

DAVIES: I think it was a bit ahead of the time for the record companies. Companies only sell records on a formula that they can understand. Possibly, it was almost, like, 10 years ahead of its time. So if video had been around, if MTV had been around, it would have been easier. It would have been perfect for early MTV. But unfortunately, like RCA once said to me, "We're not in the talent business." I don't understand that (laughs).

Q: "Low Budget" (1979) was a surprising comeback for the Kinks. Suddenly, you were headlining stadiums. You had to *be* bigger.

DAVIES: I like "Low Budget." It was a successful record. I think my favorite record — I love "Misfits" (1978), the songs and "Rock 'n' Roll Fantasy." I've still got a special place for them in my heart. I like all the stuff, but they're the records I enjoyed, because it was like a period where we weren't trying to take over the world. We were just trying to establish ourselves. They were good albums — good, solid albums. We created a real fan base. Without those albums, "Low Budget" wouldn't have been a success.

Could this be the guy who wrote "Dedicated Follower of Fashion"?

Dave Davies

Serious guitar

Dave Davies in the groovy days. Opposite: With a sweet black Telecaster on break from a sound check in 1998.

1960s publicity photo; 1998 photo by Kathy Voglesong

RIGHT PLACE, RIGHT TIME? THE KINKS' FAMOUS (and infamous) Davies brothers — Ray and Dave — came of age in Muswell Hill in North London, which had certain geographical advantages for aspiring musicians in those days.

"It was a quiet sort of suburb in the mid to late '50s," Dave Davies told me during a break from a sound check in 1998.

"It's 10 miles north of Leicester Square — like, the center of London — so it was real easy to get to town. We used to get the train, the tube train, which took like 20 minutes to get to the West End. So it was quite accessible to clubs and town.

"Coffee bars were the thing in those days. People who weren't old enough to get into pubs would hang out with coffee and play guitar. You'd spend all day with your girlfriend and your mates."

The Davies brothers would argue, but musical collaboration was part of their upbringing. Davies said he never had to tailor his guitar playing to accommodate his brother's songwriting ambitions.

"We came from a family that's very musical," Davies said, "where someone sits down and plays a piano, and someone else picks up a banjo. We were used to that. There were a lot of musicians in the family. So it was just an extension of that.

"All the good stuff kind of evolved. Like, he'd do something, I'd do something. He'd write something, I'd play something. We supported and complemented each other. It's a bit like painting, isn't it? You get a feeling, or you add a bit here, some light-and-shade there. There's quite a natural process to it. I've never been one for complications. I'm not a very complicated man."

AFTER THE KINKS SCORED THEIR FIRST HIT WITH "You Really Got Me" in 1964, life was never the same for Davies.

"It changed quite drastically, although I didn't really like it very much," the guitarist recalled.

"I wanted to keep my old mates, and frequent the local pubs where I always used to go. Couldn't do that any more, because everyone always recognized you. The change got drastic.

"I moved. I rented a house further on, in Highgate. It's just a bit nearer to town but, I mean, it was quite drastic. It was a very vibrant musical time. The fashion was exotic. There was Carnaby Street. It was a very, very exciting time."

As the Kinks' guitarist, Davies was a contemporary of George Harrison, Brian Jones and Pete Townshend. The Kinks showcased "You Really Got Me" while opening for the Beatles in 1964.

"I never really got to know the Beatles very well," Davies said.

"I knew John Lennon. I used to meet Paul McCartney a lot, because he was always hanging out in the clubs where I did as well. We talked an awful lot. But they were very private.

"We all were kind of protective of each other, of our music. We would hold it close to our chests. Although, there was a certain amount of camaraderie — having drinks with Mick Jagger and all these people at clubs. But when it came down to *music,* nobody really wanted anybody else to know what they were doing."

WITH HIS EDGY GUITAR ON "YOU REALLY GOT Me," Davies was instrumental in introducing the mainstream to guitar distortion. (He achieved this, not with a "fuzz box," but by razoring his speaker cone.) But a rumor circulated for years that Jimmy Page played the solo on "You Really Got Me." Davies told me in no uncertain terms that he, not Page, played that solo.

"Jimmy was always hanging around," Davies said.

"He was one of the session guys who was always trying to get *into* sessions. He was, like, a protegé of a guitar player called Big Jim Sullivan, who was a great guitar player in the late '50s, early '60s. Jimmy was always trying to get in on the act.

"I think he was kind of a bit jealous of the fact that I'd developed this guitar sound that nobody thought of. Although, at first, everybody was making fun of me, saying, 'This crazy kid.' Previously, they were mocking it, almost. But once we had a hit record, everybody was saying, 'Oh, yeah, what a great sound!' "

FOR DAVIES, THE 1960s WAS A TIME OF SEEMINGLY endless artistic possibilities — and immediacy.

"What was so good about the '60s was that when you thought of something, you could go and *do* it," he said. "You could go to a store and buy something the next day, the next week. Whereas today, there's always 'lead up' times and complications and all that.

"It was a similar thing with TV. (The British music program) 'Ready Steady Go!' was fabulous. It was really immediate, because it was a show that was devised the week that the music came out. You didn't have to wait a long time. It was really instant. If you got a record out, and they liked it, you could be on TV a few days later or the next week. So it had that kind of immediacy that was an important part of that whole '60s euphoria."

IT'S A FULL

The Yardbirds

Guitarist Jeff Beck, drummer Jim McCarty, bassist Chris Dreja, guitarist Jimmy Page and singer Keith Relf in 1966.

WHO ARE THE THREE GREATEST GUITARISTS TO emerge during the British Invasion period? There is only one answer: Eric Clapton, Jeff Beck and Jimmy Page.

How crazy is it that *all three* were launched by the same band?

The Yardbirds demonstrated their bluesy, edgy sound in such songs as "For Your Love" (#6), "Heart Full of Soul" (#9), "Shapes of Things" (#11) and "Over Under Sideways Down" (#13).

The band formed in London in 1963 and, lucky them, took over the Rolling Stones' residency at the Crawdaddy in Richmond.

"It was actually a clubhouse, a rugby clubhouse," Yardbirds drummer Jim McCarty told me in 2011. "They'd get about 200 or 300 people packed in there. We wondered how it would be, following the Stones, but we went down a storm straight away. It was a mad club. Everyone went mad. They'd swing on the rafters.

"We decided, first of all, not to play any of the same covers the Stones played — not to play the same Chuck Berry songs, the same Bo Diddley songs. We got a bit bored with playing 12-bar blues. We wanted to make it more interesting, so we built in these things like the bass-and-drum crescendo, which became known as the 'rave up.' And the tempo changes and elongating all the songs and, you know, trying to make them more exciting."

Once "For Your Love" hit, things changed for the Yardbirds.

"It was immediate," said McCarty. "We were just a local band 'round the Southwest London area. We played all the local clubs. You could play in these blues clubs every night of the week."

But Clapton vanished after "For Your Love." Page (born 1944 in Heston) was offered Clapton's post; in turn, Page recommended Beck (born 1944 in Surrey), who accepted the job. A year later, Page joined as bassist, then switched to guitar. It all sounds messy.

BEST-KNOWN EARLY LINEUP: Singer Keith Relf (1943-1976, born in Surrey); guitarists Eric Clapton and Chris Dreja (both born 1945 in Surrey); bassist Paul Samwell-Smith (born 1943 in London); drummer Jim McCarty (born 1943 in Liverpool)

"Well, it was a bit touch-and-go with Jimmy and Jeff," McCarty allowed. "When Jimmy came in on bass, we looked on it as a bit silly that Jimmy should play bass, being such a great session guitarist. There was no problem with him swapping with Chris Dreja. So the only aggravation might have been between Jeff and Jimmy.

"They both played lead guitar, and they'd be like dueling guitarists. One would play a solo followed by the other. Maybe some of the time, they'd be playing 'stereo' — the same parts doubled — which worked sometimes but not always. And really, underneath it all, they were probably trying to *outgun* each other."

(Beck remembered these events differently; see page 61.)

Continued McCarty: "And then, Jeff got stressed out during the touring. It was very difficult with Jeff, because he was a highly strung person. He was a brilliant player, but he had a very nervous disposition. He'd be very particular about his sound, about what amps he wanted, and if didn't get them, he'd sort of freak out. So he was very, very keyed up most of the time."

According to McCarty, the Yardbirds then dismissed Beck.

Said the drummer: "He started, you know, not to turn up at some of the gigs, and sort of wouldn't do tours and things. So we eventually decided to carry on as a four-piece."

But all's well that ends well. Beck, Page and the Yardbirds made nice in 1992, when the Yardbirds were inducted into the Rock and Roll Hall of Fame, followed by Beck's solo induction in 2009.

Eric Clapton (circled) and the Yardbirds.

"Derek." "Clapper." "Slowhand." "God." No, this isn't a sequence of mysterious clues from "The Da Vinci Code."

Blues-rock fans recognize these as nicknames for guitarist Eric Clapton from various crossroads in his career. Clapton is one of the most important guitarists to spring from the British Invasion, though only the Yardbirds (which he was in from 1963 until '65) counts as a bona fide Invasion group. Thereafter, Clapton band-hopped (in the Blues Breakers, Cream, Blind Faith, Delaney and Bonnie, and Derek and the Dominos) before going solo in 1970.

According to Yardbirds drummer Jim McCarty, Clapton had already earned a degree of notoriety when he joined the group.

"Eric was quite famous on a small level," McCarty told me in 2003. "He'd been to art school with Keith Relf and Chris Dreja, Kingston Art School (in Surrey). He'd played with a couple bands."

McCarty and his fellow Yardbirds immediately sensed that Clapton had considerable musical gifts. "When we first met him, when he first came and played, he was obviously going to be something special," McCarty said. "He sort of had a certain aura about him and a certain presence, and he certainly could play as well as we needed. And then, you know, we went from there."

But Clapton's tenure in the Yardbirds was shortlived. He didn't want to be in a pop band, and considered "For Your Love" to be a pop song. Recalled McCarty: "When Eric Clapton left — when we had our first single, 'For Your Love' — he didn't really like that song, and he thought we were selling out. You know, there was a bit of personality conflict in the band as well."

CLAPTON THEN JOINED THE BLUES BREAKERS, with whom he recorded an album that solidified his reputation and became a blues-rock touchstone: "Blues Breakers With Eric Clapton" (1966). The group's leader, singer-guitarist John Mayall, agreed that Clapton was then something of a blues purist.

"Absolutely, he was," Mayall told me in 2005. "I mean, this was the reason he departed from the Yardbirds. He didn't like the direction they were going in. Because all he wanted to play was blues. They didn't quite understand where he was coming from.

"We (the Blues Breakers) were kind of unique at the time for being into a kind of blues that nobody else was doing. So after Eric left the Yardbirds, it was a golden opportunity for me to jump in there and offer him the job. He was a little bit reluctant at first, because he'd kind of had enough of the scene. But he took it, and we got on great together. We both learned from each other. "

As for putting Clapton's name in the album title: "I think he deserved it," Mayall said. "He was such a big part of it. We were all very much into the blues. We wanted to showcase his playing."

The musician said he didn't feel betrayed when, not long after the album's release, Clapton quit the Blues Breakers.

"We carried on," Mayall said matter-of-factly.

"It was not much of a surprise, really. My bands were like a training ground in some respects. They came; they learned what direction they wanted to go in; and then they cleared off."

NEXT, CLAPTON FORMED CREAM, ROCK'S FIRST "supergroup," a powerhouse trio with bassist Jack Bruce and drummer Ginger Baker. Cream scored hits in America beginning with "Sunshine of Your Love" (#5 in 1968), but it was no British Invasion band. (There were no screaming girls.) Rather, Cream was the first of the *next* wave of groups, for whom the Invasion opened doors. Cream disbanded in 1968 after four studio albums.

Clapton's second "supergroup" would be even shorter lived. Blind Faith — with Baker, keyboardist Steve Winwood and bassist Ric Grech — recorded one eponymously titled album, played one tour and then closed shop. According to Baker, Clapton defected to Blind Faith's opening act on the tour, Delaney and Bonnie. ("Stevie and I couldn't believe it!" said the drummer.)

According to singer Bonnie Bramlett, it was George Harrison who made Clapton aware of Delaney and Bonnie in the first place.

"George took our tapes back to Eric, and Eric at that time was doing the Blind Faith tour, and the rest is pretty much history," Bramlett told me in 2004. "Then we just blew him (Clapton) right off the stage. He just loved it. He came and played with us."

The partying on that tour was legendary. Admitted Bramlett: "It was: par-TAY! Every day, all day long; every night, all night long. What can I say? We didn't hurt anybody but ourselves."

This group then morphed into Derek and the Dominos, whose song "Layla" (1970) will be heard on radio until the end of time.

Jeff Beck

Jeff Beck's sister, Annetta, heard tell of a boy in the neighborhood who, like her brother, was obsessed with playing guitar.

Without having met Jimmy Page, Annetta Beck decided Jeff and he should be introduced. She marched up to the Page homestead with her brother in tow, and knocked on the door. The first meeting of Jeff Beck and Jimmy Page, at age 13 or 14, became one of those uncanny crossroads in rock.

Page recalled that Beck brought along a homemade guitar, and had been learning songs by listening to records. That day, these kindred spirits forged a friendship that would last for decades, with careers that would occasionally intertwine.

OVER THE NEXT FEW YEARS, BECK JOINED A series of bands and got as much stage experience as he could — not that his equipment was the greatest.

"Golly, every day was a *year* back then, you know," Beck told me in 2011.

"I don't recall owning an amplifier. It was always a sob story to the band. I used to plug into a tape recorder or a radio. My first amp was a 5-watt Selmer. It probably couldn't be heard beyond the first row! Then I moved onto an El Pico, which was pretty loud. The El Pico stood up to a lot of abuse, and I'm talking about booze, getting kicked, cigarette burns. I blew that up. Then I got a Vox Twin, which sounded good, and then a Vox Super Beetle. Then I moved onto Marshalls."

Recalled Beck of the first time he ever recorded: "We were petrified. It was only a demo, but we treated it as if we were making the most amazing record of all time. We did one song; we were only allowed to do one song for the fee we were paying. So we did two mixes, one with echo and one without. I took the acetate home and played it over and over."

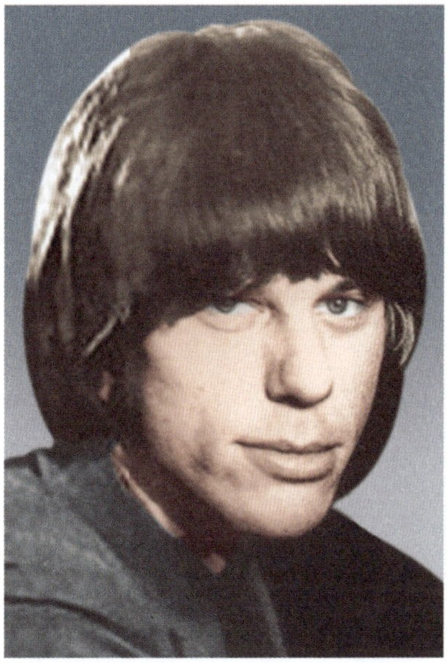

In the bowl-cut 1960s. Opposite: Beck and Strat onstage in 1999.

Publicity photo; 1999 photo by Kathy Voglesong

Beck steadily built his career, and by 1965, had played on a few professionally released recordings (including one from Screaming Lord Sutch). Meanwhile, his old buddy Page emerged as a highly sought session guitarist.

IN THE MIDST OF THIS, THE YARDBIRDS WERE looking to hire a new guitarist following the departure of Eric Clapton. They invited Page to join their group, but at the time, he was focused on becoming a record producer.

"Jimmy was a real leaning post for me, because he was always in work, I remember," Beck recalled.

"I used to go and see Jimmy as often as I could, because I had a car, at least. So I was always bugging him at his house.

"One day, he played me this live Yardbirds album. He said, 'What do you think?' He played 'Five Long Years,' which is a blues. One of Eric's best solos. And I said, 'Wow, this guy's great.' Jimmy said, 'Uh, how would you feel about replacing him if he left the band?' 'I dunno about that.' Because I already had a band which was doing really well in the local area — Richmond and Kingston area."

Beck demurred without giving a firm no.

"And then the next thing that happened was, I've got a guy standing in front of me at one of our gigs," he said.

"This guy was acting on Jimmy's recommendation. So I obviously must've appeared to Jim — at the time that he asked me to join the Yardbirds — like I was half-interested. Mind you, *he* had rejected the offer, because he wanted to stay earning money," Beck added with a laugh. "He didn't want to ditch everything he'd built up, to go on the road with a band that was not really widely known at that time."

Beck, as rock history tells us, indeed joined the Yardbirds in 1965. "And the rest is greased lightning," he said.

"Everything happened. They had a hit record ('Heart Full of Soul') just after I joined. And then the tours of America came. We did two big tours. I say 'big' tours; to *us* they were big, because we'd never been outside South London."

SURPRISINGLY, PAGE JOINED the Yardbirds as a "temporary" bassist the following year. Page would eventually slide over to guitar, and the Beck-Page lineup of the Yardbirds became famous for its two-pronged guitar approach.

"Well, it was unforeseen that Paul Samwell-Smith was going to leave; that was the bass player," Beck recalled.

"He played a huge part. I mean, he had a really wild, big bass sound. He used to play four-string chords on the bass, and just cause all kinds of earthquake sounds. Without that, the band wasn't really the same band.

"And Jimmy, bless his cotton socks, he didn't really play much bass. But it was my design to get him on double-lead. I promised, 'If you come in this band, you'll be on guitar before you know it.' And poor old Chris (Dreja) was kind of duped into playing bass. It wasn't very good. Jimmy wasn't settled in, because he'd only just swapped over onto lead, and Chris hated playing bass, as I recall. You know, you don't just switch from rhythm guitar to bass easily."

Beck intimated that this situation led to his parting ways with the band (though he couldn't say if he quit or was fired).

"Really, there was no other solution," Beck said.

"Because Chris was one of the founding members. And I was an employee. And I *remained* an employee of the band until I left — or was booted out. I can't remember what happened in '67, I think it was."

Next up for Beck was the Jeff Beck Group, the earliest lineup of which featured relative unknowns Rod Stewart and Ron Wood. But Beck found a lasting niche with the instrumental jazz-rock albums "Blow by Blow" (1975) and "Wired" (1976), which were recorded by — to bring the whole thing full circle — Beatles producer George Martin.

The Spencer Davis Group

The Spencer Davis Group, from left: Muff Winwood, "Stevie" Winwood, Pete York and Davis circa 1967. © United Artists Records

ONE DAY, SPENCER DAVIS GOT AN UNSOLICITED lesson in how little Americans know about American music.

"When I was a student — I studied languages in Birmingham in England and Berlin in Germany — I was playing a Tony Zemaitis 12-string," Davis told me in 2007. "To the guitar lovers now, they know a Zemaitis was made by Anthony Zemaitis. He's passed on, unfortunately. But they were handmade guitars.

"I was playing on the steps of *Sacre Coeur* in Paris. I was playing, 'Good Night Irene.' An American tourist said to me, 'Oh, you're playing a song by the Weavers.' I said, 'No, this song was actually composed by Huddie Ledbetter.' "

AS WITH MANY BRITISH MUSICIANS OF HIS TIME, Davis cited skiffle pioneer Lonnie Donegan as a major influence.

"Lonnie Donegan was the banjo player in the Chris Barber Jazz Band," Davis explained. "Chris Barber played a British sort of New Orleans music, the kind of stuff that George Lewis or Bunk Johnson or Louis Armstrong would have played. All of these guys were our heroes — our mentors, if you like.

"Chris Barber played trombone. He'd put down the trombone and pick up a big, full-sized bull fiddle. Donegan would go around to guitar. I always liked the music that came from them. I believe the name in America was Dixieland. We called it traditional jazz.

"Donegan actually had a hit with 'Rock Island Line' (1955), which is obviously about a train, as many of those songs are. Skiffle music reflected that sort of 'train' feeling."

Davis' passion for American music led to the formation of the Spencer Davis Group in 1963 in Birmingham. Playing keyboards was a 15-year-old prodigy then calling himself "Stevie" Winwood. The Spencer Davis Group scored hits with "Somebody Help Me," "Keep on Running" (both #1 in the U.K.) and "I'm a Man" (a #10 hit in the States written by the band, later covered by Chicago).

FOUNDING LINEUP: Guitarist Spencer Davis (1939-2020, born in Swansea); keyboardist "Stevie" Winwood (born 1948 in Birmingham); bassist Muff Winwood (born 1943 in Birmingham); drummer Pete York (born 1942 in Yorkshire)

The Spencer Davis Group's #7 hit in America in 1966, "Gimme Some Lovin'," spotlighted Winwood's soulful vocals and shimmering Hammond. Davis said that if *he* hadn't discovered Winwood, "somebody else would have."

It was the Spencer Davis Group's dream to play America.

"That's where the music *came* from," said Davis.

"There was always that strong desire to go there. Probably, the doors were opened by the Beatles and the Animals and Eric Burdon, obviously. And again, Eric Burdon — I mean, look at the hit: 'House of the Rising Sun.' The story of a brothel in New Orleans. How Americana can you get?

"In fact, one of our first singles of the original Spencer Davis Group was a song called 'Dimples' (1964), which was very similar to John Lee Hooker's 'Boom Boom.' Eric Burdon covered 'Boom Boom' in the Animals. So it all went 'round."

By the time the SDG arrived in New York, the band was in flux.

"The original band had split into twos," Davis recalled. "Steve had gone into Traffic, and Muff had gone into Island Records as an A&R guy. So I kept it going with Pete York and Eddie Hardin, the keyboard player that replaced Steve. Eddie was recommended to me by (singer) Paul Jones of the Manfred Mann band.

"Even in those days, the networking system worked, to the point where you just said, 'I need somebody.' Even Screaming Lord Sutch — God bless him — he recommended a singer to me by the name of Terry Reid, and what a singer Terry Reid is. Elton John, under the name of Reggie Dwight, did audition for the gig but didn't get it. So a lot of people say to me, 'You actually turned down Elton John!' And I say, 'Yeah? So?' "

The Blues Breakers

IN HIS INFLUENTIAL BAND THE Blues Breakers, John Mayall mentored such rock luminaries as Eric Clapton, John McVie, Mick Fleetwood, Peter Green and Mick Taylor.

"I've always thought of myself as having a great time with the musicians that turn me on," he told me matter-of-factly in 2005.

Mayall (born 1933 in Macclesfield) was inspired to play piano courtesy of his father's record collection. "It was just for my own enjoyment, because there was nobody around that I could even consider being an audience for it. So it was a personal thing," he said.

"Years later, when (guitarist) Alexis Korner and (harmonica player) Cyril Davies kicked off the blues scene in London in late '62, '63, that was pretty amazing to me. Here's something I *knew* something about. So it was a golden opportunity for me to give it a shot."

The British blues scene caught on "very quickly," according to Mayall.

"Traditional 'trad' jazz had been ruling the clubs for 10 years," he said. "When Alexis went to electric, he had this amazing band which was Blues Incorporated, which was Dick Hecktall-Smith and Graham Bond on saxophones, and (bassist) Jack Bruce and (drummer) Ginger Baker as the rhythm section. It had an extraordinary impact on the club scene, almost overnight.

"At the same time, Brian Jones and Mick Jagger were putting the Rolling Stones together. So I would say within six months of creating a scene in the clubs, it was running rampant."

Said Mayall of making the landmark album "Blues Breakers With Eric Clapton" (1966): "That was a quick thing. We were working seven or eight gigs a week, and in the afternoon for a couple of days, we went in and cut the album. We were just playing in the studio what we were pretty much doing every night in the clubs. We just wanted it to accurately reflect what we were doing. We wanted to make a good blues album."

John Mayall in 1970.

The Zombies

The Zombies were, from left, Hugh Grundy, Colin Blunstone, Paul Atkinson, Chris White and Rod Argent. © Decca Records

FOUNDING LINEUP: Singer Colin Blunstone (born 1945); keyboardist Rod Argent (born 1945); guitarist Paul Atkinson (1946-2004); bassist Chris White (born 1943); drummer Hugh Grundy (born 1945). All were born in Hertfordshire except for Grundy, who was born in Winchester.

CAN YOU IMAGINE ROD ARGENT BEING IN A BAND and *not* playing keyboards? This nearly happened in St Albans, Hertfordshire, in 1961, in a precursor of the Zombies.

"Going right back to the beginning, 1961, it really began with Rod Argent wanting to put an album together," Zombies singer Colin Blunstone told me in 2004.

"He was a sensational keyboard player. But because bands were all guitar-based, he didn't think of himself as being the keyboard player in the band. He was going to be the lead singer."

A ragtag lineup (including some future Zombies members) was assembled from around St Albans. For the group's first rehearsal, Argent was to sing and Blunstone was to play guitar.

"By the end of our first rehearsal — I have to say that it was starting to sound quite good — but there was one big change that happened," Blunstone said. "We took a break. Rod went over to a broken down old piano in the corner and he started playing 'Nut Rocker' by B. Bumble and the Stingers. I was just amazed. I went over there and said, 'You have to play keyboards in the band!' He'd never thought of that, because it wasn't the fashion at the time. So he became the keyboard player instead of the singer.

"He remembers me just singing a Ricky Nelson song and thinking, 'That was really great. You should be the singer.' It was exactly as casual as that. We just sort of moved 'round one in the band. Rod became the keyboard player and I became the singer."

By the spring of 1964, the group was poised to record its first song. Recalled Blunstone: "(Producer) Ken Jones said to all of us, he said, 'Look. There's a recording session in about three weeks time at Decca Studios in West Hampstead in London. Why don't you try and write something?' So Rod went away and he wrote 'She's Not There.' It was as simple as that. I mean, Rod was and is a sensational keyboard player. And he became a world-class writer. That was the start of it."

"I remember it being a real joy, writing that song," Argent told me in 2011. "It was only the second song I ever wrote. We had rehearsed it very thoroughly, because we knew things had to go very quickly in the recording studio. But it went great.

"It was the very first time that a guy called Gus Dudgeon ever engineered any session. But what happened was, the main engineer got drunk. He couldn't do anything."

Said Blunstone: "I think he'd been to a wedding earlier in the day. But he was outrageously drunk. And rather aggressive."

Said Argent: "We put him in a taxi. He was unconscious. We carried him out — four of us did, one on each arm and each leg.

"So this became Gus Dudgeon's very first record (as the main engineer). Of course, he later produced Elton John and many other artists. But it all went a bit like a dream, really."

"SHE'S NOT THERE" REACHED #2. WAS THERE ANY pressure from Decca for the Zombies to sound like the Beatles?

"Not at all. They just let us get on with it," said Argent.

"Particularly with Decca. They were so scared of missing out on something, because they had famously turned the Beatles down. So the creative side was a closed world to them, really."

The Animals

The Animals were, from left, John Steel, Alan Price, Chas Chandler, Eric Burdon and Hilton Valentine. © ABKCO Records

FOR SINGER ERIC BURDON, THE MOST EXCITING part of his career came *before* the formation of the Animals.

"I had more freedom then," the singer told me in 2004.

"During my years at art school, when I first met (future Animals drummer) John Steel and we started exchanging ideas about music — this was before the Animals were ever *thought* of — they were the most exciting, free times. A real taste of freedom.

"I had odd jobs. I was delivering newspapers, digging road trenches. I had more money than I thought I needed. I'd work at that for a couple of months, and then for the remaining month of the three months of holidays, I would go to Paris to buy records.

"Getting to Paris really opened up my head. Here I was, just across 21 miles of water in a different world. I met a lot of U.S. expatriates, like runaways from problems in New York with either drugs or they couldn't get cabaret licenses. I ran into people like Bud Powell, Chet Baker, Memphis Slim, Jimmy Witherspoon.

"I had wonderful insight into what America had in store for me when I was 17 years of age. I made some records with local jazz musicians before I got together with the Animals. We recorded direct to disc — no tape, just cut straight onto disc. Those records would last for about 20 plays before the shellac would turn white."

The band was an amalgam formed in Newcastle in 1962.

"The Animals came together from various bands that played in my hometown," Burdon said. "There was a lot of action in my hometown, musically speaking. There were folk clubs, jazz clubs.

"We forced rock 'n' roll down the throats of people who would not normally have been interested. Then when the Animals came to be and we became professional, it was a mixture of both excitement and pure hell — five guys and equipment following in one Econoline-type vehicle, doing one gig after the other, non-stop."

BEST-KNOWN LINEUP: Singer Eric Burdon (born 1941 in Walker); guitarist Hilton Valentine (1943-2021, born in Northumberland); keyboardist Alan Price (born 1942 in Fatfield); bassist Chas Chandler (1938-1996, born in Heaton); drummer Steel (born 1941 in Gateshead)

Among the Animals' hits in 1964 and '65 were "House of the Rising Sun" (#1), "Don't Let Me Be Misunderstood" (#15), "We Gotta Get Out of This Place" (#13) and "It's My Life" (#23).

"Then the big money surfaced and the big problems surfaced," Burdon lamented. "Consequently, the band just imploded, and we were over and done with by the time 1966 rolled around."

BUT BURDON COULD STILL LAUGH WHEN HE recalled the time the Animals first landed in the United States.

"It was all kind of silly, really," he said. "We were jetted into New York. We were supposed to land at JFK, but the authorities had problems with the Beatles, so they expected the same kind of riotous crowds. The plane was directed to La Guardia instead.

"We had this reception with all the New York press. There were these girls dressed up as animals with these strange costumes on. We drove into town, each one of us with a girl, in a Mustang car, which was the most popular car of the day.

"It was like the American businessman, the American record industry, were creating hysteria before we even arrived. They wanted us to be the Beatles. And that's not what we were about. We were deadly serious blues guys. We wanted to be taken seriously. We wanted to change the world, and turn the world onto this new religion that we'd found called the blues."

The Hollies

Clockwise from top left: Graham Nash, Allan Clarke, Tony Hicks, Bobby Elliot and Eric Haydock.

SUNNY HITS LIKE "BUS STOP," "ON A CAROUSEL," "Carrie-Anne" and "Stop Stop Stop" represented a winning streak for the Hollies in 1966 and '67. But chart success didn't make founding member Graham Nash *feel* like he was winning.

It was something he addressed in his self-reflective song "King Midas in Reverse," with the opening lyrics: *"If you could only see me / and know exactly who I am / you wouldn't want to be me."*

When the Hollies formed in Salford in 1962, three-part harmony was the group's trademark. "It was an extremely happy time," Nash told me of his tenure in the group, when we spoke in 2002.

"The Hollies had found a vehicle through music to escape what I've come to call the 'gold watch' theory — in terms of working for a company for 65 years, getting a gold watch, and then lying down and dying. I never felt that was appropriate for me, and fortunately for me, neither of my parents did.

"When the Hollies found music and went down to London and started to record and be on TV and radio and do live shows and just be appreciated, it was an unbelievably happy time in my life. I'm glad people feel happy when they put that music on. So do I."

Still, Nash felt that he needed to do more serious work.

WHEN, IN 1968, NASH QUIT THE HOLLIES TO FORM Crosby, Stills and Nash, he was replaced by Terry Sylvester (born 1947 in Liverpool). Meanwhile, another founding singer, Allan Clarke, left the group to attempt a solo career, but soon returned. The Hollies were, against the odds, having hits again. In the '70s, the group pierced the Top 10 three times, with "He Ain't Heavy, He's My Brother" (#7 in 1970), "Long Cool Woman in a Black Dress" (#2 in 1972) and "The Air That I Breathe" (#6 in 1974).

FOUNDING LINEUP: Singer Allan Clarke (born 1942 in Salford); singer-guitarists Graham Nash (born 1942 in Blackpool) and Tony Hicks (born 1945 in Nelson); bassist Eric Haydock (1943-2019, born in Stockport); drummer Bobby Elliott (born 1941 in Burnley)

The sound of the "new" Hollies was less pop-y. A case in point was the rocker "Long Cool Woman," which Clarke sang.

"That was never supposed to be a single," Sylvester told me in 2005. "It was recorded as an album track, because we'd already decided on the single; I can't remember what that was at the time. It ended up on the B-side of a single that was put out in Germany. A DJ in Germany was playing the A-side (on the radio). He switched it over and played 'Long Cool Woman in a Black Dress.' He started to get phone calls saying, 'Where can I get this?'

"So he called EMI Records and said, 'Look, we're getting a lot of calls for this song. I think you might have made a mistake here. You should have put the B-side on the A-side.' And what happened was, they did exactly that, and it became #1 in Germany. And then, obviously, all over the record companies. We were on Epic in the States. They picked up on this.

"It just shot all the way to #1. Lots of people thought it was Creedence Clearwater Revival," Sylvester laughed. "They didn't know it was the Hollies. And you know what? It's the only Hollies hit record we've ever had with no harmonies."

As for "The Air That I Breathe": "That's me singing the top harmony, and it's in real voice. It's not in falsetto," Sylvester said.

"So it's the power. There was a nice power about the Hollies. But, listen, we've been lucky. We were obviously talented. It's a bit of both — a bit of talent, a bit of luck, and I think you get there."

Graham Nash

LIKE SO MANY BRITISH ARTISTS OF THE PERIOD, Graham Nash had a childhood affected by World War II.

"I was born in Blackpool, which is about 30, 40 miles from Manchester," Nash told me. "We lived in a place called Salford, which was a suburb of Manchester. But during the end of World War II, pregnant ladies were evacuated outside the bombing area to have their babies in peace. That's how I came to be born in Blackpool, although I lived just outside of Manchester."

Nash cherished his time in the Hollies, but left the group to join David Crosby and Stephen Stills with altruistic intentions.

"I think in retrospect, in looking at the Hollies' catalog, it *is* happy. They *are* light songs," Nash explained. "They don't take a lot of thinking about. They do feel good. It's nice to put the hood down on the convertible and drive around listening to 'Carrie-Anne' and 'On a Carousel' and 'Bus Stop' and stuff.

"But what happened to me a little later was that I became a bit more serious when I realized — having hung out with David and Stephen — that maybe there was a deeper responsibility as an artist to reflect exactly what's going on around him.

"What was going on around me at the time, when I was first living in America, was the Vietnam War, the Civil Rights movement, the beginning of the environmental movement. Things were much more serious than they were with the Hollies."

Hollies founder Graham Nash performs in 2001.
Photo by Kathy Voglesong

The Hollies' Terry Sylvester shown below in 2005.
Photo by Kathy Voglesong

Terry Sylvester

THE HOLLIES' LOSS WAS TERRY SYLVESTER'S GAIN.

"My big break came when Graham Nash decided to join his friends Stills and Crosby, and then later, (Neil) Young," said Sylvester.

"That was my big break. In many ways, it helped me that I didn't, what I call, 'make it.' I didn't make it until I was 22.

"And you know what? I'd paid my dues. To replace Graham in the Hollies was a dream come true. Suddenly, I'm on all the TV shows. I'm touring America. I kind of think I got what I deserved. I hope you take that the right way, because I really worked hard to get there."

(If his statement *was* boastful, Sylvester can be forgiven. After all, prior to the Hollies, he stuck it out in two Liverpool bands that date to the early days of the Invasion: the Escorts and the Swinging Blue Jeans.)

Sylvester relished singing three-part harmonies with the Hollies.

"I was a big, big fan of the Everly Brothers," he said. "So were the Hollies. I think that our harmonies were Everlys-based. The Everlys were just two-part harmony; the Hollies were three-part harmony.

"It's a very natural thing. I can't explain it. We used to get the lead line of the song, and I would just work a harmony out in my head. I can read a little bit of music, but it was just totally off the head. That's how we did it. I think that's why it's so unique.

"It was never worked out with a musical director. Because I think what would happen there is, you wouldn't get the natural. What you would get is the obvious. I would just listen to Allan (Clarke) singing, and then I would work out a harmony that matched what he was singing. Whether it made musical sense, I don't know. Maybe I don't even care. It just sounded good."

The Small Faces

The group in 1967, from left: Ronnie Lane, Steve Marriott, Ian McLagan and Kenney Jones. "From the Beginning" © Decca Records

IAN McLAGAN DUG THE SMALL FACES. "I'D SEEN them on the telly," the keyboardist told me in 2013. "They were fantastic! Steve Marriott was great. My dad saw them (on TV) and pointed to Ronnie Lane and said, 'He looks just like *you.*' "

The group formed in London in 1965, with singer-guitarist Marriott, bassist Lane, keyboardist Jimmy Winston and drummer Kenney Jones. McLagan, too, had been in and out of bands.

"I loved the music," he said. "I wanted to be on the inside of that. I loved the blues. I loved rock 'n' roll when it came out. So it was all about: How do I get to play that music? How do I make that work? Then I got in a band."

But on the night McLagan watched the Small Faces on TV with his dad, he happened to be *between* bands. Little did McLagan know, the Small Faces were looking to replace Winston.

He recalled: "That night, which was a Sunday night, an old friend said to me, 'How's the band?' I said, 'I just quit.' He said, 'You should join the Small Faces.' I said, 'Thanks a lot!' "

Was it kismet? The next day, McLagan was summoned by Small Faces manager Don Arden, who invited him to join the band.

"I was finally in a band," he said. "Everything I wanted, they had. They wanted to play. They were fantastic people. They really loved the music. Steve and I had the same musical tastes. We worked like mother****ers. We had days off every coupla months. We played everywhere. People saw us. We made records."

In the U.K., the Small Faces' first single "Whatcha Gonna Do About It" (1965, with Winston) went to #14, followed by "Sha-La-La-La-Lee" (1966, with McLagan), which shot up to #3.

"The success was overwhelming," Jones told me in 2005.

"We were completely bowled over by it, really. We were new, fresh on the scene, and people liked our music."

At the time, Jones felt as if the world held endless possibilities.

BEST-KNOWN LINEUP: Guitarist Steve Marriott (1947-91, born in London); keyboardist Ian McLagan (1945-2014, born in Hounslow); bassist Ronnie Lane (1946-97, born in Plaistow); drummer Kenney Jones (born 1948 in London)

"Well, in the '60s, don't forget, I was a kid," Jones said.

"I was the youngest drummer in the music business. I had a hit record in the charts when I was 15, which is unbelievable. As soon as the record was a hit, I'd just turned 16. One of the most frustrating things about it was, I had enough money to buy a car, but I wasn't old enough to get a driving license. Although, I *could* drive, but I wasn't supposed to."

Said McLagan: "It was the Beatles, the Stones, the Kinks, the Who, and the next thing I knew, the Small Faces. And here we go! A whole year goes by, and I'm on TV. It happened that quickly."

BUT NOBODY WAS TAKING THE BAND SERIOUSLY, according to Jones. This particularly bothered Marriott.

"We were trying desperately not to be pop-y," Jones said.

"Because we were a proper band, you know. We could play really, really well. We could play quite heavy stuff. Nevertheless, we were thrust into the pop world, in a sense. We really wanted to shake that image. But that was an uphill battle.

"That's one of the downfalls of the Small Faces, and one of the reasons that we split up — apart from making (the 1968 concept album) 'Ogden's Nut Gone Flake,' which was: How do you follow that? Especially Steve Marriott. He wanted to be treated more as a serious professional musician. And whilst you have this pop image hanging around your neck, you couldn't do it."

Marriott quit the Small Faces in 1968 to form Humble Pie. McLagan, Lane and Jones spun off into Rod Stewart and the Faces. In 1978, Jones kicked off a two-album hitch with the Who.

The Moody Blues

From left: Denny Laine, Clint Warwick, Ray Thomas, Graeme Edge and Mike Pinder. Inset: Justin Hayward.

FROM POP STARS TO ART ROCKERS, THE MOODY Blues had two distinct incarnations. The group formed in 1964 in Birmingham and had a #10 hit with "Go Now!" (1965), on which future Wings guitarist Denny Laine sang the swoony lead vocals.

"That's, obviously, the most important period of my life musically," Laine told me in 2007. "Because everybody wants to have a hit record, or at least be recognized for the music that they do."

According to Laine, that initial chart success was hard-earned.

"It was a lot of work prior that led up to that," he said.

"We were all working for years as solo artists or in other bands. Then, certainly, you got to the stage when everything blows out of proportion, which is what happened in London. All the bands that came to London — starting with the Beatles, the Animals, the Stones, Rod Stewart, the Who — they started at the same time. We all became kind of semi-friends in those days. It was a friendly rivalry between all the bands. We went to the same clubs.

"And because we were all starting together, there was a lot of help and a lot of encouragement from each other. That's how I got to know the Beatles. That's how I became friends with Paul (McCartney), and that's how Wings came about, basically."

Not that the Moodies thought of it as "networking."

"We were so busy, a lot of it just went over our heads in some ways," Laine said. "When you look back now, you realize how important it was. But at the time, we were just having fun or working. It was this big sort of work ethic. To stay in there, the competition being what it was, you had to work like the devil."

A turning point came in 1966, when Laine and bassist Clint Warwick left the Moodies (who were showing signs of floundering). They were replaced by singer-guitarist Justin Hayward (born 1946 in Swindon) and bassist John Lodge (born 1945 in Birmingham). Newcomers Hayward and Lodge were instrumental in the reinvention of the Moody Blues — though not at first.

FOUNDING LINEUP: Guitarist Denny Laine (born 1944 in Birmingham); flautist Ray Thomas (1941-2018, born in Stourport-on-Severn); keyboardist Mike Pinder (born 1941 in Birmingham); bassist Clint Warwick (1940-2004, born in Birmingham); drummer Graeme Edge (1941-2021, born in Rocester)

"It was confusing for me and John at the time," Hayward told me in 2004. "Because we didn't really have an identity. The Moodies had been put together about 18 months before that from a number of different groups. They really based it on rhythm-and-blues, which I suppose everybody liked, but nobody was really good at except for Denny, who was there at the beginning. Then he left. That left us with some blue suits, but a rhythm-and-blues act that really didn't suit us. We did that for about six months."

The Moodies were by then drifting, according to Hayward.

"And then our price had *really* dropped down," he said. "I'd gone back to living with my parents and sold my car and all that."

Hayward then wrote the Moodies' comeback song, "Nights in White Satin," which debuted in 1967 and reached #2 in 1972. The song remains the group's most iconic. The rest is FM radio history.

FOR HAYWARD, THE BEATLES' BREAKTHROUGH in 1962 and '63 was an inspiration to young British musicians.

He recalled: "The radio was everything for me. A few pop acts would appear on British radio. You'd have a variety show, and then there'd be a pop act on. But I can't say there were any great English rock 'n' roll records. I mean, Cliff Richard's 'Move It' was a great record, and the Shadows were always fabulous.

"But it wasn't until the Beatles came along that Britain could really hold its head up high in the music world. And then we all found our identity."

Herman's Hermits

The Hermits in 1966: Derek Leckenby, Karl Green, Barry Whitwam, Keith Hopwood and Peter Noone. © Metro-Goldwyn-Mayer

"How can we be different? Let's get a name that sounds stupid. No girls are going to scream 'Herman!' We made fun of ourselves."

That's how Peter Noone — a.k.a. "Herman" of Herman's Hermits — recounted the origin story of the band behind the hits "I'm Into Something Good" (#13), "Mrs. Brown, You've Got a Lovely Daughter" (#11), "I'm Henry VIII, I Am" (#1) and "There's a Kind of Hush" (#9).

The Hermits stood out from the pack because they were younger, and took themselves less seriously, than most of the British groups who came over during the Invasion period. Also, there was something nostalgic and wistful about their songs that just didn't sound like, say, the Yardbirds or the Animals.

The group's sound was shepherded by producer Mickie Most, who recorded other Invasion acts such as the Nashville Teens, Lulu, the Seekers and, whaddaya know, the Yardbirds and the Animals. He was first drawn to the Hermits based on their looks.

"Their manager sent me a photograph of Herman's Hermits at Piccadilly Station in Manchester, and Peter Noone looked like a young Kennedy," Most once told an interviewer.

"I thought: This face is saleable, especially in the United States. All I need to do is find cute songs to go with it."

Between 1964 and '68, the Hermits scored 18 Top 40 hits, 11 of them in the Top 10. The raucous novelty song "I'm Henry VIII, I Am" — a cover of a 1910 ditty (*speaking* of nostalgia) — was touted as the "fastest-selling record in history." In 1965, *Billboard* ranked them the best-selling British group (over You Know Who).

FOUNDING LINEUP: Singer Peter Noone (born 1947); guitarists Derek Leckenby (1943-1994) and Keith Hopwood (born 1946); bassist Karl Green (born 1947); drummer Barry Whitwam (born 1946). All were born in Manchester except for Leckenby, who was born in Leeds.

The Hermits had many brushes with fellow Invasion artists. Jimmy Page and John Paul Jones, later of Led Zeppelin, played on some of their songs. (Jones arranged the lush, lovely "There's a Kind of Hush," and once toured with the Hermits as a keyboardist.) Early on, the group played on bills alongside the Beatles, the Stones, the Kinks, the Animals and the Small Faces. In 1967, the Hermits' first U.S. tour featured the Who as the supporting act!

The Hermits starred as themselves in two movies, one made in Hollywood and one in England. "Hold On!" (1966) was a clichéd American vision of the band being chased by screaming girls while scrambling from gig to gig. "Mrs. Brown, You've Got a Lovely Daughter" (1968) was a more thoughtful, authentic look at the Hermits, largely filmed in their home town of Manchester.

Peter Noone

Something good

AT SIX OR SEVEN YEARS YOUNGER THAN MANY of his contemporaries, Peter Noone was the antithesis of the rock front man. His comically large front teeth — which Noone proudly didn't have "fixed" — made him more teddy bear than Teddy Boy.

Noone had already achieved fame as a child actor, but his first love was rock 'n' roll. He studied (and occasionally joined) bands that played in clubs. One night, Noone filled in for the lead singer of a band called the Heartbeats. This led to a *new* group with a most unlikely name. I spoke with the singer in 2003 and 2011.

Q: You were a child star in England. How did your childhood pave the way for the musical career that followed?

NOONE: It's all connected. All of show business is connected. I'm lucky that I've done all these other things. It started out that my dad was a sort of almost-famous musician. You know, he *almost* was famous. He was a good trombone player. I think he wanted to make sure I was a good musician, so he sent me to a school of music. At this class at my school — St. Bede's Jesuit College For Boys — I was better than the teacher at music. He was a really good priest, you know, because there are lots of those. He said, "You're better at this than me. You should go to college."

Q: How old were you at the time?

NOONE: I think I was 13. He signed me up for the Manchester College of Music when I was 13 instead of 18. They threw me into this class of all these geniuses who made me look like an idiot. I just didn't know as much as they did. But because I was so afraid, I joined every class. And the only class I liked was the room where the people were playing the Chuck Berry songs. They were all 18-year-olds with beards, you know? I just watched them for a while.

I got into the elocution class. My dad thought it would be important — if I ever was gonna be in show business or *any* business — to speak properly. Because none of us did that. We all had these terrible accents. I've *still* got mine. It was like a thrown-in class. I did it at night. It wasn't full-time. I still had to do my work. You go to a school of music, you're with musicians. My life just changed. I got on all these TV shows. I got my first acting job because I could play the piano.

"Every day was a new adventure," said Peter Noone (shown in 2005).
Photo by Kathy Voglesong

Q: What was your first professional acting job?

NOONE: They wanted a kid who could sing and play the piano at the same time in this show called "Knight Errant." I sang "The Holly and the Ivy" with, like, three chords, right? And then any time they wanted a kid on a television show, they'd call me.

Meanwhile, I was doing all that to support being a musician. It never occurred to me to be an actor. I didn't like actors; I liked musicians. The actors were all, like, reject male hairdressers to me. So I wasn't into the acting as much as I was into making the *money* from the acting to buy a van, so I could be in a band.

Q: But you actually won fame as an actor. How did that happen?

NOONE: I got on this TV series, which was a big one, called "Coronation Street." Even kids at my school watched it. Suddenly, I was famous as this actor. But I was making money and keeping it in supporting the band. And in the first band, it was like I was this rich little singer, you know? Because there's always some kid in every band who's got a bit more money, who buys the amps and the P.A. That's the way bands are made. It all just sort of worked out.

Q: So you band-hopped for a time.

NOONE: For years and years, we went around in the bands. We went from being absolutely horrible to being quite good to being, basically, the only unsigned band in town. You know, everybody gets that turn. We were the only unsigned band in town.

Q: On that fateful night when you filled in as a singer with the Heartbeats — which transmogrified into Herman's Hermits — was there chemistry from the very beginning?

NOONE: Yeah, there really was. Because I knew all the songs they did. I had never seen this band before, but I had a bit of a record collection. I never collected English records; I didn't have any Cliff Richard records. That was my sister. And this band, the Heartbeats, did Bobby Rydell tunes. They were called the Heartbeats because the singer fancied himself as a bit of a crooner. So they had all these sort of "I'll Never Dance Again If You Don't Love Me" kind of songs. I just knew them all and I parodied them. So instead of being the serious 14-year-old sex symbol, I kind of gave everybody a bit of a break from that. The world needed a break from all those, you know, Billy Furys.

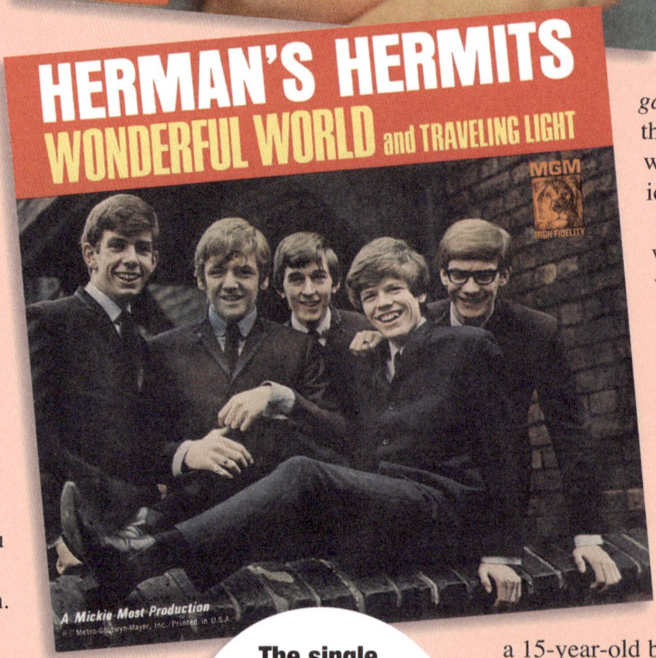

The single "Wonderful World" (1965) and a Datebook cover story (1967).
© MGM Records; © Young World Press, Inc.

And (singing like Elvis Presley) *"Since my baby left me."* All that stuff was really getting old. You know, American high-school sweater crap was just overwhelming the world.

Q: Did it succeed? Did this irreverent kind of approach get you noticed?

NOONE: We became the flavor of the month. We were completely different from every other band before us. That was the plan. We didn't do the same kind of material as every other band in town. They all did the same material, which was quite odd. They all did three Beatles songs, a Chuck Berry song. We didn't do any of that. We did "I'm Henry VIII, I Am" and "My Boy Lollipop" and "Sea Cruise" — all songs that nobody else did. So old songs instead of, *"This pullover that I gave you, baby."* We didn't do any of that stuff. We did silly stuff, which was kind of a send-up of the teen idols of the time.

The idea of Herman's Hermits was that we were different. We can't write songs as good as the Beatles. We can't play rhythm-and-blues as good as the Stones. We don't have as good a drummer as the Dave Clark Five. We didn't have this sort of sexy, pop-star, lead singer. We had a guy called Herman who was not sexy at all, do you know what I mean? We played *against* that. We didn't do Billy Fury. We did (the Ernie K-Doe song) "Mother-in-Law," because it was so odd that a 15-year-old boy would sing a song called "Mother-in-Law." I thought, "Let's go and, like, mix a bit of the dramatic in with it." So "Mrs. Brown, You've Got a Lovely Daughter" is kind of a dramatic idea, you know? I could dress up and be the character. So I dressed up as a 14-year-old schoolboy and sang, "Mrs. Brown, You've Got a Lovely Daughter."

Q: Did any of the other bands at the time get the joke?

NOONE: Funny you should ask that. To tell you the truth, we were only *really* trying to impress the Beatles. We'd do a song in the hopes that they'd be impressed by it (laughs). I mean, the Beatles came along specifically to get rid of — what was his name? That guy from Philadelphia there? — Frankie Avalon. "What can we do to make those people look ridiculous? Let's do the Beatles!" Do you know what I mean?

Above: The 1968 movie "Mrs. Brown, You've Got a Lovely Daughter." Overleaf: A 1966 illustration by Frank Frazetta. © MGM

Q: Where did the name "Herman's Hermits" come in?

NOONE: We were rehearsing in a pub. I was wearing these big horn-rimmed glasses. The man who runs the pub walks up and he says, "What are ya *doin'?"* I said, "Buddy Holly." He said, "You look nuthin' like Buddy Holly! You look like Herman from the 'Bullwinkle' show." He meant Sherman, the boy in the glasses with Mr. Peabody on the cartoon. He says to the band, "What are *you* laughin' at? You should call yourselves the bloody Hermits!"

Q: I suppose that the legend isn't true — that the Hermits recorded "Mrs. Brown" as a lark, and then American radio picked up on it, which led to your novelty song "I'm Henry VIII, I Am."

NOONE: Well, in those days, when a band made its first studio album, everybody just went in — like the Beatles' first album — you went in and recorded your stage act as quickly as possible. "Mrs. Brown You've Got a Lovely Daughter" was one of the songs that we did on stage. By the way, nobody *wanted* us to record "Mrs. Brown, You've Got a Lovely Daughter." Everyone said, "Oh, bloody hell, let's not have *this* on the album." So (producer) Mickie Most said, "Just hide it on the second side. No one will ever get that far anyway." You know what I mean? Everybody listens to the first two songs, and if they're crap, they just make a cassette or something. But it was the song that jumped out. It was really a unique song, that's all.

Same thing with "There's a Kind of Hush." The record company didn't like it. So we hid it. We put it on Side 2, Track 3. We knew nobody would get that far. If the record company had anything to do with it, we never would have had *any* hits.

Q: The Hermits came to America to make a movie, "Hold On!" (1966). What do you remember about the experience?

NOONE: I remember everything. It was an odd experience. What happened was, we were in a rock 'n' roll band, and we were very lucky because we got to go to Hollywood. We were on MGM Records. They decided that if they put us in a movie, a la Elvis Presley, it would help to sell records. So it seemed to be all packaged. But we just made fun of the whole idea.

We got to MGM, and the driver of our limo was the guy who worked for Cary Grant full-time! When we got there, he said there were more fans outside of the studio than *Elvis* got. Because, this was at the height of the whole British Invasion thing.

Q: What *is* your take on what we Yanks call the British Invasion?

NOONE: That was when the old-timers suddenly *became* old-timers. With the British groups, that was the end of that "West Side Story" world. Kids went out on their own; they weren't taken by their moms and dads anymore. They went to Shea Stadium.

Q: How did it feel to be chased by screaming girls?

NOONE: It was all right. We saw "A Hard Day's Night" and "Help!" and the Dave Clark Five in "Catch Us If You Can." We just couldn't run quite as fast as the Beatles.

Q: Did you mind being called Herman?

NOONE: It was unavoidable. *Everyone* called me Herman in those days. Even my mom — just so her friends would know who she was talking about.

HERMANS
HERMITS

6

Pink Floyd

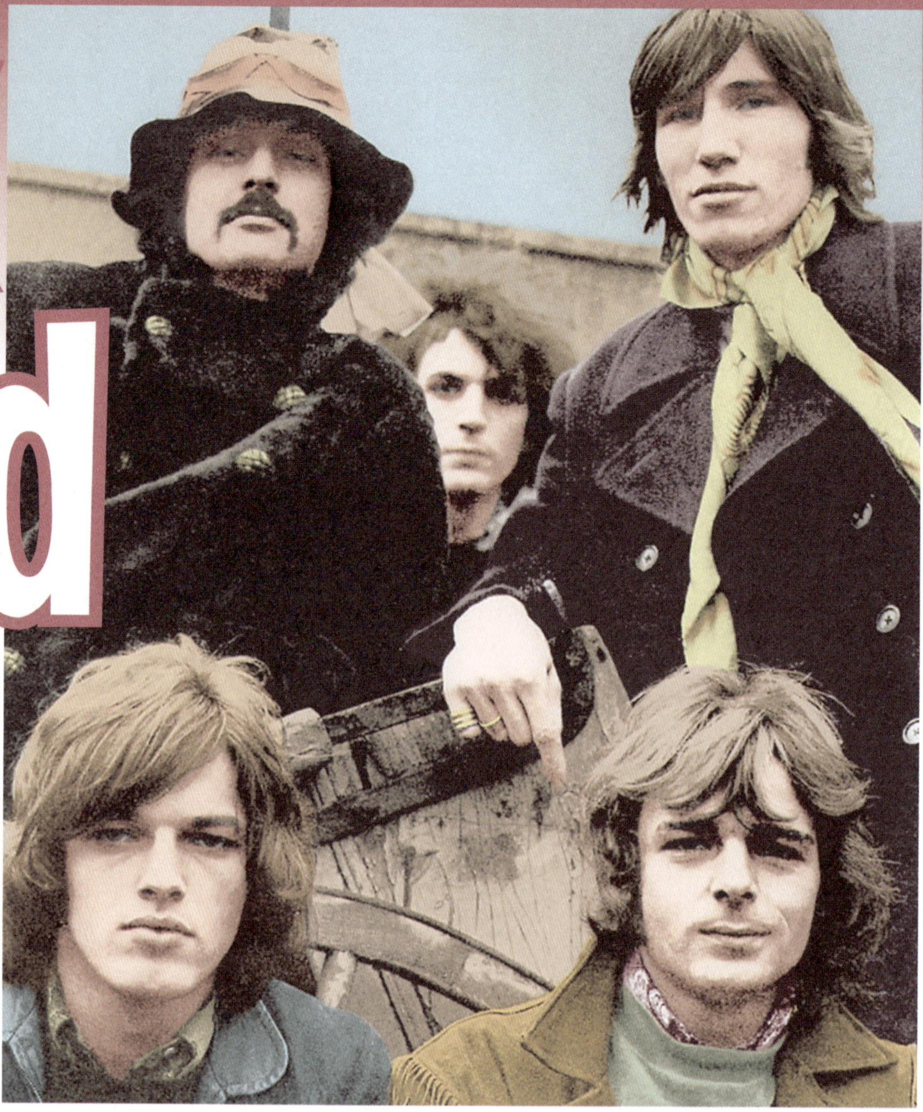

Pink Floyd circa 1968 was, clockwise from top left, Nick Mason, Syd Barrett, Roger Waters, Richard Wright and David Gilmour. © Columbia Records

MANY THINK OF PINK FLOYD as the band behind "Dark Side of the Moon" and "The Wall" — art-rock albums with ponderous themes and spacey arrangements that go well with, let's say, illicit enhancements.

These records often sound like they have roots in psychedelia, and they *do*.

Surprise! Floyd formed in London in 1964, not 1972, and for certain fans, the group's golden period came with "Arnold Layne" (#20 in the U.K.) and "See Emily Play" (#6 in the U.K.), songs from 1967 that sounded quite different from the pop pack. These songs can be attributed to the singular genius of Syd Barrett, the band's singer, main songwriter ... and tragic figure. He proved a frail person whose reign was not sustainable, and whose post as leader was assumed by bassist Roger Waters.

"It's well documented, the fact that Syd left under a cloud, and then we had the big bust-up with Roger," drummer Nick Mason told me in 2005. "One almost gets the impression that Pink Floyd has been at war since the dawn of time. The fact is, I was in a band where most of the time, we got on really well. We came from slightly similar backgrounds, and actually spent a lot of time together having fun. Most of the time, we had a terrific time."

Mason felt the popularization of the period obscured its depth.

"One of the aspects of the whole psychedelic era, which people forget, was that it was about much more than music and fashion. Music is what became the big *commercial* success," he said.

"But in fact, the London underground was led by poetry reading, initially. They had some of the Americans, the sort of Beat poets, come and give a reading at the Albert Hall. There was a huge turnout for it. People wanted this. So it was much more sort of general culture than just music and flared trousers."

Pink Floyd were teenagers. Were they just looking for kicks?

"I suppose I'll answer particularly on my behalf," Mason said. "Because Roger, I think, sometimes thinks that he had a longer-term view of it. Certainly, as far as I was concerned, we were a college band just doin' it for fun. When it looked like it actually might *do* something, I certainly assumed it would only last a year.

BEST-KNOWN EARLY LINEUP: Singer Syd Barrett (1946-2006, born in Cambridge); bassist Roger Waters (born 1943 in Great Bookham); guitarist David Gilmour (born 1946 in Cambridge); keyboardist Richard Wright (1943-2008, born in Hatch End); drummer Nick Mason (born 1944 in Birmingham)

"I actually had to prepare, in rather a cheating way, the background that ensured that I actually could return to college a year later," Mason added with a laugh. "You know, I *still* haven't been back, so I don't think my place is still being held."

It's possible that Mason's long career in music was spurred by his interest in language as a boy growing up in Hampstead.

"I always liked reading when I was a kid, and I read all sorts of unsuitable books, like (Charles Hamilton's series) 'Billy Bunter' and (author) Arthur Ransome and stuff like that," Mason said.

"I had very good English teachers when I was at school. I can even remember their names: Michael Camp and Allan Humphries. There was a lot of reading at school. Probably from that period, English was always a favorite subject of mine. Math and French and Latin seemed like work. English didn't seem like work."

THE PINK FLOYD FAITHFUL PUTS BARRETT ON an altar alongside other casualties of rock who were enormously creative but consumed by their recreational pursuits — paying dearly for the privilege — such as Brian Jones and Jimi Hendrix.

But Barrett rated some deification. His unique songwriting approach paired saturnine wordplay with peculiar melodies. An early user of noise to create aural spaces, Barrett took chances in the studio. And he had a look that just *screamed* Rock Martyr.

By 1968, Barrett — who used LSD and possibly suffered from schizophrenia — could no longer be counted upon to even show up at gigs, let alone lead Pink Floyd. That year, he was fired from the band, an unhappy situation for both parties.

After his solo albums "The Madcap Laughs" and "Barrett" (both 1970), on which Floyd members Richard Wright, David Gilmour and Waters appeared, Barrett withdrew from performing by degrees. He became a recluse, a shell of his vibrant old self, sometimes approached by paparazzi or curious fans. Barrett was often spoken of in the past tense, as if he was already dead.

There were tributes. David Bowie covered "See Emily Play" on his album "Pin Ups" (1973). Pink Floyd's song "Shine On You Crazy Diamond" (1975) was about their onetime bandmate.

Barrett died at 60 of pancreatic cancer in Cambridge in 2006.

AMERICAN "SHOCK ROCKER" ALICE COOPER GOT to know Barrett and Pink Floyd in 1968, when Cooper and his band were still unknowns (before charting with such songs as "School's Out," "I'm Eighteen" and "No More Mr. Nice Guy").

"Well, they used to *live* with us," Cooper told me in 1997.

"When they first came over to the States, they literally moved in. We had a house in Venice (Calif.) that we were just barely able to pay the rent on. They came into town, and *they* didn't have any money either. So I said, 'Why don't you guys move in with us for a while?' So it was Alice Cooper and Pink Floyd living in the same house. Isn't that bizarre?

"Syd Barrett would just sit there, like ..." (Cooper stared into space for a few seconds.) "Hel-*lo?* He was, like, really gone. I mean, it was a lot of acid damage, I think. Even then. And that was '68, so you can just imagine."

Mason, of course, knew Barrett before the deterioration.

"He was absolutely charming, absolutely delightful," said the drummer. "When I first met him, I felt, 'What a great guy.' After a time, I don't know if he wanted to *be* in a rock band any more.

"You know, it *is* a sad story. One of the elements of Syd is that sort of James Dean thing: What could he have achieved if he'd carried on? And that sort of sad thing of a genius unfulfilled."

'What could he have achieved if he'd carried on?'

— Nick Mason on Syd Barrett

The Troggs

As definitive and cool as Jimi Hendrix's version of "Wild Thing" is, it doesn't hold a candle to the Troggs' in-your-face version, which went to #1 in 1966. Founded in Andover, Hampshire, the foursome also charted in the States via the pop-y "With a Girl Like You" (#29) and the hippie-ish "Love is All Around" (#7). Need you be told that the root of the band's name is "troglodyte"?

Manfred Mann

Named for Johannesburg-born keyboardist Manfred Lubowitz — who quit jazz to play pop, but still *looked* jazz — the band had two singers. Paul Jones sang "Doo Wah Diddy Diddy" (#1), "Sha La La" (#12) and "Pretty Flamingo" (#29); Mike D'Abo sang "Mighty Quinn" (#10). In 1976, spinoff Manfred Mann's Earth Band scored a #1 with Bruce Springsteen's "Blinded by the Light."

The Merseybeats

They're called the Merseybeats, so naturally, they are four lads from Liverpool who played the Cavern Club and were once managed by Brian Epstein. The Merseybeats never charted in the U.S., but between 1963 and '65, the group had quite a few hits in the U.K., including "I Think of You" (#5), "Don't Turn Around" (#13), "Wishin' and Hopin'" (#13) and "I Love You, Yes I Do" (#22).

The Mindbenders

Named after a science-fiction film, the Mindbenders were founded in Manchester in 1963 by singer Wayne Fontana. They scored a #1 hit with "The Game of Love" (1965). Fontana then quit — reportedly in the middle of a show — and guitarist Eric Stewart sang the band's #2 hit, "A Groovy Kind of Love" (1966). The Mindbenders are seen playing a dance in the movie "To Sir With Love" (1967).

The Nashville Teens

No, they weren't teens from Nashville. The sextet formed in Surrey in 1962, and scored a #14 in the U.S. with their harmony-driven version of "Tobacco Road." The Teens honed a specialty backing American rock 'n' roll pioneers like Jerry Lee Lewis, Chuck Berry and Carl Perkins. Lewis' album "Live at the Star Club, Hamburg" (1964) is just Lee backed by the Teens!

Them

Two things for which to thank Them: introducing Van Morrison, and the group's super raw 1964 garage-rock classic "Gloria" (a Morrison composition later covered by the Doors and Patti Smith). Them formed in Belfast in 1964, and charted in the U.S. with "Here Comes the Night" (#24) and "Mystic Eyes" (#33). Hear also Them's cover of Big Joe Williams' "Baby Please Don't Go."

The Swinging Blue Jeans

Four *more* lads from Liverpool formed in the early '60s ... played the Star-Club in Hamburg and the Cavern Club back home ... covered "Long Tall Sally" by Little Richard ... *and they're not even the Beatles*. The Swinging Blue Jeans formed in 1962 and scored a #24 in the U.S. with "Hippy Hippy Shake" and, speaking of Little Richard, a #43 with "Good Golly Miss Molly."

Freddie and the Dreamers

Buddy Holly made it cool for a nerdy-lookin' guy in glasses to front a rock 'n' roll band. Freddie Garrity of Freddie and the Dreamers took full advantage of this exemption. The group formed in 1963 in Manchester, and had hits with "I'm Telling You Now" (#1), "I Understand Just How You Feel" (#36) and "Do the Freddie" (#18), a song built around the group's "funny" choreography.

The Searchers

Another four lads from Liverpool (was there an endless supply?) formed in 1959 and named themselves after the John Wayne western. They transitioned from skiffle to pop, and scored hits with covers of American artists such as Jackie DeShannon, the Drifters, the Orions and the Clovers. Their catchy version of DeShannon's "Needles and Pins" reached #1 in the U.K. and #13 in America.

The Fortunes

In 1965, in the thick of the British Invasion era, the Fortunes charted in the U.S. with "You've Got Your Troubles" (#7) and "Here It Comes Again" (#2). But the quintet, which formed in 1961 in Birmingham, proved it had staying power with the 1971 hit "Here Comes That Rainy Day Feeling Again" (#15), a pop confection which blended xylophone and strings like a dream.

The Tremeloes

How many bands can say they beat out the Beatles? It happened when the Tremeloes and the Fab Four auditioned for the same gig with Decca Records. "They just didn't do the right songs that day," Tremeloes singer Brian Poole later explained on why his group prevailed. The Tremeloes formed in 1958 in Essex, and scored a #11 hit in the U.S. with "Silence is Golden" (#11).

Dave Dee, Dozy, Beaky, Mick & Tich

Stylish DDDBM&T formed in Salisbury in 1964, and had a killer song in "Hold Tight!" (Quentin Tarantino put it in 2007's "Death Proof.") In 1969, when the Beatles recorded their very last song while John Lennon was away in Denmark, George Harrison said on mic: "You will have read that Dave Dee is no longer with us. But Micky and Tich and I would like to carry on the good work."

Not every British act could be the Beatles. Some had U.S. hits but weren't as "sexy." Some had hits in England but not in the U.S.

The Ivy League scored two Top 10 hits in the U.K., but none in the States. Cliff Richard, Adam Faith and Jonathan King all had many hits in the U.K., but only one Top 40 apiece in the States during the British Invasion period.

There are acts we Yanks remember because the careers of Invasion bands somehow intersected with theirs, such as Remo Four, Pretty Things, the Fourmost, the Mojos, the Undertakers, Billy Fury, Screaming Lord Sutch, Georgie Fame, Long John Baldry, Zoot Money, Tommy Quickly, the Roadrunners, Derry and the Seniors, Rory Storm and the Hurricanes, Cliff Bennett and the Rebel Rousers, and Billy J. Kramer and the Dakotas. (Exactly *how* their careers intersected is the stuff of rock history.)

Bands that made ripples among hardcore Anglophiles who somehow got their hands on *New Musical Express* or *Pop Weekly* were the Action, a Band of Angels, the Applejacks, the Banchees, the Beatstalkers, the Black Knights, the Blackwells, the Boys, the Brook Brothers, the Brumbeats, the Clique, Dean Ford and the Gaylords, the Dennisons, Downliners Sect, the Easybeats, the Gamblers, the Honeycombs, the Hullaballoos, the Kestrels, the Koobas, the Mockingbirds, the Mods, the Primitives, the Roulettes, the Syndicats and the Untamed.

Launching pads for future stars included the Artwoods (with Jon Lord); the Cheynes (Mick Fleetwood); the Paramounts (Robin Trower); the V.I.P.s (Keith Emerson); the Senators (John Bonham); and the Rockin' Vickers (Lemmy).

THE IMAGINATION REELS. I'VE always wondered about local bands throughout the U.K. from the period, who perhaps never recorded, nor played beyond the regions from whence they hailed. But these groups indeed played pop or rock or blues or skiffle in pubs or halls or cafes or schools. People followed them. You could say they were on the cusp of history.

While perusing an old issue of *Rave,* I came upon the endorsement of such a group from a female fan on the letters page. The group was known as Buddy Francis and the Blue Starrs, this fan wrote, and they played in a place called Bury, which is just northwest of Manchester.

It's kind of a romantic thing to ponder. Who *were* Buddy Francis and the Blue Starrs? What did they sound like? What were their day jobs? What were their hopes and dreams?

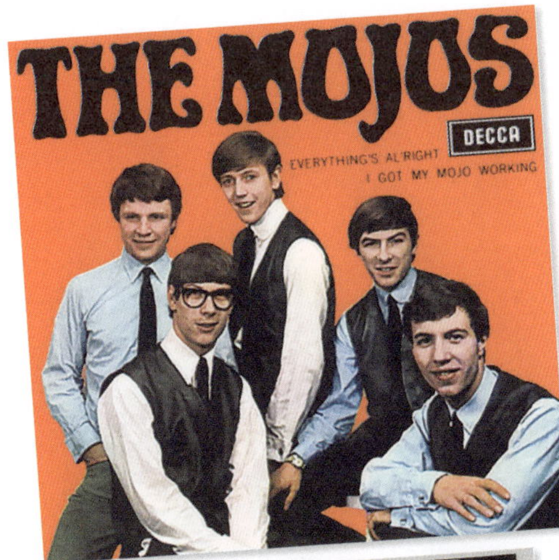

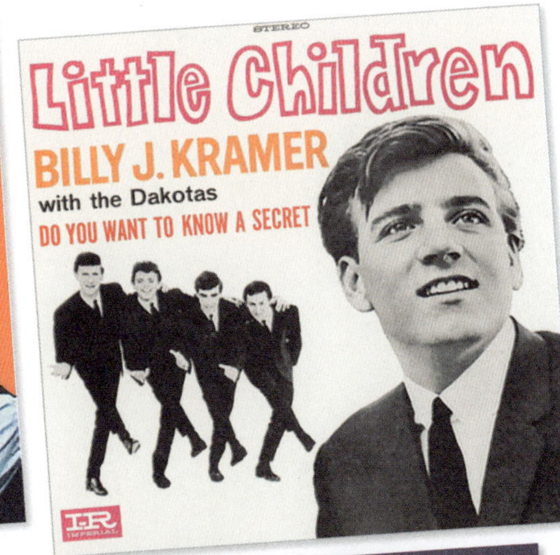

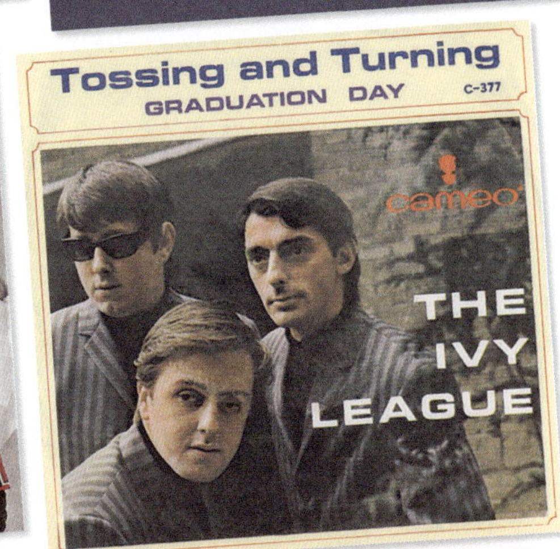

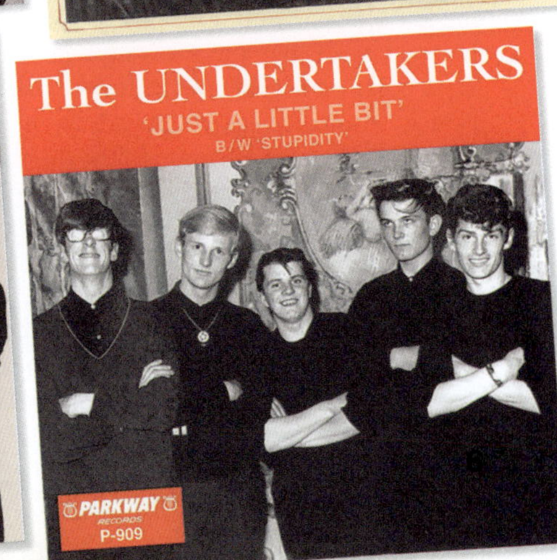

There's much music from British artists of the period that warrants rediscovery.

Solo artists made some noise, too. From left above: Dusty Springfield, Cilla Black and Lulu. Below: Sandie Shaw.

Guitar-strumming bands weren't the only Brits to conquer America.

Solo artists likewise made some noise, er, music on our shores.

London native Dusty Springfield (1939-1999) scored 10 Top 40 hits in the States. Springfield's bouncy debut single, "I Only Want to Be With You" (#12 in 1963), made her only the second British Invasion-era artist to chart in the U.S. (after the Beatles, natch). Springfield also charted with "Wishin' and Hopin'" (#6), "You Don't Have to Say You Love Me" (#4) and "The Look of Love" (#22).

Cilla Black (1943-2015) was chummy with her fellow Liverpudlians the Beatles and Gerry and the Pacemakers, and all were represented by Brian Epstein. Black (born Priscilla White) had 19 Top 40 hits back home (with two at #1), but just one in America with "You're My World" (#26). Still, the song was enough to show us Yanks that Black had some pipes on her, in a performance that begins with a smoky, wounded voice and ends as an all-out belter.

Dagenham native Sandie Shaw (born 1947) was only 17 when she scored her first of three #1 hits in the U.K. with the Burt Bacharach/Hal David composition "(There's) Always Something There to Remind Me." That song and "Girl Don't Come" pierced the Top 100 in the States. In October 1964, Shaw appeared on an episode of the American TV show "Shindig!" that also featured the Beatles.

London native Marianne Faithfull (born 1946) scored a #22 in America with "As Tears Go By," written by the Rolling Stones' Mick Jagger (then Faithfull's boyfriend) and Keith Richards. Faithfull had three more Top 40 hits in the States.

Glasgow native Lulu (born Marie Lawrie in 1948) topped the charts for five straight weeks with "To Sir, With Love," theme song of James Clavell's 1967 British film of the same title starring Sidney Portier as a teacher of troubled youths. Lulu played a student in the film.

MORE BRITISH SOLO ARTISTS WERE Middlesex native Adam Faith (1940-2003), whose "It's Alright" went to #31 in 1964; Kent native Crispian St. Peters (1939-2010), who scored a #4 with "The Pied Piper" in 1966; Wales native Tom Jones (born 1940), whose debut "It's Not Unusual" featured Jimmy Page and went to #10 in 1965; Glasgow native Donovan, who had a dozen Top 40 hits between 1965 and '69; as well as Dave Berry (seven U.K. Top-40s, but none here), Julie Driscoll, Brian Auger, Elkie Brooks, Kiki Dee, Erkey Grant, David Macbeth and Twinkle.

Which brings us to Islington native Chris Farlowe (born 1940). His raspy, soulful vocal on "Out of Time" (#1 in the U.K. and produced by Jagger) is better than the Stones' version.

Petula Clark

At the time of her first U.S. hit, Petula Clark was no teenager.

"I was married with two small children when all of this started," she recalled with a laugh when we spoke in 2011.

Clark (born 1932 in Ewell) was a child actor in movies, and released her first single in 1949. Despite all that experience, her life changed at age 31 when "Downtown" went to #1 in America in 1964, followed by such hits as "I Know a Place" (#3), "A Sign of the Times" (#11) and "Don't Sleep in the Subway" (#5).

"I was living in Europe and working in Europe and I had all of these different contracts," Clark said. "And then America happened, which was a very exciting thing to happen. When America calls, you don't just say, 'Sorry, I can't make it.'"

Clark made her American TV debut on — where else? — "The Ed Sullivan Show," in a hastily booked appearance.

She recalled: "When 'Downtown' became a #1 hit in the States, I started getting calls. 'You've gotta get here!' I was on tour in French-speaking Canada, which really wasn't that far. But I couldn't just drop everything. Then, about three (American) dates came up on a Sunday."

But *getting* here was a problem for the singer.

"I flew in from Paris," Clark said. "I got to the (television) studio in New York. I was absolutely jet-lagged out of my brain. I mean, I'd had a show the night before in Paris!

"I walked straight into the studio, into a dress rehearsal, which was done before a live audience. I had not rehearsed with the band. They suddenly started playing my music — a bit too fast, I might add. And the place went crazy! It was remarkable.

"So I had to do a lot of traveling. There were a lot of separations. We took the children around with us as much as we could. I never actually lived in the States ever, except when I was doing (the 1968 film) 'Finian's Rainbow.'"

BUT THERE WAS NOTHING EXTRAORDINARY, NO particular sense of urgency, while recording "Downtown."

"I was living in Paris when I heard 'Downtown' for the first time," Clark said. "(Composer) Tony Hatch came to my apartment and played it for me on piano. It was not finished yet, but it was a very good tune with one or two good lyrics. I said, 'This is a great song. Finish it as well as you started it, and I'll record it.'

"I was in London a couple of weeks later, and we recorded it. We just did it straight-ahead. There was no fooling around, no electronic twiddly bits," Clark added, laughing again. "I just sang the song. We did three takes and used the second one. The orchestration was wonderful. That was the key.

"He (Hatch) wrote many songs for me after that — 'Don't Sleep in the Subway,' 'I Couldn't Live Without Your Love,' all of those. It was great fun singing these great songs in the studio."

As for Clark's long-ago movie career: "I was a child. Later on, I did a film with Alec Guinness. I gave him his first screen kiss, and he gave me mine. It was not particularly earth-moving for either of us. We were both very shy."

Petula Clark was a child actor in movies.
Photo courtesy of Clark

Chad and Jeremy

"We should have been voted 'Least Likely to Succeed as a Pop Duo.' He wanted to be an actor. I was to become a magnificent arranger."

That was Chad Stuart, on his and Jeremy Clyde's ambitions before teaming up as Chad and Jeremy. "It goes to show you," he continued, "life is what happens when you're making plans."

Windermere native Stuart (1941-2020) and Dorney native Clyde (born 1941) scored seven Top 40 U.S. hits in 1964 and '65, including "Yesterday's Gone" (#21) and "A Summer Song" (#7).

"The whole thing was a very strange example of serendipity," Stuart told me. (We spoke in 2005 and 2011.)

"We had a band in college. You usually do, if you're halfway musical. It wasn't a very good band, but never mind."

Stuart explained that Clyde was embarking on a theatrical career when the actors' union went on strike. "Actors couldn't work," Stuart said, "so Jeremy was at a loose end. He came back to London. We started playing again, just for fun. We played at this Italian restaurant near his apartment. They'd give us a free dinner and 10 shillings, which is half a pound, which is not much. We ate a lot of spaghetti in those days," he added with a laugh.

"So had there been no strike — Jeremy was acting, and I was in all sort of different bands playing keyboards — things would have turned out differently."

THE DUO WAS DISCOVERED by John Barry, then a record producer who went on to score 11 James Bond films, including "Goldfinger."

Recalled Stuart: "I was working my day job. I had hot-footed down to this club where we used to sing during lunch hour, and then at night I would work with pickup bands. I just remember feeling rather exhausted and thinking, 'God, something good's gotta come out of this.'

"Sure enough, John Barry came and heard us singing at the lunch hour at this folk-club cellar kind of place. The rest was history, pretty much."

But Stuart recalled that their debut single, "Yesterday's Gone," did not exactly take England by storm. "The song got to #45 with an anchor, and stayed for a few weeks," he said. "Then it sunk out of sight."

Owing to the British Invasion's momentum, the song fared better in the States, breaking the Top 40 and launching C&J in America.

Chad (left) and Jeremy

FULL-BLOWN CHAD-AND-JEREMY-MANIA occurred during the group's second trip to the United States, according to Stuart. "When we finally arrived in L.A. on our second visit, I mean, neither Jeremy nor I will ever forget that," he said. "The record company and the DJs all got together and made *sure* that all the kids knew when our flight was.

"And, you know, it was the usual story — like the Beatles at JFK, except obviously not on such a grand scale. To us, it was incredible. Of course, it was manufactured in the sense that if the DJs hadn't told them we were coming, those girls wouldn't have been there. But, I mean, *was* that manufactured? I don't know. I think there was a definite misplaced hysteria. If they couldn't have a Beatle, they would take a Chad or a Jeremy.

"This was in the days before airport security. It was a school day, but all the girls came anyway. There was an arrival lounge full of girls playing hookey from school, stacking the place floor-to-ceiling. On the stairs, on the balcony. It was just the most ear-splitting, mind-boggling noise I've ever heard."

That's a sound, Stuart was told, that many a young fella would sell his soul to hear. "Right," he laughed again. "Any young fool who believes in his own immortality. Definitely, it stoked the testosterone, I think, at that point. It was craziness."

WAS STUART ABLE TO, shall we say, cash in on any of this feminine attention? "Oh," he said, "Jeremy did enough for both of us.

"I was married to a fellow drama student (Jill Gibson) who then became an Eileen Ford model and made it into that silly magazine that says, 'The 10 Most Beautiful People in the World.' So I was a married guy. And interestingly enough, that was considered to be a huge challenge in those days. Remember when they tried to hide John Lennon's marriage to Cynthia Lennon?

"We diffused that problem by making (Gibson) the intermediary for the girls. She became the 'Secretary of the Fan Club,' sort of thing. I think it worked because Jeremy was Studly Stud Muffin and I was Mr. Nice Guy."

THE DUO BECAME TV STARS, TOO, IN America, by playing themselves (or versions of themselves) on "The Dick Van Dyke Show," "The Patty Duke Show" (both 1965) and "Batman" (1966).

"The most exciting one was 'Dick Van Dyke,' for two reasons," Stuart said. "One, it was the first. But to wake up one day and find yourself sitting at the table on a Monday morning, reading the script for the first time with Dick Van Dyke, Mary Tyler Moore, Carl Reiner, (screenwriters) Bill Persky and Sam Denoff — I mean, these were Hollywood legends. It was like, 'Pinch me, I'm dreaming,' wasn't it?

"Dick and Mary reinforced the theory that the bigger they are, the sweeter they are. You don't find the Dick Van Dykes and Mary Tyler Moores being anything other than helpful, kind, considerate, full of good advice, and realizing that you're probably a nervous kid out of a coal-mining town in the North of England who happened to go to drama school and knows a few things but not much, and you're feeling very much out of your depth. They went out of their way to make us feel at home. It was an unforgettable experience."

As for "Patty Duke": "It was kind of a stupid show, wasn't it? It wasn't going to win an award for scriptwriting. Don't get me wrong, Patty was great."

And "Batman": "The show was legendary at the time. Everyone wanted to do it. It was the 'in' thing, the flavor of the year. We didn't have to do anything except stand around and be pathetic. I know Jeremy was very enamored of Julie Newmar, but he didn't get anywhere with her. Oh, lordy."

"WHEN YOU THINK ON THOSE DAYS, you're a piece of meat, aren't you?" Stuart concluded. "You're just a tool to be exploited. I'm not p***ed off about it. They weren't hurting us. You just went along for the ride.

"The press would always ask us, 'What are you going to do when the bubble bursts?' And we would be offended. Because, we would say, 'Well, it's not *gonna* burst, man.' Which, of course, it did."

Alas, chart success didn't translate into monetary success for the duo, according to Stuart.

"To this day, we don't know if anyone paid anyone," the singer said. "Three #1 hits and no money — what's wrong with this picture? But that's the thing, isn't it? You can either spend your life being bitter, or say, 'Hey, it's too late now.' After all that time, you've gotta laugh."

Pop duo Chad Stuart (left) and Jeremy Clyde were still cozy in 2005.

Photo by Kathy Voglesong

Peter and Gordon

How duo narrowly avoided becoming folk singers

BEING THE GIRLFRIEND'S LITTLE BROTHER HAD its privileges for Peter Asher of the pop duo Peter and Gordon.

His sister was model-actress Jane Asher, who dated Paul McCartney from 1963 until '68. When Peter Asher and Gordon Waller won a recording contract, McCartney wrote their first hit, "A World Without Love," which went to #1 in 1964. Peter and Gordon went on to score 10 Top 40 hits, including "Nobody I Know," "I Go to Pieces," "Lady Godiva" and "True Love Ways."

Scotland native Waller died at 64 in 2009. London native Asher (born 1944), once a dead ringer for Austin Powers, reported that yes, he and Waller were chased by girls. We spoke in 2011.

Gordon Waller and Peter Asher with Ed Sullivan in 1964. Courtesy of Peter Asher

Q: You and Gordon met at Westminster School, a boys' school in London. It's the origin story for many groups of your generation.

ASHER: It's always something like that, because you spend most of your time in school during that time of life. In the case of Gordon and myself, we were both attending Westminster, which is a very posh public school. That's the British gift for understatement — it isn't "public" at all. It costs a lot of money to go there. So that's where we met. At the time, there were not a lot of people playing guitar and singing, believe it or not. We might have been *it*.

I was a big folk fan. I liked Woody Guthrie and Cisco Houston. I was also big into jazz, but I couldn't *play* jazz, because I didn't have the genius for it. On the other hand, folk songs, I could play. Gordon was more of a rocker. He was into Elvis (Presley) and Buddy Holly. So we did a mixture of music that we both liked, though our voices were quite different. Gordon had this big sort of Elvis-y, rock 'n' roll voice; he remains one of my favorite singers. I had this choir-ish voice. But to our surprise, they worked together. They did seem to form some kind of an entity.

Q: Of course, Paul McCartney was dating your sister, Jane. When did Paul first play "A World Without Love" for you?

ASHER: Paul, he became a friend. He was actually living in my family home. Since he was going with my sister, and we were all friends as well, he used our house when they (the Beatles) weren't on tour. He had the room on the top floor next to mine, so he and I would hang out. At some point, Paul played me "World Without Love," but it was unfinished. There was no bridge.

Q: It's such a great song. No offense intended, but why did he give it to you guys?

ASHER: He said the Beatles decided not to record it. I quite liked the song, and I remembered it. Some months later, we (Peter and Gordon) were offered a record deal by EMI. At the time, they imagined us being the English answer to the Kingston Trio or Peter, Paul and Mary. In their minds, we were going to be part of the folk boom. We had a song called "Five Hundred Miles" that they liked, so they signed us.

As the date for the first recording session was approaching, the search was on for what tunes we should record. I said to Paul, "Remember that song you played for me? Can you finish that for us?" Paul said he would. It took quite a bit to get it done. He finished writing the bridge at the last minute. So he wrote that bridge, and we recorded the song. "World Without Love" became the universal choice for the first single. So we weren't folk singers any more (laughs).

Q: Peter and Gordon had 10 Top 40 hits. You were on television and radio. Were screaming girls chasing you and trying to tear your clothes off?

ASHER: Yes. Screaming girls trying to tear your clothes off is highly recommended. It's great fun. It happened in Britain as well. But American girls were more determined.

Q: You and Gordon played "The Ed Sullivan Show" nine months after the Beatles debuted. What do you remember about that night?

ASHER: Ed Sullivan was fun. We knew what a big deal that was. It was very formal. Everyone in studio would be very reverential to him — *"Oh, yes, Mr. Sullivan"* — whispering and bowing and scraping. We didn't meet him at all before we played. The great thing about it was that we played live. Half of the other shows in America were done with lip-synching, which is boring. On Sullivan, you sang live with his orchestra, which was very good. They told us, "When you're done playing, look over to Mr. Sullivan. If he holds out his arms encouragingly, you walk over to him. If he doesn't, you don't." Well, he *did,* or I might not be telling you that part.

Q: You were a child actor. Were you really in an episode of "Colonel March of Scotland Yard," which starred Boris Karloff? Did you work with Karloff?

ASHER: Yes and yes. Boris Karloff played a detective in this series in England. I did get to meet him. He was charming. I remember he had to smash a glass of milk out of my hand (in the episode). I was sitting at a table with my parents, and he was there. Someone was trying to kill us with poison or something. He took his walking stick and smashed it out of my hand. Yes, Boris Karloff seemed very nice.

Q: Were you disappointed when your acting career came to an end?

ASHER: Yes. I believe that being a child actor faded away for me because of school. When you go to Westminster, you take it seriously or not at all. So I started turning things down. As you know, with actors, once you start turning things down, they stop calling you. In my case, interest waned. But I honestly did miss it.

Q: After Peter and Gordon disbanded in 1968, you got into producing. You produced "Fire and Rain" by James Taylor (#3 in 1971), among many songs. Was becoming a producer the musical equivalent of an actor who wishes to direct?

ASHER: It was, in a way. All the time we'd been singing and making records, I just loved the studio process. I was fascinated by it all. I loved watching what could be done and learning from the engineers. I owe a debt to Paul Jones, who was the lead singer for Manfred Mann — a fantastic singer and one of best harmonica players in the world. He asked me to produce his record ("And the Sun Will Shine," 1968), so I owe him a debt. I loved doing it, and the whole process of casting musicians and working with the singer to bring out his best performance. Then Paul McCartney became aware that I was doing this, and asked if I'd produce some records for Apple and become their A&R guy. So that's how I drifted into it. But I didn't really "drift." I made a decision and then I aimed for it.

From top: "Nobody I Know" sleeve; Asher in 1964; Asher the producer. Courtesy of Peter Asher

Living room rock

Pudding-bowl haircuts? Nov. 18, 1963, brought us, as the expression goes, a first draft of history in the Beatles saga, at least in America.

"Dispatches from Britain have been talking about a new sound," reported Chet Huntley, co-host of NBC's "The Huntley Brinkley Report." "For a while," Huntley continued, "we thought the new sound was Prime Minister Douglas-Home describing himself as a simple man of the soil, but that's not what they meant."

Huntley then introduced a segment by Edwin Newman, who reported: "The hottest musical group in Great Britain today is the Beatles. That's not a collection of insects, but a quartet of young men with pudding-bowl haircuts who spell 'Beatles' B-E-A-T-L-E-S.

Jack Paar © NBC Television

"They were all born during the Blitz in the Merseyside section of Liverpool, the toughest section of one of the toughest cities in the world. It's anybody's guess why the Beatles emerged from its cellar nightclubs to national prominence — but emerge, they did."

This was one of at least two Beatles-themed segments on American television that preceded the band's historic first appearance on "The Ed Sullivan Show."

On Jan. 3, 1964, a month before "Sullivan," "Tonight" host Jack Paar wrapped a segment about the Beatles by quipping: "It's nice to know that England has finally risen to our cultural level."

POST-"SULLIVAN," PROGRAMMERS LEARNED THAT booking just about any British pop act translated into ratings. Dean Martin introduced the Rolling Stones on the June 13, 1964, "Hollywood Palace" with: *"I've* been rolled while I was stoned myself." Jimmy O'Neil introduced the Beatles on the Oct. 7, 1964, "Shindig!" as the "entertainment phenomenon of the century."

It was a Brit-nanza when American shows packed a given episode with Invasion acts. The Feb. 17, 1965, "Shindig!" had the Moody Blues, Peter and Gordon, Herman's Hermits, and Sandie Shaw. David McCallum hosted the Sept. 27, 1965, "Hullaballoo" with Peter and Gordon (performing "Yesterday") and the Animals.

The two-parter "Shindig! Goes to London" (taped at the Fifth National Jazz and Blues Festival in Richmond) aired in December 1965, and boasted quite a few "firsts" for American television.

Part 1 featured the Animals (with Eric Burdon in dark specs howling "Rosie"); the Moody Blues (with singer-guitarist Denny Laine doing "I'll Go Crazy"); and Georgie Fame. The finale, "I Feel Alright," brought together Burdon, Stevie Winwood of the Spencer Davis Group, and Steampacket's Long John Baldry, Julie Driscoll and — dancing crazy and singing scat — Rod Stewart.

Part 2 featured the Yardbirds (with guitarist Jeff Beck); Manfred Mann (with singer Paul Jones); the Graham Bond Organisation (with bassist Jack Bruce and drummer Ginger Baker in a precursor to Cream); and the Who (with Pete Townshend gouging his Union Jack-decorated amplifier with his guitar).

PETER NOONE OF THE HERMITS RECALLED DOING "Sullivan," "Danny Kaye" and the Martin-hosted "Hollywood Palace." "It was a fad, remember," Noone told me in 2005. "All of the old-timers, to this day, think it's a fad. The music you hear today, people still say, 'Oh, it'll never last.' So we were a fad. We were replaced by the Monkees, who were replaced by the Osmonds.

"But I think they had a strange kind of respect for us, because we were more talented than they expected. Dean's son was a fan of the band. Danny Kaye's daughter was in the fan club. He showed up in a Herman's Hermits T-shirt and shorts. We showed up in suits, and *he* was in a T-shirt. Ed Sullivan took me to church! He said, 'It's Sunday, church day. Meet me at Delmonico's on Park Avenue.' That's where he lived. So we went to church."

Dave Clark of the Dave Clark Five hits the skins; Mick Jagger sings "Satisfaction"; Peter Noone and his fellow Hermits.

"The Ed Sullivan Show" © CBS Television

Photo illustration

Live from New York

ADDING TO THE EXCITEMENT of the Beatles' debut on "The Ed Sullivan Show" was the fact that what you saw in your living room was happening *right now*.

"Remember, this was live," said newscaster Larry Kane. "You couldn't go anywhere. You couldn't 'fix' it. The performance was amazing. They looked great, they felt great. They proved once and for all that they could replicate their recorded sound as well as any artist in the world."

The first of five songs played by the Beatles — essentially the genesis of the Invasion — was "All My Loving." There's something sweet about the candid moment when Sullivan reintroduced the group for "I Saw Her Standing There," cracking up when he couldn't even get the band's name out over the sudden burst of screaming.

Sullivan knew a good formula when he stumbled onto one. After scoring ratings gold with the Beatles, he brought on more Invasion acts, one after another.

And so, sharing the stage with the Marquis Chimps and Señor Wences were the Dave Clark Five (18 shows, a record); Petula Clark (13 shows); the Stones (six shows); the Animals and the Hermits (four shows each); Dusty Springfield, Peter and Gordon, and the Searchers (one show each).

Sullivan liked to refer to the Beatles as "clean-cut" boys. But the British acts were maturing, with lyrical themes that no longer fit in with Sullivan's family-friendly vision.

Still, he clung to those almighty ratings like grim death. The Beatles' films that Sullivan gratefully aired — the band was *through* with live performances — didn't really jibe with what he presented on his New York stage. The Stones' final appearance on "The Ed Sullivan Show" on Nov. 23, 1969, was a study in twains-not-meeting. Sullivan brought out Topo Gigio, and the Rolling Stones — with Brian Jones dead and buried — sang, *"Oh, see the fire is sweepin' / Our very streets today."*

'The Beatles' (1965-67)

TRY AS YOU MIGHT, YOU CANNOT HATE THE Saturday-morning animated series titled, simply, "The Beatles." Yeah, it's lame. Yeah, the voices don't sound a whit like the Beatles (with the possible exception of Ringo). Yeah, sometimes the wrong Beatle sings a given tune.

But the songs are terrific. (It's the Beatles, yo!) And though the series is an easy target for ridicule, once the cartoon Beatles plug in and play, it's ... it's ... *charming*.

The series was produced by Al Brodax, the animator behind the series "Beetle Bailey" and "Barney Google and Snuffy Smith" — not exactly Disney-level stuff. Though the Beatles initially disliked the series, they later OKed Brodax to produce their 1968 movie "Yellow Submarine."

The episodes are named after song titles. The formula has John, Paul, George and Ringo thrown into various settings such as a jungle, a cruise ship, a rodeo, a movie studio, the ruins of Rome. There is always a gig to get to, and the ongoing problem of being chased by screaming girls. (Of course, this kiddie show never alludes to the fact that these screaming girls represent the brink of sexual awakening.)

Sometimes the boys land in the realm of classic literature, such as Victor Hugo's "The Hunchback of Notre Dame" or Alexandre Dumas's "The Three Musketeers." Sometimes they are dropped into an alternate universe, and encounter leprechauns or monsters. (The Beatles meet Dracula in an episode set at a wax museum in Piccadilly.)

For fans of the great voice artist Paul Frees, "The Beatles" is a treasure trove. Still, John and George are inappropriately voiced. John has the posh "I say" accent. George sounds like an Irish farmer — nothing against Irish farmers. Ringo's approximated Liverpudlian accent is, eh, passable.

But, to give the devil his due, the likenesses are outstanding. These deceptively simple caricatures are instantly recognizable. Brodax's team truly captured the Fab Four.

Inveterate TV watcher John Lennon later called the shows "a blast." Mused George Harrison: "They were so bad or silly that they were good, if you know what I mean."

Ya see? It couldn't have been all *that* terrible.

BEATLES

Kiddie show shenanigans

Even children's fare was affected by the British Invasion. From far left: The Flintstones and the Rubbles donned prehistoric Beatle wigs; Jack Wild won pop-star-level fame on "H.R. Pufnstuf"; the stylish British import "Thunderbirds."

"THE BEATLES" CARTOON SERIES, DOPEY AS IT was, had one profound and lasting effect on Saturday morning television. After "The Beatles," many characters on the Saturday roster formed singing groups — electric guitars and all — and/or original pop tunes were heard during their slapstick montages.

Such shows included "The Archie Show," "The Banana Splits Adventure Hour," "Scooby-Doo, Where Are You!," "Josie and the Pussycats," "Lancelot Link: Secret Chimp" and "The Jackson 5ive." (The Archies' "Sugar Sugar" was the #1 song of 1969!)

Hanna-Barbera's "The Flintstones" (1960-66) — a comedy set in the caveman days with more than a passing resemblance to "The Honeymooners" — often commented on current events. The Beatles did not escape the notice of the "modern Stone Age family."

In a 1965 episode, the "Flintstones" ensemble of Fred, Wilma, Barney and Betty don Beatle wigs, gather around a microphone and, as Fred strums along on guitar, sing "Bug music." The lyrics: *"I said, Yeah, yeah, yeah! He said, Yeah, yeah, yeah! She said, Yeah, yeah, yeah!"* The foursome is joined by the Gruesomes, a neighboring family of monsters, who sing the same song while likewise wearing — I hate to ruin the surprise — Beatle wigs.

THE WEIRD AND WONDERFUL THING ABOUT THE "supermarionation" shows created by British puppeteers Gerry and Sylvia Anderson and imported to American TV ("Fireball XL5," "Supercar," "Stingray," etc.) is how superbly crafted and "acted" the stories are. Before long, you get caught up in the action and drama — and forget that you're watching puppets.

During the height of the British Invasion period came the Andersons' "Thunderbirds" (1965-66), which follows the exploits of the Tracy family. They live on a lush private island in an ultra-chic abode with floor-to-ceiling windows overlooking a shimmering ocean vista. There's a pool with a high diving board and an inviting patio. The spread is a marvel of modern architecture, a veritable vacation home for jet-setters. So ... what's the *catch?*

The Tracys can never relax. They're a family, yes, but they're also a highly skilled, well-funded, top-secret agency known as International Rescue. When disaster strikes anywhere in the world, this family must answer the call. The house itself transforms into their vehicle for dispatch. Chairs sink into the floor, swiftly delivering occupants into emergency vehicles. A wall poster flips around to deposit agents into a chute for rapid deployment. Beneath the home is a vast, multi-level, underground depot with monolithic emergency vehicles, including planes, rockets, and an aquacar. A rocket ship blasts off from beneath the swimming pool. The pool slides aside, chlorinated water included, to make room.

The Tracys' father, Jeff — a fit, silver-haired former astronaut — stays home and monitors the missions of his five adult sons. Scott, John, Virgil, Gordon and Alan each have a specialty. (I don't want to cast aspersions on Jeff's late wife, but his sons look like they all have different fathers.) There hangs a portrait of each son; when one of the boys reports from the field, the eyes light up on his corresponding portrait, which turns into a video screen.

"Thunderbirds" is, at heart, a parody of the James Bond films, and an exceedingly clever one. Composer Barry Gray's movie-ready score is worthy of 007. Even as a child, you sensed that this was *not* American television. That this was British to the core.

Then there was Lancashire boy Jack Wild who, following his Oscar-nominated turn as the Artful Dodger in "Oliver Twist," was exported to star in "H.R. Pufnstuf" (1969-70). With his magazine-ready looks, Wild emerged as not just a guy who interacts with a talking flute on Saturday mornings, but a bona fide teen idol. Wild wouldn't be the *last* Brit to star on American TV during the period.

Chad and Jeremy were everywhere! From top: "Batman," "The Dick Van Dyke Show" and "The Patty Duke Show."

WHEN AMERICAN SITCOMS DID THEIR RIFFS ON the British Invasion, and the Beatles were too busy (and expensive) to take part, Chad and Jeremy happily became TV's go-to Brits.

Chad Stuart and Jeremy Clyde played thinly veiled versions of themselves on "The Dick Van Dyke Show" and "The Patty Duke Show" (both 1965), and played themselves outright on "Batman" (1966). Screaming girls figure in each episode, and real-life songs by Chad and Jeremy are heard — excellent product placement.

On "Dick Van Dyke," the boys play Ernie and Fred, members of a pop group called the Red Coats who are constantly on the run from female fans. When they are booked to perform on "The Alan Brady Show," head writer Rob Petrie (Van Dyke) and his wife Laura (Mary Tyler Moore) are elected to host the duo in their suburban abode. Sworn to secrecy, the Petries are dying to tell neighbors about their famous visitors. ("It's like being Clark Kent," grouses Rob.) A clever "meta" moment comes when Ernie and Fred introduce a song "recorded by Chad and Jeremy, friends of ours back in England. They're very close to us, you might say."

On "Patty Duke," they play Nigel and Patrick, a duo "discovered" by high schooler Patty Lane (Duke), who volunteers to be their manager and get them a recording contract. Patty impersonates her twin cousin Cathy (also played by Duke), who has a classical radio show, in order to play Nigel and Patrick's demo on the air.

On "Batman," Chad and Jeremy stay at Wayne Manor, stately home of millionaire Bruce Wayne (Adam West), alias Batman. Catwoman (Julie Newmar) uses a high-tech gizmo to steal their voices, demanding that England cough up an 8-million-pound ransom. Her rationale: "Chad and Jeremy pay so much income tax to their native land, that if it were to stop, the whole empire might crumble." Spoiler alert: C&J get their voices back.

Later, while attending a Chad and Jeremy show, Commissioner Gordon (Neil Hamilton) complains: "A bit on the groovy side, aren't they?" Counters Bruce in a voice that sounds *exactly* like Batman: "Every era has its own music, Commissioner."

The Beatles gambled that an unscripted travelogue with quirky costumes and props could coast on charm. © Apple Corps

'Magical Mystery Tour' (1967)

IT'S LIKE FELLINI WITHOUT THE EXISTENTIALISM. Or Monty Python without the punchlines.

Such was the Beatles' uncanny Midas touch that for years, it looked as if the group could do no wrong. Then came their rambling, "avant-garde" 1967 TV special "Magical Mystery Tour."

With only a vague outline concerning a tour bus filled with a zany cast of characters including the Beatles, the largely improvised "Magical Mystery Tour" is a mess, honestly. (The diminutive wrestlers were probably funnier on paper than in practice.)

But there *are* moments. The songs — always the Beatles' strong suit — proved that the group was still breaking ground.

John Lennon's psychedelic masterpiece "I Am the Walrus" anticipates the music-video form, with visuals that are just as trippy as the song (which says a lot). Paul McCartney's "Your Mother Should Know" conjures Busby Berkeley with its art deco-inspired sets; pretty people in period dress; and the boys doing light choreography as they descend a grand staircase wearing white tuxedoes.

Alas, not every song is successfully visualized. Early in the special comes "Fool on the Hill," in which a glassy-eyed McCartney skips in slow motion and mugs unabashedly.

There are a few laugh-out-loud moments, such as when Lennon and Harrison patronize a gaudy strip club, where an Elvis impersonator act (actually the Bonzo Dog Doo-Dah Band) plays a downtempo "Death Cab For Cutie" while a stripper struts her stuff.

We Yanks got the album titled "Magical Mystery Tour," if not the TV special itself. As we paged through the photo album that came with the record, we could only wonder: Why is John Lennon dressed as a waiter, serving spaghetti with a shovel to a fat lady?

The TV special gathered the cream of rock, as it captured one Stone on the ascent and another in decline. © ABKCO Films

'Rock and Roll Circus' (1968)

THE DECISION NOT TO AIR THE ROLLING STONES' TV special "Rock and Roll Circus" — taped in December 1968 but unseen for decades — is the subject of several theories. **(1.)** The shoot ran too long, and the Stones were exhausted. **(2.)** Brian Jones, always a handy scapegoat, was less than cogent. **(3.)** The Who upstaged the Stones. **(4.)** Taj Mahal upstaged the Stones.

I don't buy any of it. My theory — based on nothing — is that once Mick Jagger saw the edited special, he was aghast at his own unexpurgated narcissism. An over-the-top Jagger gets in the camera's "face," maintains eye contact (often to the exclusion of the studio audience) and acts *super* weird. At one point, Jagger strips off his shirt to reveal temporary tattoos on a scrawny torso, and then dances like a chicken. His freaky new stage persona would serve him well for decades, but in 1968, it still needed polishing.

This makes "Rock and Roll Circus" the missing link between the Stones' 1966 and 1969 tours. Alas, we never got to witness it.

For rock fans, "Rock and Roll Circus" is heaven on Earth. Early Jethro Tull! The Who in their prime! A one-shot, one-song, once-in-a-lifetime lineup performing "Yer Blues" from the Beatles' "White Album"! Namely John Lennon, Eric Clapton, Keith Richards and Mitch Mitchell! It doesn't get any better.

Which brings us back to the sad, lovely Mr. Jones, who had less than seven months to live, in his final live appearance with the Stones. This man who contributed so much exotic instrumentation to immortal songs gave us a fitting final musical moment. When Jones plays exquisite slide on a plaintive version of "No Expectations," it just rips your heart out. Especially as Jagger sings, *"I got no expectations / to pass / through here / again ..."*

From top left: "The Scarecrow of Romney Marsh," "The Avengers," "Secret Agent," "The Saint" and "Man in a Suitcase."

IF THE WAIT BETWEEN JAMES BOND MOVIES seemed like an eternity, fans could get their fix by tuning in to British TV imports for suave protagonists in fashionable attire saving the world with quick wits and the odd karate chop.

Patrick McGoohan ruled the British imports with three shows from across the pond. The period thriller "The Scarecrow of Romney Marsh" (1963) — a three-part Walt Disney production filmed in England — first aired in the U.S. opposite the Beatles' debut on "The Ed Sullivan Show" (good luck!) on NBC's "Walt Disney's Wonderful World of Color." "Scarecrow" starred McGoohan as Dr. Syn, leader of a ring of do-gooding vigilantes.

CBS aired "Secret Agent" (1965-67), titled "Danger Man" in the U.K., starring McGoohan as John Drake, who vanquished baddies throughout Europe without carrying a gun. The series' theme song, cooked up specially for the U.S. market, was Johnny Rivers' "Secret Agent Man" (#3), with its catchy 007-esque guitar riff.

McGoohan also created and starred in "The Prisoner" (1968-69) as Number 6, an operative who is gassed and awakens in a bizarre, colorful village populated by a secretive society. The 17-episode series is like a "Twilight Zone" marathon. The final episode dovetails into the first, so "The Prisoner" can be viewed in an endless loop. The cult that grew around the show did just that.

ABC aired "The Avengers" (1966-69), which co-starred Patrick MacNee and Diana Rigg as urbane agents John Steed and Emma Peel. Dapper Steed wore tailored suits topped with a bowler tilted at a jaunty angle, and he carried an umbrella that concealed a saber. Alluring Peel wore a snug, gleaming black catsuit, the better to launch into the martial arts in which she specialized.

Their droll banter was as vital to the show as the action and intrigue. Subtle sexual overtones colored Steed and Peel's teasing interplay, but were never acted upon. Linda Thorson later replaced Rigg; alas, MacNee and Rigg's chemistry could never be equaled.

Future screen 007 Roger Moore honed his espionage chops as author Leslie Charteris' Robin Hood-like thief Simon Templar, a.k.a. "The Saint" (1967-69), which aired on NBC.

ABC aired "Man in a Suitcase" (1968) starring Richard Bradford as MacGill, an enigmatic ex-agent for British Intelligence who, in the wake of his wrongful termination, goes freelance. No longer protected by the system, MacGill finds himself at odds with the Brits, the Americans and, of course, the Russians.

Brits on American TV, from top left: Series regulars Davy Jones, Richard Dawson, Judy Carne, Noel Harrison and Maurice Evans; and "guest villains" Boris Karloff (in drag), George Sanders and Joan Collins. Below: Tom Jones in studly mode.

WOULD DR. BOMBAY'S DIAGNOSES SEEM as trustworthy, if not for Bernard Fox's authoritative British accent?

As the mania for All Things British continued to hold its grip on America, TV showrunners turned to a practice known since the dawn of talking pictures: that a well-placed British accent (so long as it is authentic, mind you) lends a ring of class or pizzazz to a production. Suddenly, British actors were popping up in the casts of American TV shows as regular or recurring characters.

The two "U.N.C.L.E." shows wisely installed Brits, the better to evoke the 007 franchise they were emulating.

On "The Man From U.N.C.L.E." (1964-68), David McCallum (born in Glasgow) played fair-haired spy Illya Kuryakin, causing hysteria approaching Beatlemania level among teenage girls.

On "The Girl From U.N.C.L.E." (1966), Noel Harrison (born in London) was Stefanie Powers' soft-spoken wingman. The young actor's famous father was Rex Harrison.

In the World War II comedy "Hogan's Heroes" (1965-71), Richard Dawson (born in Hampshire) played Newkirk, a Cockney-accented hustler who helped keep the Gestapo in the dark about Allied missions from the confines of Stalag 13.

Lest we forget, the fictional pop band in "The Monkees" (1966-68) was one-quarter British. Davy Jones (born in Manchester) played the vertically challenged heartthrob in the group called ... *Davy*.

The hipster comedy "Laugh-In" (1968-73) had several Brits in its ensemble, including Judy Carne (born in Northampton), as the mini-skirted "Sock it to me!" girl, and post-"Hogan" Dawson.

Besides Fox (born in Wales) as top-hatted medico Bombay on the supernatural sitcom "Bewitched" (1964-72), there was Maurice Evans (born in Dorchester) as playboy warlock Maurice, and Estelle Winwood (born in Kent) as the spell-casting Aunt Enchantra.

A HAVEN FOR BRITS WAS THE campy action comedy "Batman" (1966-69). Series regular Alan Napier (born in Birmingham) played proper Alfred the butler. "Guest villain" roles were filled by George Sanders (Mr. Freeze), Roddy McDowall (the Bookworm), Evans (the Puzzler), Michael Rennie (the Sandman), Joan Collins (the Siren) and Glynis Johns (Lady Penelope Peasoup).

Speaking of villains, horror icon Boris Karloff (in a hideous bouffant) was a riot as murderous Mother Muffin on "The Girl From U.N.C.L.E."

Singer Tom Jones (born in Wales) busted moves on his variety show "This is Tom Jones" (1969-71). There's no polite way to put this: The tighter Jones' trousers were, the better American ladies liked it.

With open arms, Jones welcomed fellow Brits the Dave Clark Five, Petula Clark, Donovan, Lulu, Lonnie Donegan, Herman's Hermits, the Hollies, Mary Hopkin, the Moody Blues, Sandie Shaw, Dusty Springfield, the Who and, dancing like a madman — would you expect less? — Arthur Brown.

DAVID McCALLUM (Illya)

LIFE SIZE PIN-UP... only $1

It's the newest, it's the wildest, greatest ever . . . A super pin-up of Illya. It's life size (over 38″x50″). And what's more it's exclusive, no one else has it, not even the fan mags. IT'S THE OFFICIAL PHOTO CHOSEN BY THE FAN CLUB. Wait till your friends walk into your room. Won't they flip! THERE IS ILLYA— life size and so real they'll think for a minute he's there. It's real fab for your bedroom, den or playroom. It's like nothing you've ever seen before. You'll really be the envy of the crowd. And remember it's personally autographed, and it's official.

FREE Rush your order now and receive FREE your official membership card in the Man from U.N.C.L.E. Fan Club. PLUS your very own U.N.C.L.E. Agent card. So c'mon. Don't Delay.

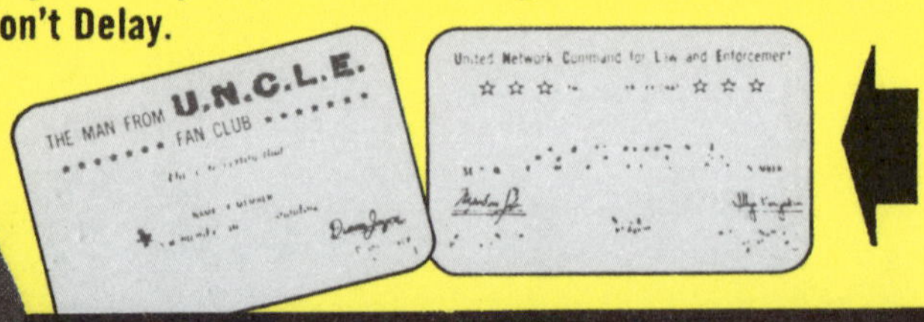

RUSH BACK THE COUPON NOW!

MAN FROM U.N.C.L.E. FAN CLUB, Dept. 7DM24
35 Wilbur Street, Lynbrook, N.Y.
Rush me my life size David McCallum pin-up plus official Man from U.N.C.L.E. Fan Club membership card and U.N.C.L.E. card I must really flip or I may return everything for a full purchase price refund. I enclose $1 plus 25¢ (to cover shipping charges).

Name ______________________

Address ______________________

City ____________ State ________ Zip Code ________

☐ Send Robert Vaughn Life Size pin-up too! I enclose an additional $1.

It's Illya-mania!

He didn't sing, but David McCallum was chased by screaming girls.

"I once took refuge in a ladies' toilet (restroom) on the campus of Louisiana State University," the Glasgow native (born 1933) told me in 1995. "The police barred the door so that nobody would get in. And they all came in through the windows! I was trying to get out, but the police wouldn't *let* me out. I got pretty badly torn about. I wasn't like being kissed. It felt like you were being killed."

In his blond, Beatle-esque haircut and black turtleneck, McCallum often stole the show from the more conventionally heroic Robert Vaughn on TV's "The Man From U.N.C.L.E." (1964-68). As quiet Russian agent Illya Kuryakin, McCallum lent the espionage thriller (some call it a spoof) a sensitivity uncommon to the era's preferred concept of the superspy as a stop-at-nothing stud.

Illya was *deep,* man.

AN UNWITTING TEEN IDOL, McCallum found himself on the cover of teen magazines alongside fellow Brits like the Beatles and Herman's Hermits.

I recalled an article in one such mag in which McCallum was mobbed by girls, one of whom asked his then-wife, Jill Ireland, for permission to kiss him. When she said yes, a kissing frenzy followed.

"I think that's apocryphal," he said with a laugh. "That sounds like the MGM publicity department. As you know, every publicity department manipulates those occasions to the hilt.

"Things like that did happen, yes. Absolute insanity at that time. But those scenes were manageable most of the time."

During the height of his "U.N.C.L.E." fame, McCallum released four instrumental albums on Capitol Records such as "Music: A Part of Me," and "Music: A Bit More of Me." (Factoid: In 2009, Dr. Dre and Snoop Dogg rapped over a sample from McCallum's track "The Edge.")

IN 1965, McCALLUM FOUND HIMSELF HOSTING "Hullaballoo" in character as Illya. He even "rapped" a song (sample lyric: *"That's why they call me Agent Double-O-Soul, baby!"*)

"I got to meet the Animals; they were doing 'We've Gotta Get Out of This Place if it's the Last Thing We Ever Do' (sic)," he said of the experience. "And I did, during that time, Andy Williams' show, Dean Martin's, Carol Channing, all those shows and specials. To meet them and to work with people like Judy Garland, Herb Alpert and the Tijuana Brass, shaking hands with Willie Mays and Hank Aaron — I've always been the ultimate fan of those people. I mean, the whole of my life has been such a pleasure, in terms of meeting people."

Was it weird for McCallum to see his likeness on, for instance, the Illya doll?

Said the actor: "It wasn't until we did 'Return of the Man From U.N.C.L.E.' in 1983 that I was on Melrose Place going past one of those bric-a-brac shops, and I saw one in the window. It said 'The Man From U.N.C.L.E.' all over it, and it was this sort of blond creature in a black turtleneck. I figured, 'That's probably me.' I just went in and bought it. I *had* to, right?"

David McCallum as Illya Kuryakin amid Illya collectibles.

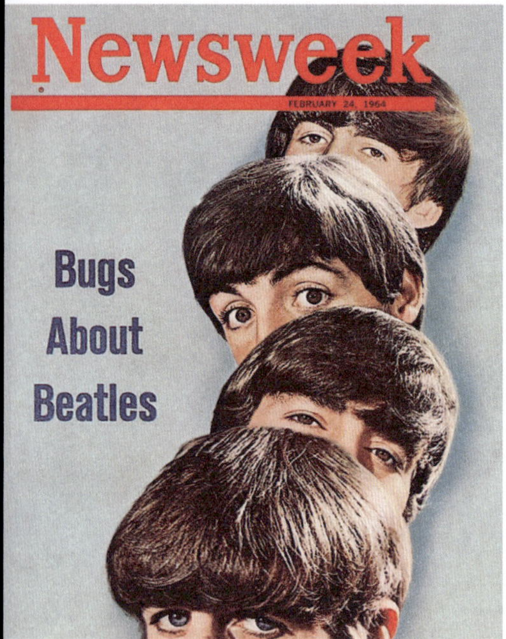

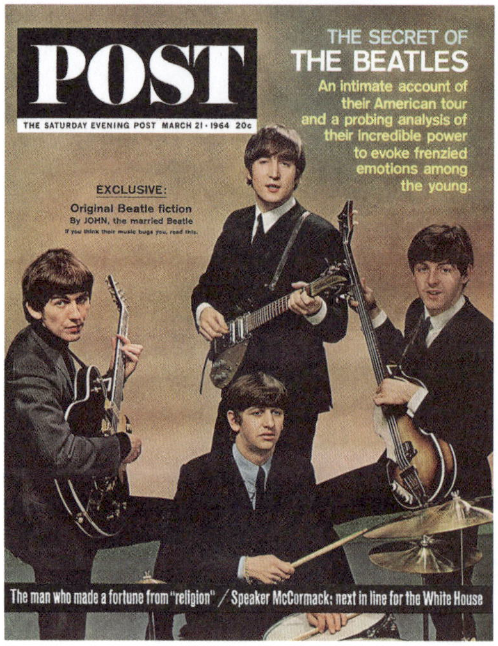

Even respectable magazines cashed in. At right, the Beatles clowned as Brit "twits" for the Saturday Evening Post.

Darlings & demons

"VISUALLY, THEY ARE A NIGHTMARE; TIGHT, *dandified, Edwardian-Beatnik suits and great pudding bowls of hair. Musically, they are a near-disaster: guitars and drums slamming out a merciless beat that does away with secondary rhythms, harmony, and melody. Their lyrics ... are a catastrophe, a preposterous farrago of Valentine-card romantic sentiments."*

There are few better examples of how the establishment media initially disrespected and derided the Beatles than that introduction to the cover story in the Feb. 24, 1964, edition of *Newsweek.*

There's lots more. From the cover of the March 21, 1964, *Saturday Evening Post:* "Exclusive: Original Beatle fiction by John, the married Beatle. If you think their music bugs you, read this."

(Can you think of another instance in which cover type actually warns potential purchasers that something inside is not worth reading?)

OK, so the old guard was hostile toward the Beatles. This was obvious. But media gatekeepers found that putting John, Paul, George and Ringo on their covers guaranteed a boost in circulation. And circulation is the golden calf to magazine publishers.

THIS UNPRECEDENTED SITUATION PUT MAINstream American magazines in an inconvenient position. They wanted to maintain their position of moral superiority. But more so, they wanted to sell magazines. Thus the Beatles became both the darlings and the demons of the print-media machine.

The *Saturday Evening Post* double-dipped with two covers five months apart. (The Post's second Beatles cover had a come-on worthy of *16 Magazine:* "THE BEATLES — 8 Pages in Color.") When the Beatles made their pilgrimage to India in search of enlightenment in 1967, *Life* made it a cover story.

Beatle business was so good, lesser publishers began to crank out one-shots with suggestive come-ons ("A date with George, John, Paul & Ringo," "A Message to you from the Beatles themselves," "The girls they want," "The love code they follow," "What it's like to be married to Ringo," "The Beatles answer your most intimate questions"). These were often transparent cash-grabs filled with photos and foldouts.

This 1966 edition contained John Lennon's "more popular than Jesus" quote.

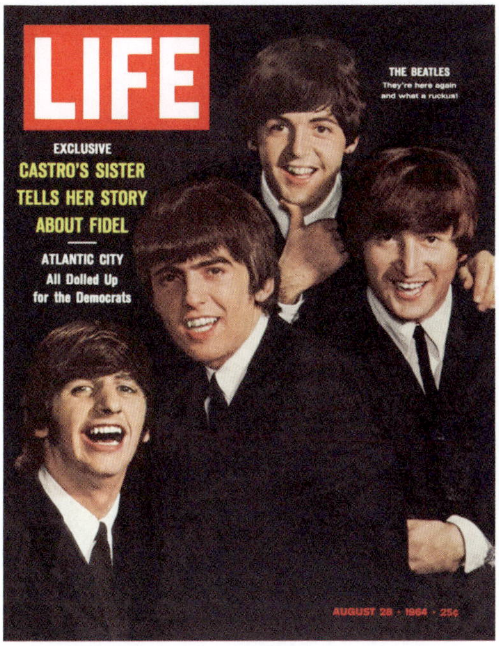

Life chronicled three phases: Beatlemania; the boys in psychedelic fashion; Paul McCartney's retreat to a Scottish farm.

JOHN LENNON'S CONTROVERSIAL COMMENT THAT the Beatles were "more popular than Jesus" first came to the attention of Americans in the Sept. 1966 issue of *Datebook.* (Lennon originally made the comment to Maureen Cleave of the *London Evening Standard.*) The outrage was instantaneous. Beatles records were burned in bonfires, radio stations boycotted Beatles songs.

"If I'd have said television is more popular than Jesus, I might have got away with it," Lennon said at a press conference, to reporters' laughter. "I'm not sayin' we're better or greater, or comparin' us with Jesus Christ as a person, or God as a thing, or whatever it is."

In the same *Datebook* edition, Paul McCartney likewise courted controversy by taking Americans to task over ongoing Civil Rights abuses: "It's a lousy country where anyone Black is a dirty n*****."

Humor magazines like *Mad, Sick, Cracked* and *Help!* had a field day lampooning the group. (The Beatles were good sports, and answered with a cameo of the paperback "Son of Mad" in their debut movie "A Hard Day's Night.")

When *Rolling Stone* debuted in 1967, its first cover boy was Lennon as Private Gripweed from Richard Lester's comedy "How I Won the War."

To teen magazines like *16, Flip, Teen Screen, Teen Talk* and *Teen World,* the Beatles were their meat. Unlike the more respectable publications, *16* and company actually put other British Invasion faces on their covers such as Mick Jagger, Peter Noone, Chad and Jeremy, Peter and Gordon — as long as they were *cute,* natch.

IN THE UNITED KINGDOM, FAN MAGAZINES WERE sometimes more earnest and democratic in their coverage.

There really was no American equivalent of *Pop Weekly,* which took a slightly more serious, less teeny-bopper-ish approach to covering the music scene. The same can be said for *Beat Monthly* (later *Beat Instrumental Monthly*), which reported about instruments and equipment. You would see Charlie Watts or Keith Moon as *Beat Instrumental* cover boys, something that just wouldn't happen in America.

Lennon graced the cover of the premiere issue of Rolling Stone, dated Nov. 9, 1967. The price was 25 cents.

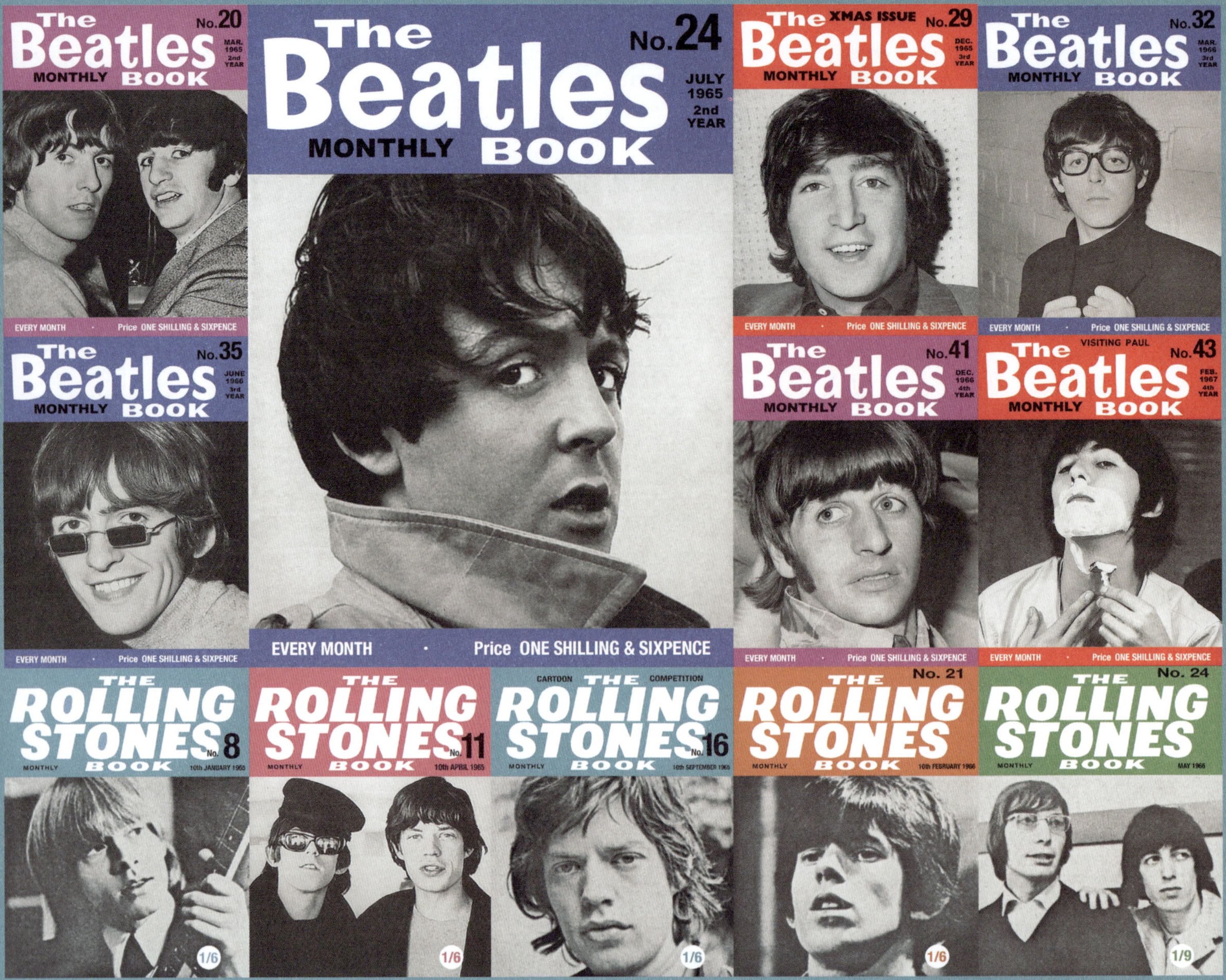

Two "sister" publications, The Beatles Book and The Rolling Stones Book, gave fans a monthly fix.

Sister tabloids Fabulous and Fabulous 208 cast a wider net in the artists they covered.

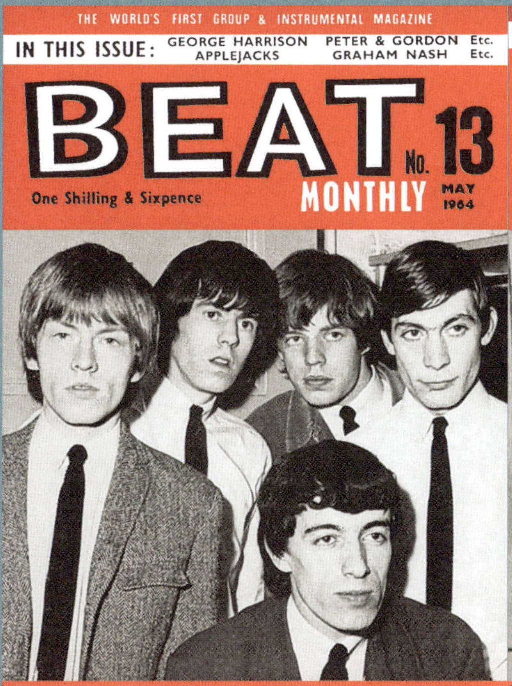

Billing itself as "the world's first group and instrument magazine," Beat Monthly (later Beat Instrumental) was as much about the gear as the "gear groups." (Good one!) Shown are the early Rolling Stones, a dapper Charlie Watts and a manic Keith Moon. Pop Weekly was earnest and informative. The Northern Beat Scene featured the Swinging Blue Jeans, while Pop Shop featured Herman's Hermits.

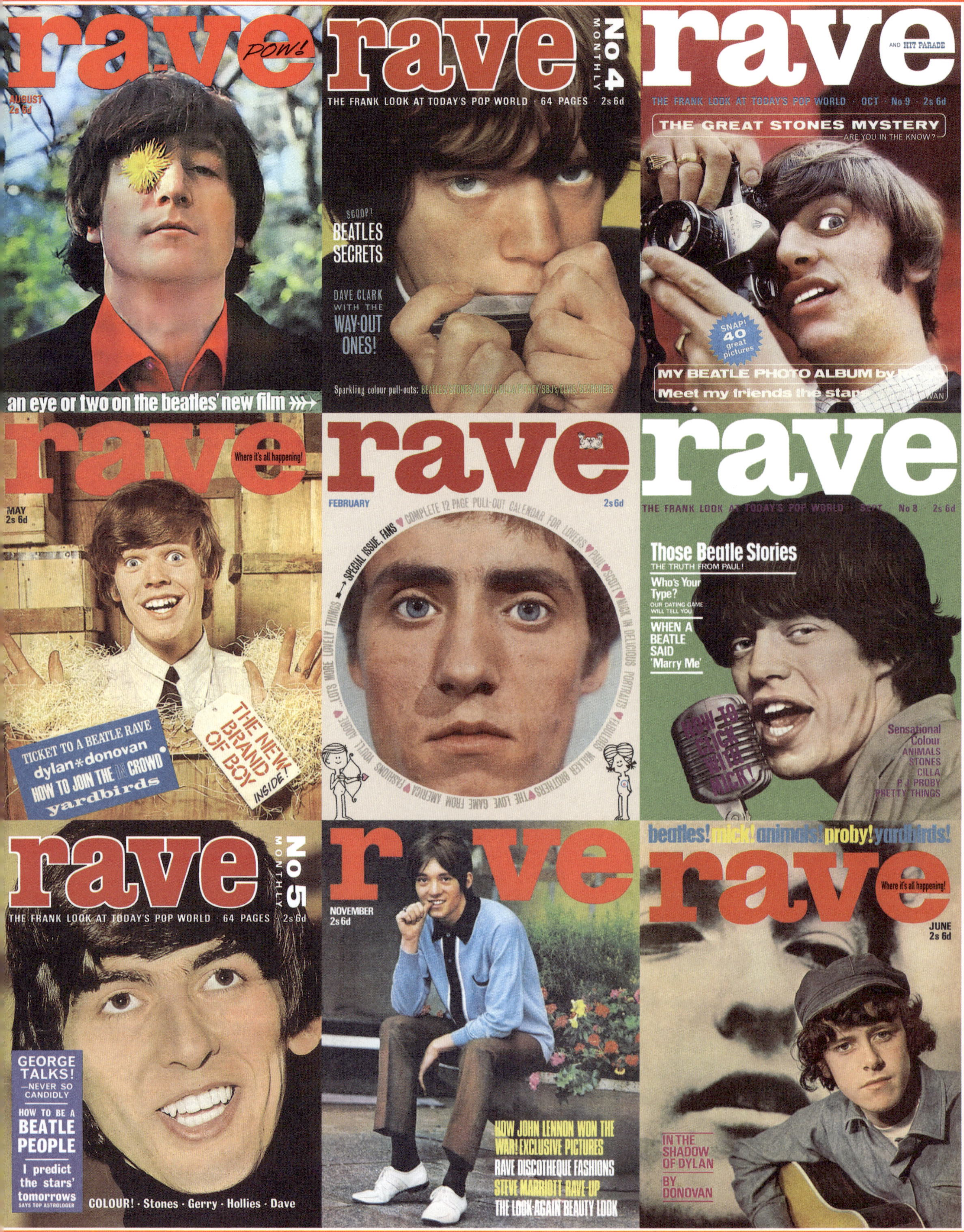
rave
POW!
AUGUST 2s 6d
an eye or two on the beatles' new film
rave
No 4 MONTHLY
THE FRANK LOOK AT TODAY'S POP WORLD · 64 PAGES · 2s 6d
SCOOP! BEATLES SECRETS
DAVE CLARK WITH THE WAY-OUT ONES!
Sparkling colour pull-outs: BEATLES/STONES/BILLY J/CILLA/PITNEY/SBJ's/ELVIS/SEARCHERS
rave
AND HIT PARADE
THE FRANK LOOK AT TODAY'S POP WORLD · OCT · No 9 · 2s 6d
THE GREAT STONES MYSTERY
ARE YOU IN THE KNOW?
SNAP! 40 great pictures
MY BEATLE PHOTO ALBUM by
rave
Where it's all happening!
MAY 2s 6d
TICKET TO A BEATLE RAVE
dylan*donovan
HOW TO JOIN THE IN CROWD
yardbirds
THE NEW BRAND OF BOY INSIDE!
rave
FEBRUARY
2s 6d
SPECIAL ISSUE, FANS ♥ COMPLETE 12 PAGE PULL-OUT CALENDAR FOR LOVERS ♥ PAUL ♥ SCOTT ♥ MICK IN DELICIOUS PORTRAITS ♥ FABULOUS WALKER BROTHERS ♥ THE LOVE GAME FROM AMERICA ♥ FASHIONS YOU'LL ADORE ♥ LOTS MORE LOVELY THINGS
rave
No 8 · 2s 6d
Those Beatle Stories
THE TRUTH FROM PAUL!
Who's Your Type?
OUR DATING GAME WILL TELL YOU
WHEN A BEATLE SAID 'Marry Me'
Sensational Colour
ANIMALS
STONES
CILLA
P. J. PROBY
PRETTY THINGS
rave
No 5 MONTHLY
THE FRANK LOOK AT TODAY'S POP WORLD · 64 PAGES · 2s 6d
GEORGE TALKS! —NEVER SO CANDIDLY
HOW TO BE A BEATLE PEOPLE
I predict the stars' tomorrows
SAYS TOP ASTROLOGER
COLOUR! · Stones · Gerry · Hollies · Dave
rave
NOVEMBER 2s 6d
HOW JOHN LENNON WON THE WAR! EXCLUSIVE PICTURES
RAVE DISCOTHEQUE FASHIONS
STEVE MARRIOTT RAVE-UP
THE LOOK-AGAIN BEAUTY LOOK
beatles! mick! animals! proby! yardbirds!
rave
Where it's all happening!
JUNE 2s 6d
IN THE SHADOW OF DYLAN
BY DONOVAN

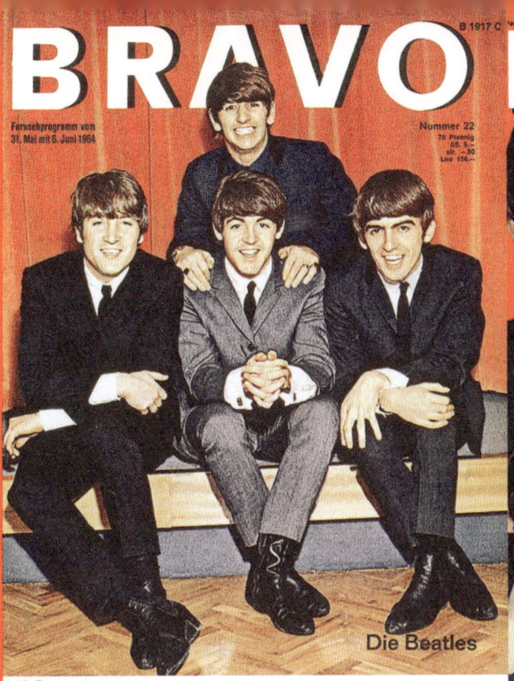

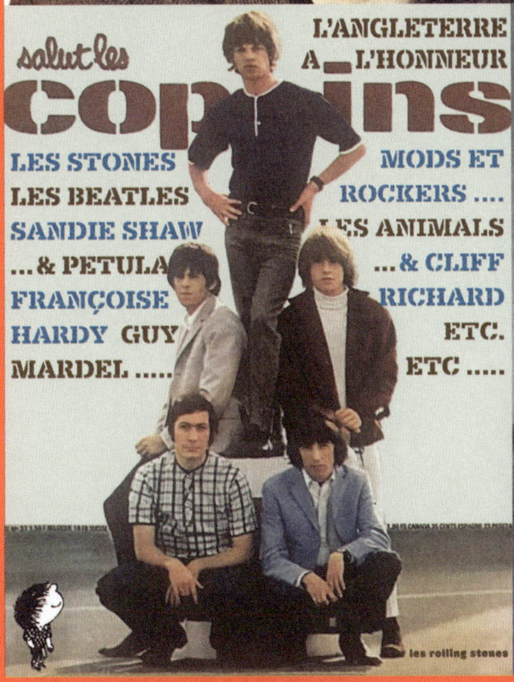

Perhaps owing to British bands' Hamburg residencies, German mags Bravo (der Beatles!) und Musik Parade took interest, while France gave us Salut Les Copains, with cover stories on the Rolling Stones and the Beatles. Opposite: Rave was democratic in the artists it covered. Peter Noone, Roger Daltrey, Steve Marriott and Donovan, for example, graced its covers in addition to the Beatles and Stones.

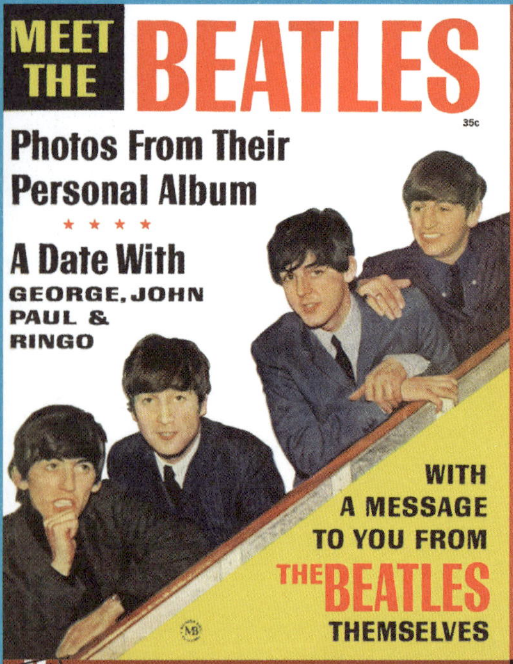
MEET THE BEATLES
35c
Photos From Their Personal Album
A Date With GEORGE, JOHN PAUL & RINGO
WITH A MESSAGE TO YOU FROM THE BEATLES THEMSELVES

THE BEATLES
PERSONALITY ANNUAL 50¢
JOHN, PAUL, GEORGE & RINGO-
The Girls They Want
The Love Code They Follow
The Words To 4 Secret Songs

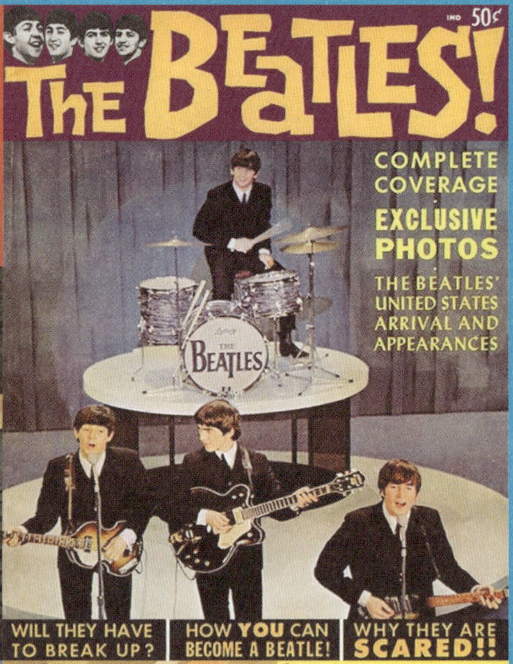
50¢
The BEATLES!
COMPLETE COVERAGE
EXCLUSIVE PHOTOS
THE BEATLES' UNITED STATES ARRIVAL AND APPEARANCES
BEATLES
WILL THEY HAVE TO BREAK UP?
HOW YOU CAN BECOME A BEATLE!
WHY THEY ARE SCARED!!

POP PICS SPECIAL
EXCLUSIVE BEHIND THE SCENES STORY AND PHOTOS
BEATLES Film
Wonderful SOUVENIR For Film Fans
60c

BEATLE MANIA
THE AUTHENTIC PHOTOS
BONUS!
50¢
FULL COLOR GIANT PINUPS AND WALLET PIX
FLASH! 1st PICTURES OF THE BEATLES HERE!

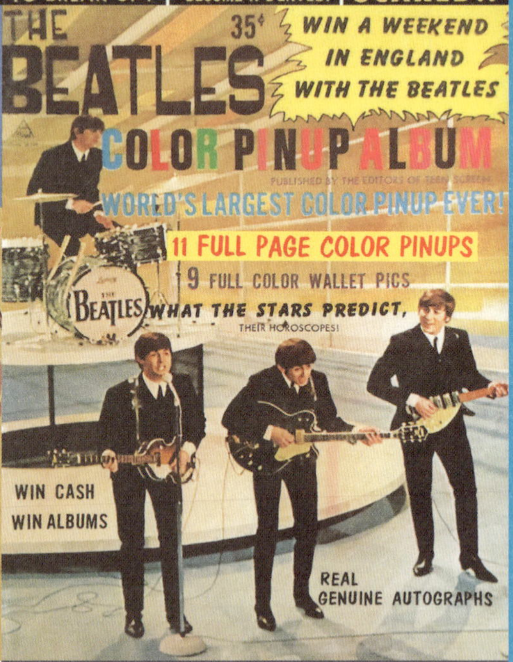
THE BEATLES
35¢
WIN A WEEKEND IN ENGLAND WITH THE BEATLES
COLOR PINUP ALBUM
WORLD'S LARGEST COLOR PINUP EVER!
11 FULL PAGE COLOR PINUPS
9 FULL COLOR WALLET PICS
BEATLES
WHAT THE STARS PREDICT, THEIR HOROSCOPES!
WIN CASH
WIN ALBUMS
REAL GENUINE AUTOGRAPHS

GEORGE
35¢
GEORGE'S HOME ADDRESS!!!
Published by the editors of Teen Screen
GEAR CONTESTS:
BONUS: FULL COLOR PICS!!!
WIN A LETTER FROM GEORGE
EVERYBODY WINS WALLET PICS
WHERE TO SEE GEORGE IN PERSON!
How to Start a Fan Club
9 FULL PAGE PINUPS
George goodies!
record labels album labels bookmarks jigsaw puzzle

36 WALLET PICS! COMPLETE LIFE STORIES!
DAVE CLARK FIVE
EXCLUSIVE: FULL COLOR PINUPS!
35¢
WIN A WEEKEND in LONDON with the DAVE CLARK FIVE!
PUBLISHED BY THE EDITORS OF TEEN SCREEN
NEW D.C.5 HAIRDO HOW TO COMB AND SET SWEEP POUF SPIKE
WIN CASH

FREE! STICKERS!
PHOTOS!
EXCLUSIVE
1ST PHOTOS IN THE USA
50¢
ROLLING STONES
FREE! MEMBERSHIP CARDS IN THE
OFFICIAL FAN CLUB
THE GREATEST YET!
Plus THE DAVE CLARK FIVE THE BEATLES GERRY & THE PACEMAKERS

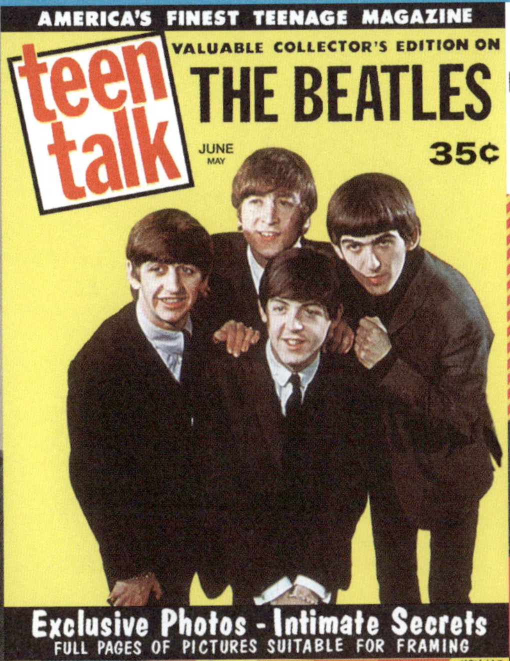

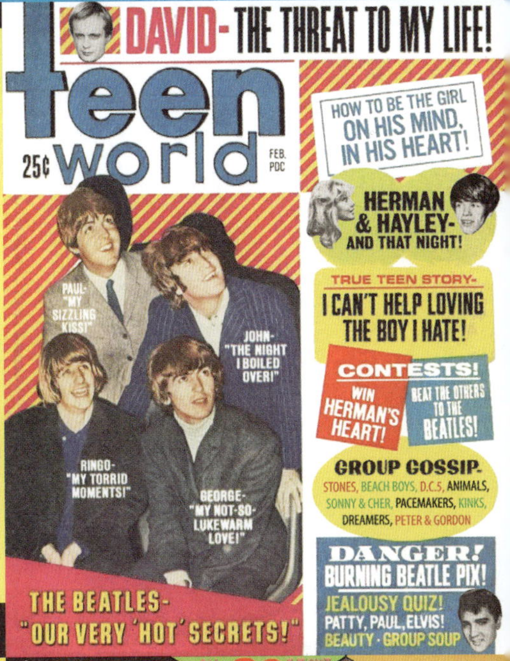

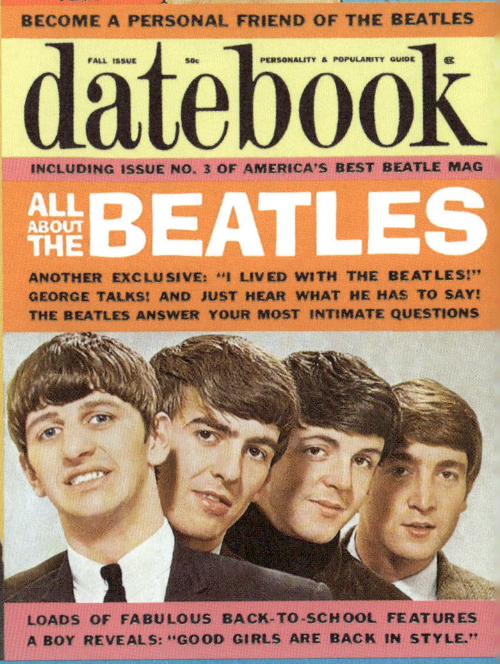

American teen-targeted magazines exploited the craze with one-shot editions about the Fab You-Know-What. Teen Screen, Teen Talk, Teen World, Flip, Dig and Datebook touted the Beatles, the Rolling Stones, Herman's Hermits, Marianne Faithfull, the Troggs and David McCallum, putting an emphasis on pinups and come-ons that practically encouraged stalking ("The Beatles' Secret Address," "Become a Personal Friend of the Beatles").

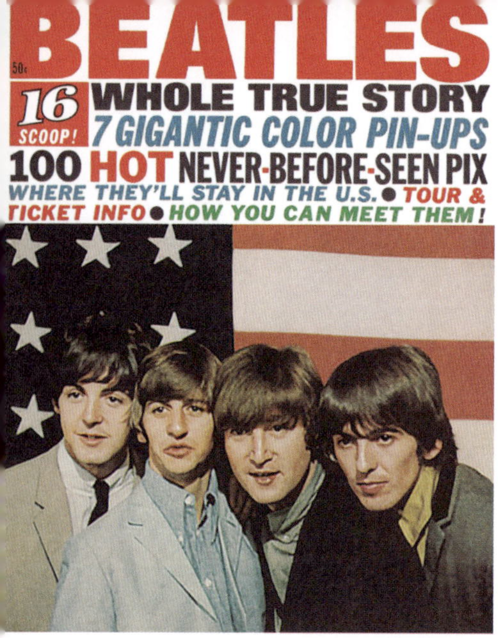

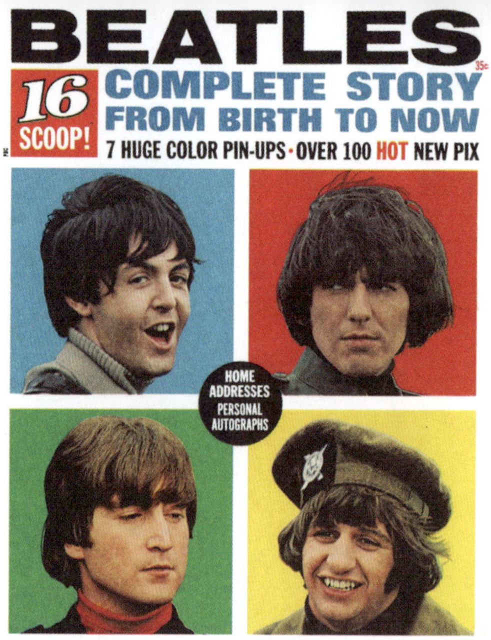

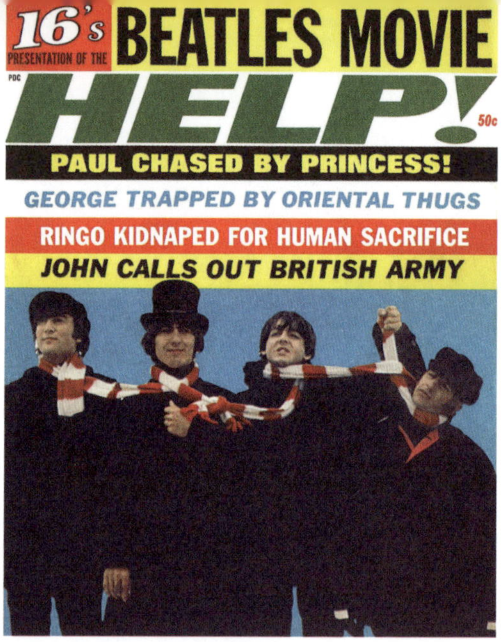

Above: 16 Magazine flogged the Beatles in special editions. Below: A John Lennon family tree, a Pattie Boyd profile and a single-panel cartoon were random inside features.

meet PATTIE BOYD

Blonde - haired, blue - eyed Pattie Boyd is 20 years old. She is a well-known London model and has been dating George Harrison steadily since they met while he was filming A Hard Day's Night. *Pattie, whose real name is Patricia Ann Boyd, is 5 feet 5 inches tall and weighs 110 lbs. Pattie has taken two vacations with George, and was his guest while he and the Beatles were recently on location in Austria for their new movie. George insists he won't be getting married for a long, long time.*

"It's from Brian Epstein's office — the Beatles can't make it to our dance!"

Getting heady on 16 Magazine covers

A playful cover gimmick put star heads on 'toon bodies. From top left: Mick Jagger, Jeremy Clyde, Peter Noone, Keith Richards, John Lennon, Petula Clark, Paul McCartney, Noone, George Harrison, Jagger, Chad Stuart, David McCallum, Stuart, Gordon Waller and Lennon.

VOGUE
ITALIA
UNA FAVOLOSA
CROCIERA
IN GRECIA:
TUTTA
UNA MODA
IN BIANCO
CALCE
VIVERE NEL MARE
FUORI DAL MARE:
I NUOVI
COSTUMI E
COPRICOSTUMI
GIVENCHY
E MINI GIVENCHY
INTERVISTA CON
FRANCO ZEFFIRELLI

JULY 27 1968 ONE SHILLING
THE NEW YOUNG WOMAN
PETTICOAT
Last-minute-rush
dresses; low price
high fashion
How to buy a
man a tie
What's
going pop?

VOGUE
JUNE 1965 3/-
WHERE THE
ACTION IS
an
entertaining summer

Au courant

RIPPLE EFFECTS FROM THE LONDON FASHION SCENE were felt far and wide. Fashion had an effect on British Invasion bands as well. Many of the musicians dated models. Can you blame them?

George Harrison met wife Pattie Boyd on the "Hard Day's Night" shoot. Paul McCartney's girlfriend was model-actress Jane Asher. Mick Jagger's was Marianne Faithfull, a model-turned-singer-turned-actress. Brian Jones and Keith Richards both had relationships with another model-actress, Anita Pallenberg. (It got a bit messy in the Stones camp.)

Right: Faithfull in shiny black leather in Jack Cardiff's "The Girl on a Motorcycle" (1968), also seen in censored form as "Naked Under Leather." Below: Asher in a publicity photo from Roger Corman's Poe adaptation "Masque of the Red Death" (1964). Bottom left: The Lady Penelope puppet wears an up-to-the-minute Mondrian print on TV's "Thunderbirds" (1965-66). Bottom right: Pallenberg in Donald Cammell and Nicholas Roeg's "Performance" (1970).

Opposite, from top left: Twiggy on *Vogue Italia* (1967); Jean Shrimpton on *Vogue* (1965); Boyd on *Petticoat* (1968); and two views of Peggy Moffitt in Michelangelo Antonioni's exploration of the dark side of the fashion world, "Blow-Up" (1966).

Rock and droll

Yock books chronicled cultural movement

IT WAS A SYMPTOM OF THE TIMES: THE EDITORS of American humor magazines in the 1960s were usually older gents who viewed British pop bands as a flash in the pan. And yet, the Beatles were catnip to the guys at *Mad, Cracked, Sick*, et al.

The magazines frequently riffed on two things about the band: their "long" hair and Ringo Starr's big honker. (A recurring device had doctored photos depicting the Beatles with bald heads.)

But said magazines fulfilled their important function — not to mention, enhanced their circulation — by the sheer act of chronicling the fad. After it became clear that the British bands were here to stay, social commentary crept into the humor magazines' coverage. If nothing else, the eye-candy artwork by masters like Frank Frazetta, Mort Drucker, Jack Rickard, John Severin and Norman Mingo was well worth the cover price.

The single most affecting image of a British pop star from a humor magazine remains Frazetta's deadpan portrait of Starr for *Mad* #90 (1964), a parody of Breck shampoo's then-current advertising campaign, here called "Blecch" ("Make your hair 'Blecch'! Yeah! Yeah! Yeah!"). Frazetta — renowned for his painted illustrations in the fantasy and sci-fi genres — made the first of a handful of contributions to *Mad* with this illustration.

A bottomless pit of talent, Frazetta reconciled the grotesque and the beautiful in an unblinking portrait that neither flatters nor ridicules its subject. Though Frazetta lightens Starr's hair (in reflecting Breck's ad campaign, which favored blondes), there's really no gag here.

The "Blecch" Ringo caught the eye of United Artists, who hired Frazetta to illustrate his first-ever movie poster, for "What's New, Pussycat?" (1965) starring Peter Sellers.

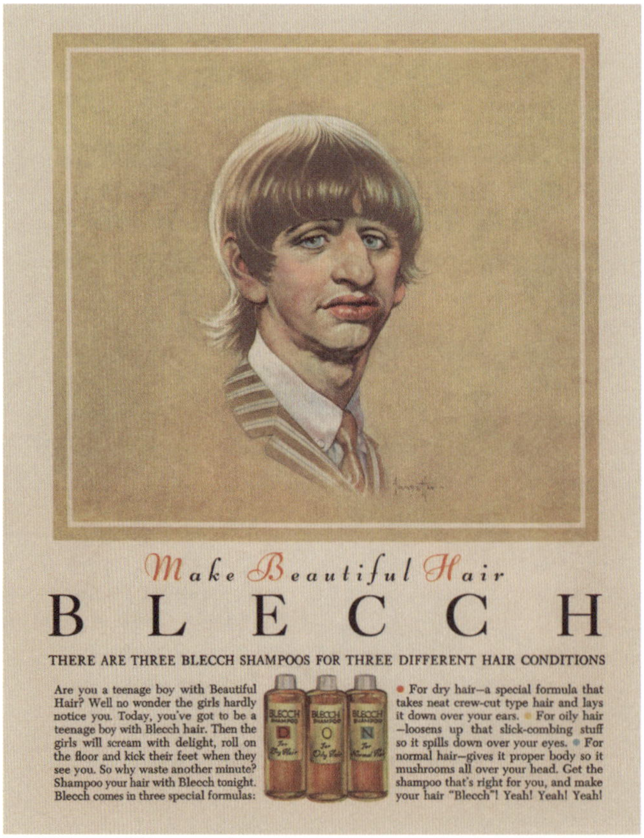

Frank Frazetta's deadpan portrait of Ringo Starr for Mad #90 (1964) remains the single most affecting image of a British pop star in a humor magazine.

The gig represented a turning point in the artist's career. Frazetta went on to illustrate posters for "Mad Max" and "The Gauntlet"; album covers for Herman's Hermits, Nazareth and Molly Hatchet; and paperback covers for Ace/Lancer's Conan series. But the "Blecch" Ringo remains a rare instance of a Frazetta illustration adorning the bedrooms of ... adolescent girls.

MAD OPTED NOT TO PARODY THE BEATLES' FILM debut, "A Hard Day's Night," upon its release in 1964. Then again, who ever thought a Beatles movie would be a hit?

The oversight was corrected in *Mad* #93 (1965). The five-pager "The Flying Ace" — written by Dick DeBartolo and illustrated by Drucker — was a parody of World War II epics "starring" John, Paul, George and Ringo, "co-starring" Natalie Wood, with "cameos" by Ed Sullivan, Barry Goldwater and Jimmy Stewart.

Later that year, the second annual *Mad Follies* featured Frazetta's calendar illustration of dozens of celebs (Barbra Streisand, Nikita Krushchev, Woody Allen, Fidel Castro), in which the Beatles surround an annoyed Elvis Presley.

Drucker and Frazetta *nailed* the Beatles, but not every artist could be bothered — again, likely owing to the old guard's expectation that the boys' popularity would expire.

The cover of the June 1964 issue of *Sick* featured a Jack Davis illustration of a Beatle-esque quartet, but not recognizably "the" Beatles. In the same issue, Angelo Torres' illustrations of the Beatles have the same problem: Except for Starr, the "Beatles" don't *look* like the Beatles. (Given Davis' and Torres' well-earned reputations as caricaturists *par excellence,* this just seems wrong.)

As for those bald jokes: The Beatles were hairless in Al Jaffee's foldout for *Mad* #88 ("Premature loss of the Beatles' hair ends this wild madness") in 1964. The boys are likewise shorn inside the June 1964 *Sick* ("Unwanted hair painlessly removed"), and on the Jan. 1965 *Help!* cover.

It might have been funny, were it not so (yawn) predictable.

The Beatles gave Mad a shoutout in their debut film, "A Hard Day's Night." In this scene, Shake (John Junkin) reads "Son of Mad" as fellow Beatles wrangler Norm (Norman Rossington) looks on. Movie © United Artists; book © Warner Bros.

Mad about Brits

From left: A Beatles broadcast in "Shakespeare Up-to-Date" from *Mad* #92 (1965). Art: Jack Rickard. John Lennon (or is that George Harrison?) sermonizes in "When Teenagers Take Over TV Completely" from *Mad* #101 (1966). Art: Rickard. Moe Howard writes to Ringo Starr in "A Celebrity's Wallet" from *Mad* #91 (1964). Art: Bob Clarke. © Warner Bros.

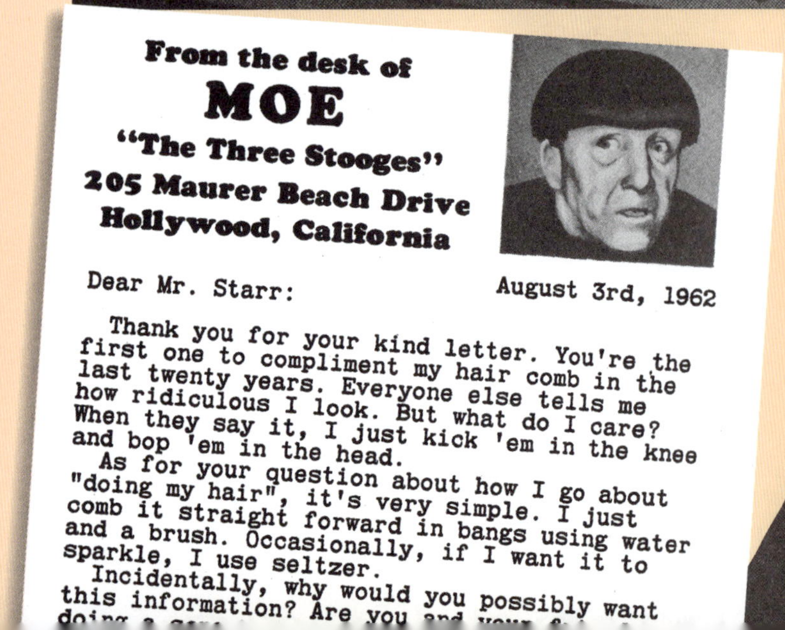

From the desk of
MOE
"The Three Stooges"
205 Maurer Beach Drive
Hollywood, California

Dear Mr. Starr: August 3rd, 1962

Thank you for your kind letter. You're the first one to compliment my hair comb in the last twenty years. Everyone else tells me how ridiculous I look. But what do I care? When they say it, I just kick 'em in the knee and bop 'em in the head.

As for your question about how I go about "doing my hair", it's very simple. I just comb it straight forward in bangs using water and a brush. Occasionally, if I want it to sparkle, I use seltzer.

Incidentally, why would you possibly want this information? Are you

After skipping "A Hard Day's Night," Mad assigned caricaturist Mort Drucker to a parody of old-timey war movies "starring" the Fab Four and Natalie Wood, in Mad #93 (1965).

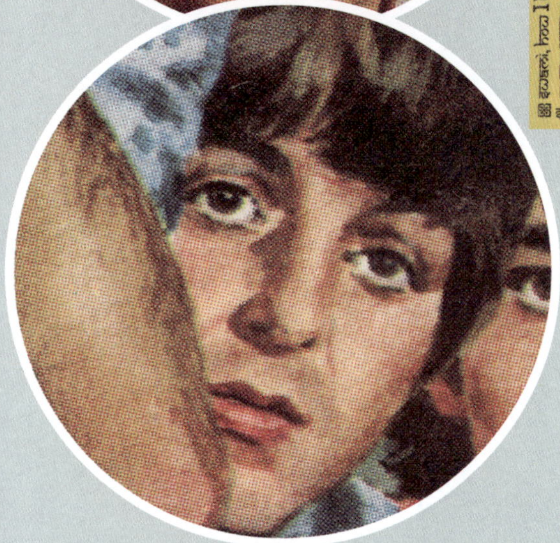

Whatta trip

The Beatles' much-publicized 1968 trip to seek enlightenment in India is spoofed on the cover of *Mad* #121 (1968), with —who else? — Alfred E. Neumann as an exalted guru. Also depicted are actress Mia Farrow and real-life guru Maharishi Mahesh Yogi. Art by Norman Mingo.

Barbra Streisand and Ringo Starr, and their noses, in Mad #111 (1967). Art by Bob Clarke.

The claim "Paul Writes Our Beatle Movie Spoof!" on the cover of Sick #33 (Dec. 1964) was not spurious; it was penned by gagman Paul Laiken. Help! featured bald Beatles on its Jan. 1965 cover. Sick © Headline Publications, Inc.; Help! © General Promotions Co.

THE BEATLE BUGGY

The Beatle Buggy from Super Cracked Annual #1 (1968). The artist is unidentified; perhaps a John Severin quickie?
© Major Magazines

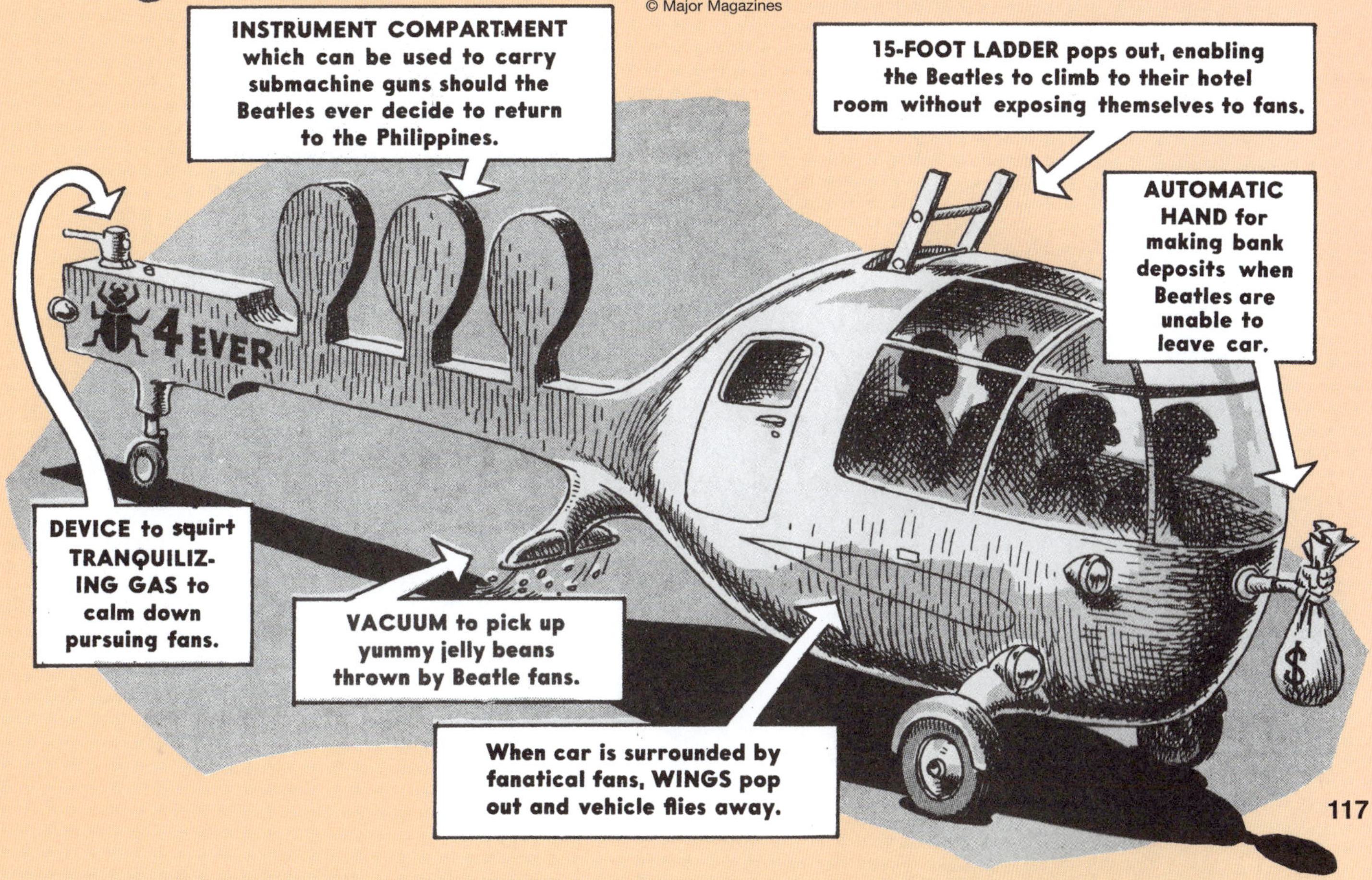

Sick over singers

Below: Honestly, do they look like the Beatles to you? From the cover of *Sick* (June 1964). Art: Jack Davis. Right: Yet another "bald Beatles" gag from the same edition. Below right: An outraged reader responds to same, in *Sick* #33 (Dec. 1964). Bottom: In 1964, Louis Armstrong knocked the Beatles out of the #1 chart spot with "Hello Dolly," hence this topical gag from *Sick* #33. (In real life, George Harrison seems an unlikely person to disrespect ol' Satchmo.)

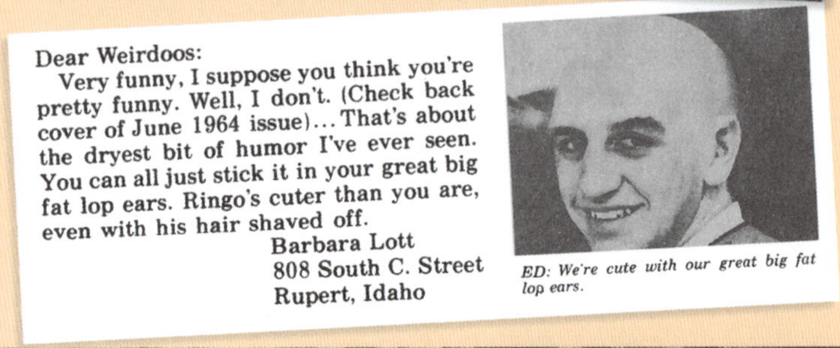

Dear Weirdoos:

Very funny, I suppose you think you're pretty funny. Well, I don't. (Check back cover of June 1964 issue)... That's about the dryest bit of humor I've ever seen. You can all just stick it in your great big fat lop ears. Ringo's cuter than you are, even with his hair shaved off.

Barbara Lott
808 South C. Street
Rupert, Idaho

ED: We're cute with our great big fat lop ears.

Toon time

Engaging caricatures of, from top left, the Dave Clark Five; Maureen Starkey (wife of Ringo); the Stones; the Hermits (with the Beach Boys); and the Animals are believed to be from 1966-68 issues of *Teen World* and *Movie Teen Illustrated,* artist unknown.

12¢
GIRLS' ROMANCES
JUNE NO. 109
APPROVED BY THE COMICS CODE AUTHORITY
SUPERMAN DC NATIONAL COMICS
BUT, PENNY--YOU PROMISED YOU'D GO OUT WITH US WHEN WE CAME OVER!
SORRY, FELLOWS--BUT I ALREADY HAVE A DATE FOR TONIGHT!
WHAT HAPPENED TO ME--WHEN MY DREAM LIFE BECAME MORE IMPORTANT TO ME THAN MY REAL LIFE...

New kind of comic hero

LIVERPUDLIANS. ROCK 'N' ROLLERS. COMIC-BOOK HEROES.

It's little wonder that the creators of comics used the Beatles as characters in their work. After all, these four living, breathing human beings were always perceived as "characters" anyway. "A Hard Day's Night" is sometimes like a live-action cartoon.

Readers in the 1960s saw the Fab Four enter the four-color realm and rub elbows with comic-book characters — typically lovestruck teenage girls and costumed heroes.

One of the Beatles' earliest appearances in the comics happened in *Betty and Veronica* #104 (1964). In an essay titled "Here Come the Beatles," an uncredited writer notes of the Fab Four: "As a group they are very talented, haven't changed with their terrific popularity and acclaim, have an impish philosophy and are very articulate."

The boys are shown in an illustration that looks to be good light-table work, based on a 1963 publicity photo. (John Rosenberger has been suggested as the likely illustrator.)

Before long, the Beatles became part of the illustrated stories — "cast members," if you like. But, as was the case with humor magazines, care was not always taken by comic-book artists to get the Beatles' likenesses strictly correct. (At the time, these artists were usually World War II veterans who viewed the Beatles as a passing fad.)

A happy exception was Dell's *The Beatles* (1964), an "official" comic book depicting the Beatles' rise. Dell — and Beatles fans — hit the jackpot with artist Joe Sinnott.

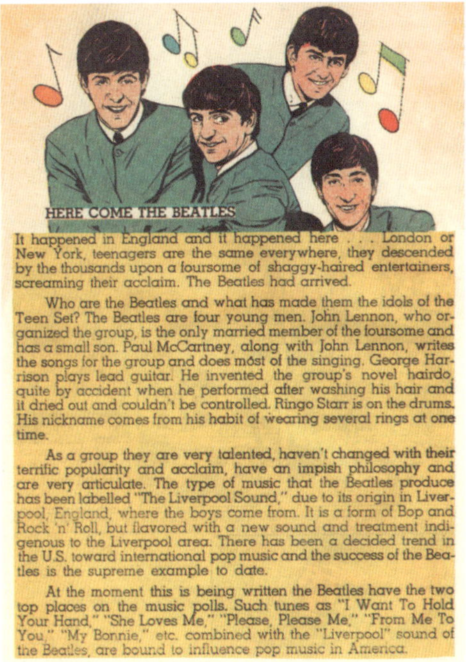

HERE COME THE BEATLES

It happened in England and it happened here . . . London or New York, teenagers are the same everywhere, they descended by the thousands upon a foursome of shaggy-haired entertainers, screaming their acclaim. The Beatles had arrived.

Who are the Beatles and what has made them the idols of the Teen Set? The Beatles are four young men. John Lennon, who organized the group, is the only married member of the foursome and has a small son. Paul McCartney, along with John Lennon, writes the songs for the group and does most of the singing. George Harrison plays lead guitar. He invented the group's novel hairdo, quite by accident when he performed after washing his hair and it dried out and couldn't be controlled. Ringo Starr is on the drums. His nickname comes from his habit of wearing several rings at one time.

As a group they are very talented, haven't changed with their terrific popularity and acclaim, have an impish philosophy and are very articulate. The type of music that the Beatles produce has been labelled "The Liverpool Sound," due to its origin in Liverpool, England, where the boys come from. It is a form of Bop and Rock 'n' Roll, but flavored with a new sound and treatment indigenous to the Liverpool area. There has been a decided trend in the U.S. toward international pop music and the success of the Beatles is the supreme example to date.

At the moment this is being written the Beatles have the two top places on the music polls. Such tunes as "I Want To Hold Your Hand," "She Loves Me," "Please, Please Me," "From Me To You," "My Bonnie," etc. combined with the "Liverpool" sound of the Beatles, are bound to influence pop music in America.

Top and right: Archie's early foray into Beatle territory, from Betty and Veronica #104 (1964). Opposite: Girls' Romance #109 (1965).

Art by Joe Sinnott from the one-shot Dell giant, The Beatles (1964). Above: The pre-fame Beatles hone their act at the Cavern Club in Liverpool. (Although, don't those dancing kids kinda look like Yanks?) Right: The Beatles meet with the Queen Mother following their Royal Command Performance in 1963. Opposite: The Beatles land in America.

It's official! Sanctioned comics

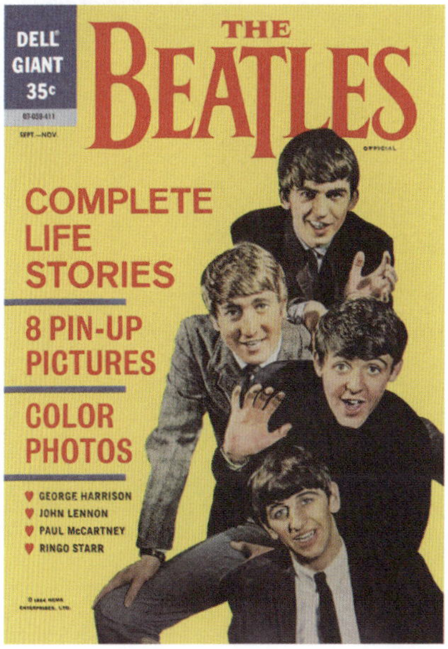

What really sets Dell Publishing's "official" 35-cent giant comic book *The Beatles* apart is the fact that its artist made the effort to capture the likenesses of John, Paul, George and Ringo.

That artist was Joe Sinnott (1926-2020), a prolific inker for Marvel Comics who delineated more than 200 issues of *Fantastic Four,* chiefly pencilled by Jack Kirby and John Buscema.

Sinnott explained that his penchant for likenesses is what landed him the Beatles gig.

"I secured an account over at Dell and also at *Treasure Chest,*" Sinnott told me in 2004. "I was fairly fortunate to be able to capture likenesses, so the companies used to give me a lot of biographical stories, which I certainly enjoyed. I did the lives of (Douglas) MacArthur and (Dwight) Eisenhower and John Kennedy and Babe Ruth and the popes and J. Edgar Hoover.

"Dell liked the way I did likenesses. So for Dell, I did the life of the Beatles. That was a 64-page book, a lot of work," added Sinnott (who drafted Dick Giordano to do some pages).

Capturing the look of the Beatles took some hustle on Sinnott's part, the artist recalled. "As far as references, I was given nothing," he said. "I relied on photos in magazines."

It was a point of pride for Sinnott to draw the Beatles' locations, and their gear, correctly. "I felt it was important to get the instruments right," he said. "I didn't want to just fake it."

Um, should Penny seek psychiatric treatment? In the fantasy world of this Ann-Margret lookalike, she is dating five men — four Beatles, and Jeff. From Girls' Romance #109 (1965). Artwork by Gene Colan. © DC Comics

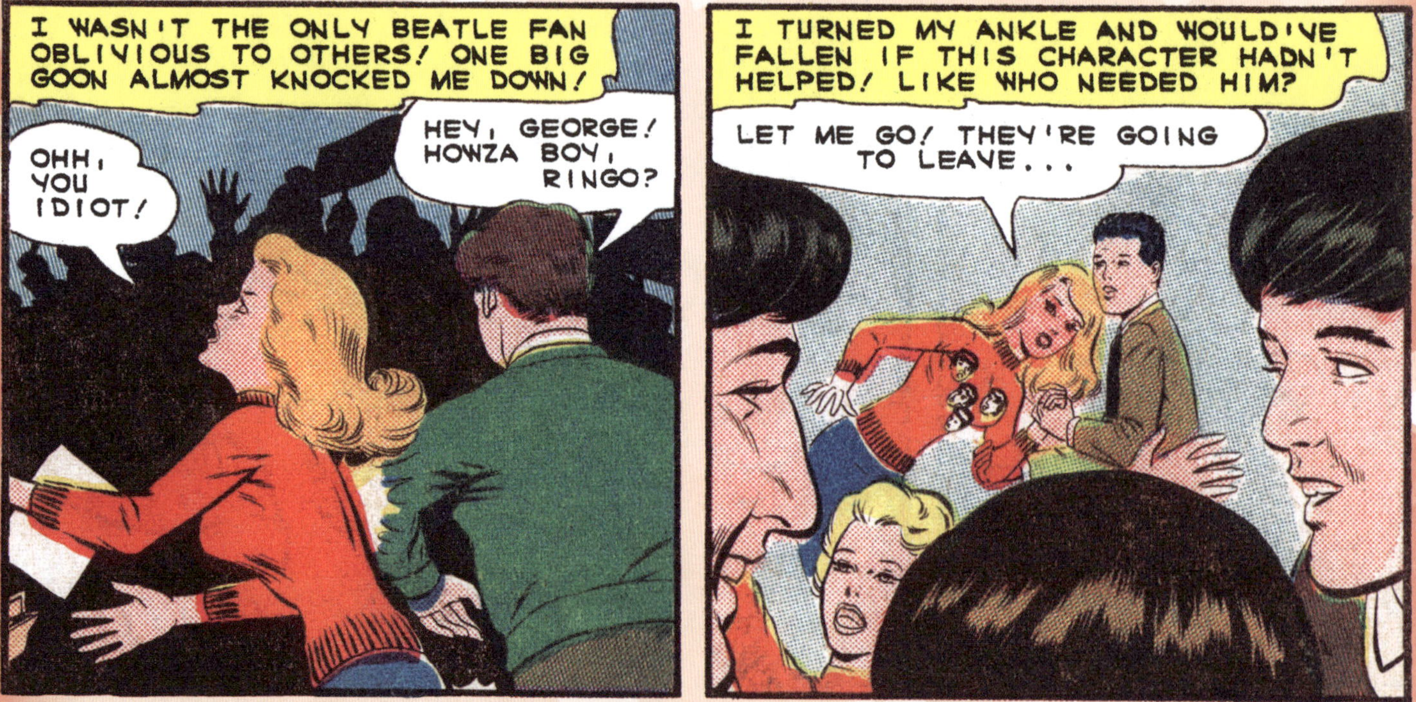

When the president of the Beatles fan club is jostled at a show, a good-looking boy comes to her rescue. "Who needed him," she thinks, but we suspect otherwise. From Summer Love #46 (1965). © Charlton Comics Group

Ah, romance

CHARLTON SHAMELESSLY PLAYED the Beatles card in its romance titles. In stories like "The Beatles Were My Downfall" (from *Summer Love* #46, 1965) and "The Beatles Saved My Romance" (from *Summer Love* #47, 1966), the heroines learn not to put their unattainable idols ahead of the actual flesh-and-blood fellows who are right in front of them. Ain't that sweet?

Publishers of romance comics sometimes shoe-horned the Fab Four onto its covers. The poster for a Beatles "record hop" on the cover of Charlton's *Teen Confessions* #31 (1964) appears to be an afterthought. The cover of DC Comics' *Heart Throbs* #101 (1966) depicts a young lady tearfully discovering that her boyfriend is cheating on her ... while attending a Beatles movie.

In the Archie Comics line, Betty and Veronica went gaga over the Fab Four. On the cover of *Laugh* #166 (1965), they swoon over the group. In *Betty and Veronica* #105 (1965), they attend a Beatle wig sale. Meanwhile, in another Archie Comics title, *Josie* #28 (1965), Josie's well-decorated bedroom is a tribute to Herman's Hermits.

EVEN ODDER THAN THE ROMANCE comic book appearances were the Beatles' crossovers and tie-ins with superheroes.

In DC Comics' *Superman's Pal Jimmy Olsen* #79 (1964), Jimmy is hijacked to the distant past, where he manufactures and sells Beatle wigs to peasants. When Superman sees Jimmy in his red wig playing a ram's horn and drum, he exclaims, "You've really started a 'Beatle' fad here, Jimmy! You seem to be as popular as Ringo, the Beatle drummer!" (You could always count on editor Mort Weisinger to spell it out for you.)

Jimmy's second Beatles-related — or, at least, Beatles-adjacent — adventure happened in *Jimmy Olsen* #88 (1965). Despite the promise of a Beatles connection on the cover, there are no Beatles — just Rick Rock and His Rolling Romeos, which Olsen challenges with his own combo, Jimmy Olsen and His Carrot-Top Cut-Ups. Jimmy arranges a front-page story about his group in *The Daily Planet.* So journalistic ethics did not exist in 1960s Metropolis.

In *Metal Men* #12 (1965), the Beatles' dialect sounds more Knightsbridge than Liverpool. I say!

In Marvel Comics' *Strange Tales* #130 (1965), the Human Torch and the Thing pursue a trio of thieves who abscond to Coney Island with the band's payroll — wearing Beatle wigs.

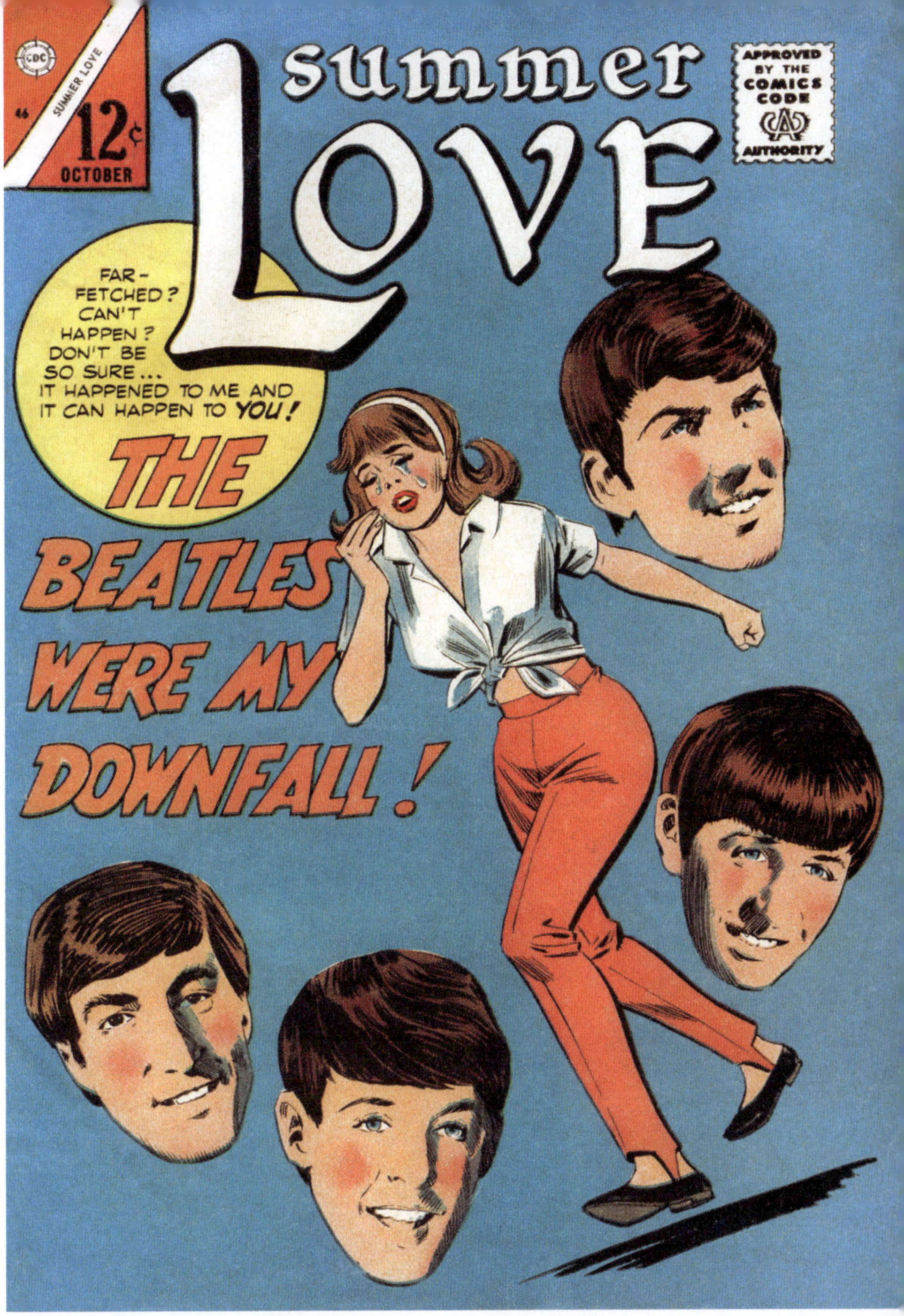

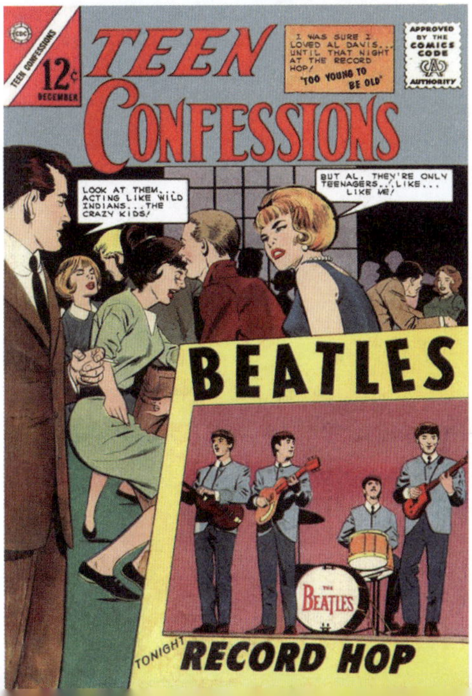

Charlton Comics Beatles tie-ins, from top: Summer Love #46 (1965), Teen Confessions #31 (1964) and Summer Love #47 (1966).

ARCHIE SERIES
AUG.
NO. 28
Josie
by DAN 'N' DICK
APPROVED BY THE COMICS CODE AUTHORITY
12¢
MAC
JOSIE, WHY WON'T YOU JOIN OUR FAN CLUB FOR THE MONKEES?
GOSH! I'D LIKE TO... BUT IT'D COST ME A FORTUNE TO REDO MY ROOM!
HERMAN'S HERMITS
HERMAN'S HERMITS ALBUM
PETER NOONE
THE MONKEES
THE MONKEES
HH
I'M HIP ON HERMAN'S HERMITS
HERMAN'S HERMITS
HERMAN'S
HERMITS
HERMAN'S HERMITS
HERMAN'S HERMITS ALBUM

Rocking out in Riverdale

If Archie Andrews needed a breather from the long-running rivalry between Betty Cooper and Veronica Lodge for his affections, he got one. The girls (along with another Archie Universe dweller, one Josie McCoy) turned their attention to ... British pop stars. From left: Pandemonium during a Beatle wig sale in *Betty and Veronica* #105 (1965); a bust of Peter Noone from the cover of *Josie* #28 (1965); the girls sample new technology at Pop's Chock'lit Shoppe in *Archie's Joke Book* #93 (1965); dreaming of Beatles in a cover detail from *Laugh* #166 (1965). Opposite: The *Josie* #28 cover by Dan DeCarlo.

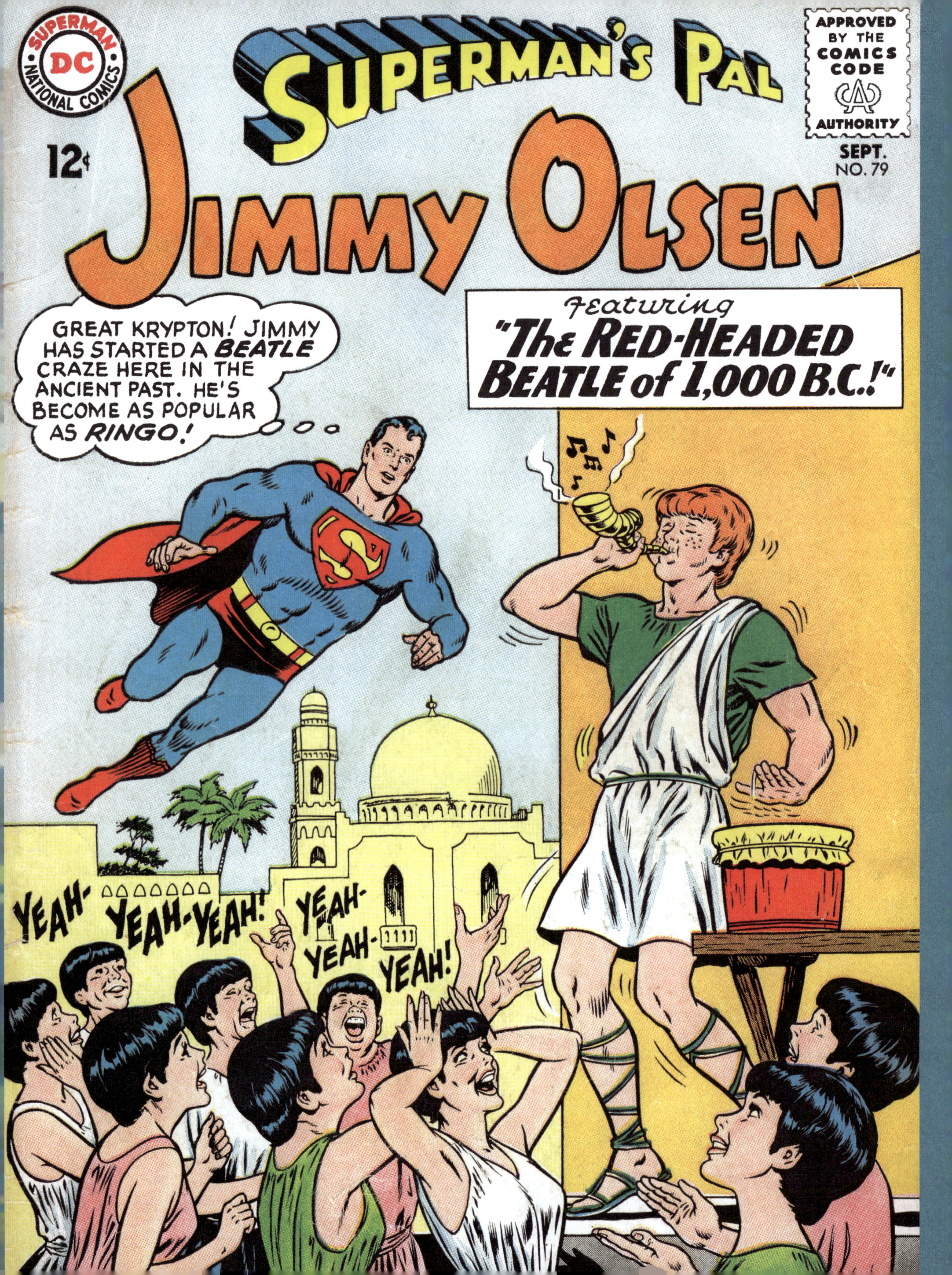
SUPERMAN DC NATIONAL COMICS
12¢
SUPERMAN'S PAL
JIMMY OLSEN
APPROVED BY THE COMICS CODE AUTHORITY
SEPT.
NO. 79
GREAT KRYPTON! JIMMY HAS STARTED A BEATLE CRAZE HERE IN THE ANCIENT PAST. HE'S BECOME AS POPULAR AS RINGO!
Featuring "The RED-HEADED BEATLE of 1,000 B.C.!"
YEAH-YEAH-YEAH!
YEAH-YEAH-YEAH!

Beatles in the DCU

Above: The most famous band in the world meets the least famous superteam in the world, in *Metal Men* #12 (1965). This really *is* an alternate universe, in which the Beatles, in their first flush of world fame, beg the Metal Men — who were not exactly the Justice League of America — for their autographs. (Tina, then the Metal Men's sole female member, asks the all-important question: "Is your hair real?") Story by Robert Kanigher; art by Ross Andru and Mike Esposito. Opposite and right: In *Superman's Pal Jimmy Olsen* #79 (1964), the first panel of "The Red-Headed Beatle of 1000 B.C.!" encapsulates the head-scratching weirdness of the *Jimmy Olsen* comic book series. Jimmy wears a red Beatle wig and dances as he watches the Beatles on TV, exclaiming, "I always seem to enjoy their music more when I wear my personal Beatle wig!" Story by Leo Dorfman; cover by Curt Swan and George Klein; interior art by George Papp.

Sinister swinger

Left: That brazen British baddie, the Mad Mod, ensnares Kid Flash in a panel from *Teen Titans* #7 (1967). In "The Mad Mod, Merchant of Menace," the Titans are enlisted to accompany Wonder Girl's favorite English pop star, Holly Hip, and break up a smuggling operation spearheaded by the Mad Mod, a haberdasher for London's swinging set who says things like "Jolly good show!" and "Cheerio!" Story by Bob Haney, art by Nick Cardy. The Mad Mod returned in *Teen Titans* #17 (1968), taunting the Titans, "Aye, me duckies, it's your old friend!" Haney and Cardy were reteamed.

SUPERMAN DC NATIONAL COMICS
SWING WITH SCOOTER
NO. 1
JULY
APPROVED BY THE COMICS CODE AUTHORITY
12¢
THAT LOVER-DOLL!
DAHLINGS-- SCOOTER'S THE ABSOLUTE END!
COOKIE
SCOOTER'S MY DISCO-BUDDY! HE'S A-OKAY-- WITH ME!
PENNY
SYLVESTER
ZIPPSVILLE! HE DOESN'T TURN ME ON!
I'LL TELL YOU WHAT I THINK OF THAT ENGLISH IMPORT... HE'S A... CENSORED
CYNTHIA
MALIBU
THAT FINK'S GOT ALL MY CHICKS TUNED INTO HIS FREQUENCY!
KENNY
JOE ORLANDO

Brit interloper

In the inaugural *Swing With Scooter* story written by Jack Miller and Barbara Friedlander and illustrated by Joe Orlando, our hero is a British pop star nicknamed after his preferred mode of transportation. He emigrates to a small town in America called Plainsville — ha, ha, *Plainsville!* — hoping to trade the hectic London scene for a life of peace and quiet in suburbia. This scheme doesn't quite pan out. (Scooter must never have read American teen-genre comics.) As the series plodded along, Scooter's British-isms became less and less frequent.

Copycat guitar-clad heroes

The Maniaks, a band of zany rockers, debuted in DC Comics' "tryout" anthology title *Showcase* with issues #68, 69 and 71 (all 1967). The group wasn't expressly identified as Brits, but the British influence was obvious in their lingo ("fab," "luv") and fashion sense (Pack Rat wore a newsboy cap and granny glasses). Stories by E. Nelson Bridwell, art by Mike Sekowsky. Speaking of Sekowsky, when the artist-editor took over *Metal Men,* he re-imagined two robotic characters Lead and Tin as "Ledby Hand and Tinker," a pop duo not unlike Chad and Jeremy or Peter and Gordon.

Top: Maniak-mania in Showcase #69 (1967). Right: Scooter and guitar in Scooter #11 (1968). Opposite: #1 cover (1966). Maniaks art by Mike Sekowsky; Scooter art by Joe Orlando and Jerry Grandenetti.

From screen to page

Above: The TV sitcom "My Little Margie" (1952-55) was *long* off the air by 1964, but Charlton Comics continued publishing a comic book based on the series, thus Margie's Beatle moment. Right: Another officially sanctioned Beatles comic book was Dell's "Yellow Submarine" movie adaptation of 1968. Below: The "Sgt. Pepper"-era Beatles meet Forbush-Man in Marvel Comics' superhero parody comic book *Not Brand Ecch* #8 (1968), in artwork by Tom Sutton.

Fab 4 meets Fantastic 2 In Marvel's *Strange Tales* #130, the girlfriends of Johnny (the Human Torch) and Ben (the Thing) — Dorrie and Alicia, respectively — have a chance encounter with the Beatles. Characteristically gruff Ben professes to be a fan of John, Paul, George and Ringo; dons a Beatle wig; and gushes, "It's them! My ever-lovin' idols!! Be still, my patterin' heart!" Interior art above by Bob Powell and Chick Stone; cover art elements below by Jack Kirby and Stone; story by Stan Lee.

MODELING with MILLIE
MARVEL COMICS GROUP
12¢ IND.
54 JUNE
APPROVED BY THE COMICS CODE AUTHORITY
THIS ISH IS POSITIVELY A ROOF-ROCKIN' HAPPENING!
THE FASHIONS ARE GO-GO... THE BEAT IS BOSS... THE MUSIC IS GONESVILLE... "AND THIS BIRD CAN SING!"
THEY'RE BACK... THOSE MADCAP MUSICIANS WITH THE HARD-DRIVING LIVERPOOL SOUND! THE EVER-BOPPIN' NEVER-STOPPIN'... GEARS!

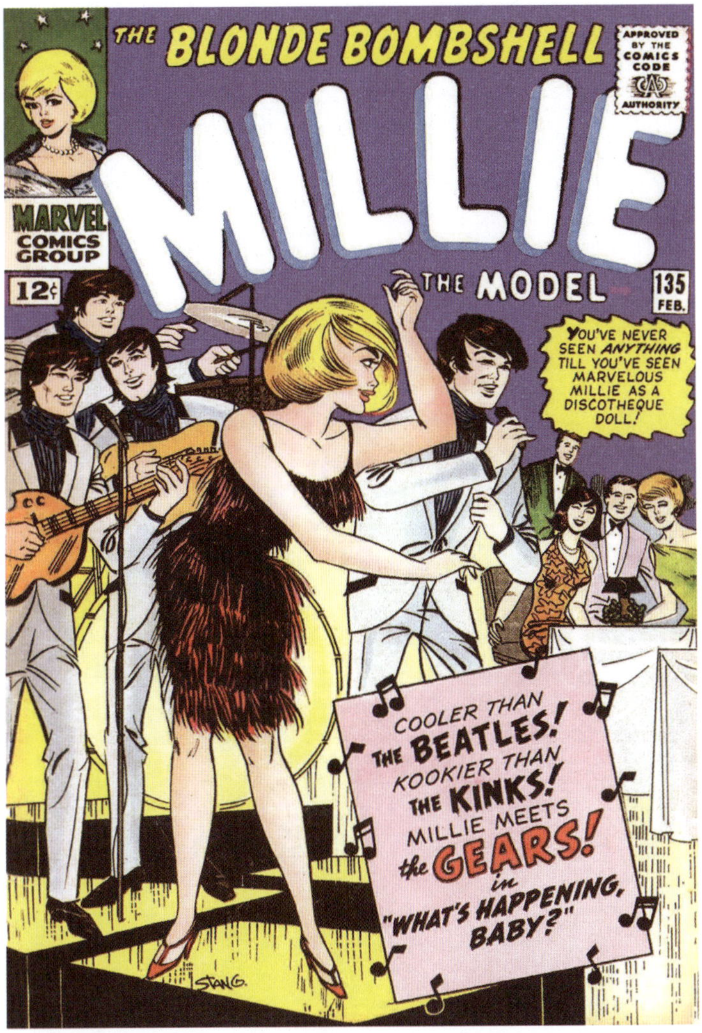

The Gears are ... gear!

Cooler than the Beatles? Kookier than the Kinks? That's what the cover type of *Millie the Model* #135 (1966) promised regarding the Gears, Marvel's fictional quartet based on real-life British Invasion bands.

Writer Roy Thomas (creator of the Gears with artist Stan Goldberg) said he didn't recall discussing the Gears with Marvel Comics editor Stan Lee "in any way, shape, or form," when we corresponded in 2021.

"It was an idea I brought up to Stan Goldberg, who was the penciler and had been, I suspect, basically doing the plotting on the *Millie* comics for some time," he said.

"Stan G. liked the idea, so we went ahead with it. In later contacts with him, he often brought up (the Gears) as one of the things he most liked doing in *Millie*."

As for the band's moniker: "The name 'Gears' came from 'Hard Day's Night' — some producer saying a line like, 'Gear, fab, and all the other pimply hyperboles.' "

The Gears debut in Millie the Model #135 (1966), top left, and return in Millie #141 (1967), top right and panel left. Art: Stan Goldberg. Opposite: More Gears in Modeling With Millie #54 (1967). Art: Ogden Whitney and John Romita.

PAUL McCARTNEY
RINGO STARR

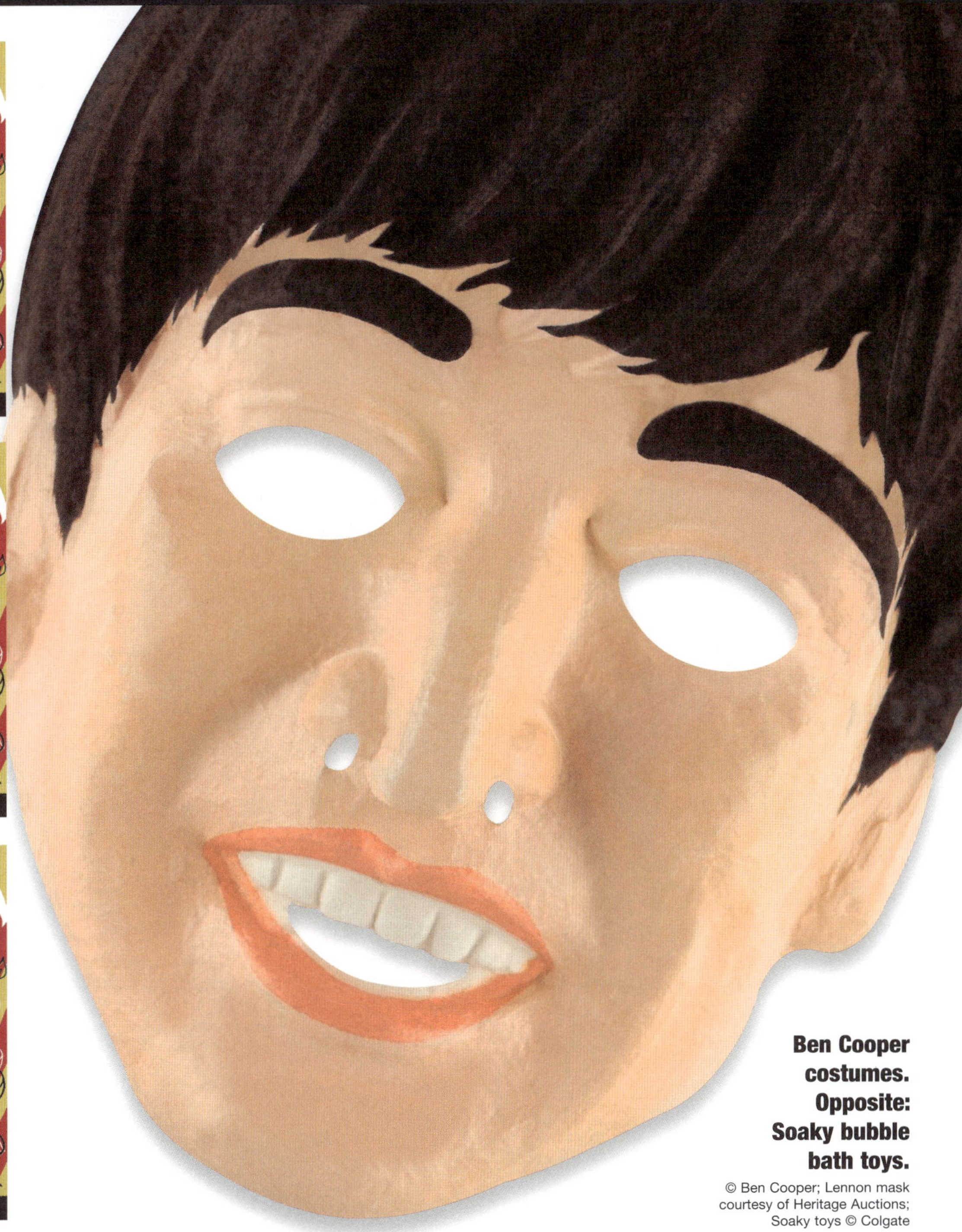

Ben Cooper costumes. Opposite: Soaky bubble bath toys.

Take a bath with Paul and Ringo

When Ben Cooper — purveyors of chintzy (but enchanting) Halloween costumes — did the Beatles, they did 'em right. The boys were represented in good likenesses on BC's crackly, rigid, nostril-blocking, sweat-trapping masks. (The "costumes," glorified aprons in "rayon taffeta," had the same striped vest for all four.)

But Colgate only rolled the dice on *two* Beatles in its Soaky line of bubble-bath toys. (Soakys were plastic figures filled with bubble-bath solution; the heads popped off to reveal a twist cap.) The two Beatles released by Colgate will hardly be a surprise: the Cute One, and the One With the Big Nose. (Pity those who wanted to take a bath with John or George.)

Another non-surprise: British Invasion-inspired collectibles overwhelmingly favored the Fab Four. But not *all*.

There were fan club buttons for the Rolling Stones, the Dave Clark Five, Herman's Hermits, etc. Remco put out Dave Clark Five figures; Hasbro released a Peter Noone doll; and Play Pal released Rolling Stones dolls of ... we can't say for sure.

Meanwhile, England was much more democratic than we Yanks when it came to rock collectibles. Selcol's Stones-themed musical toys are like something from an alternate universe.

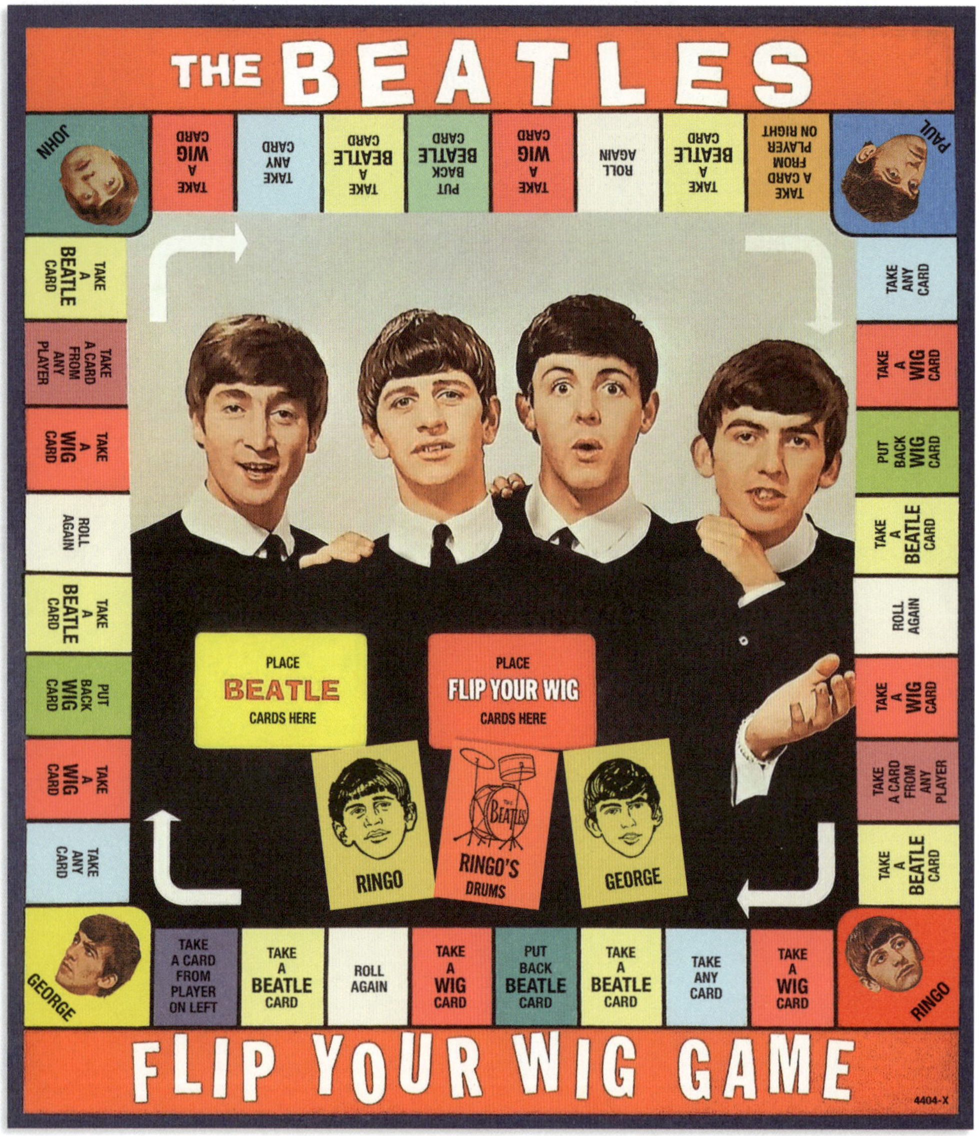

Game on!

The title of Milton Bradley's "Flip Your Wig Game" focused on Beatle haircuts. But a photo of the boys *before* they perfected the hairstyle was used as the board's main image. Like the band itself, MB's game works best with four players. Participants play as John, Paul, George or Ringo, collecting cards with autographs, instruments and a "hit record" of whichever Beatle you represent. (Stratego, this ain't.) Opposite: Band-emblazoned buttons.

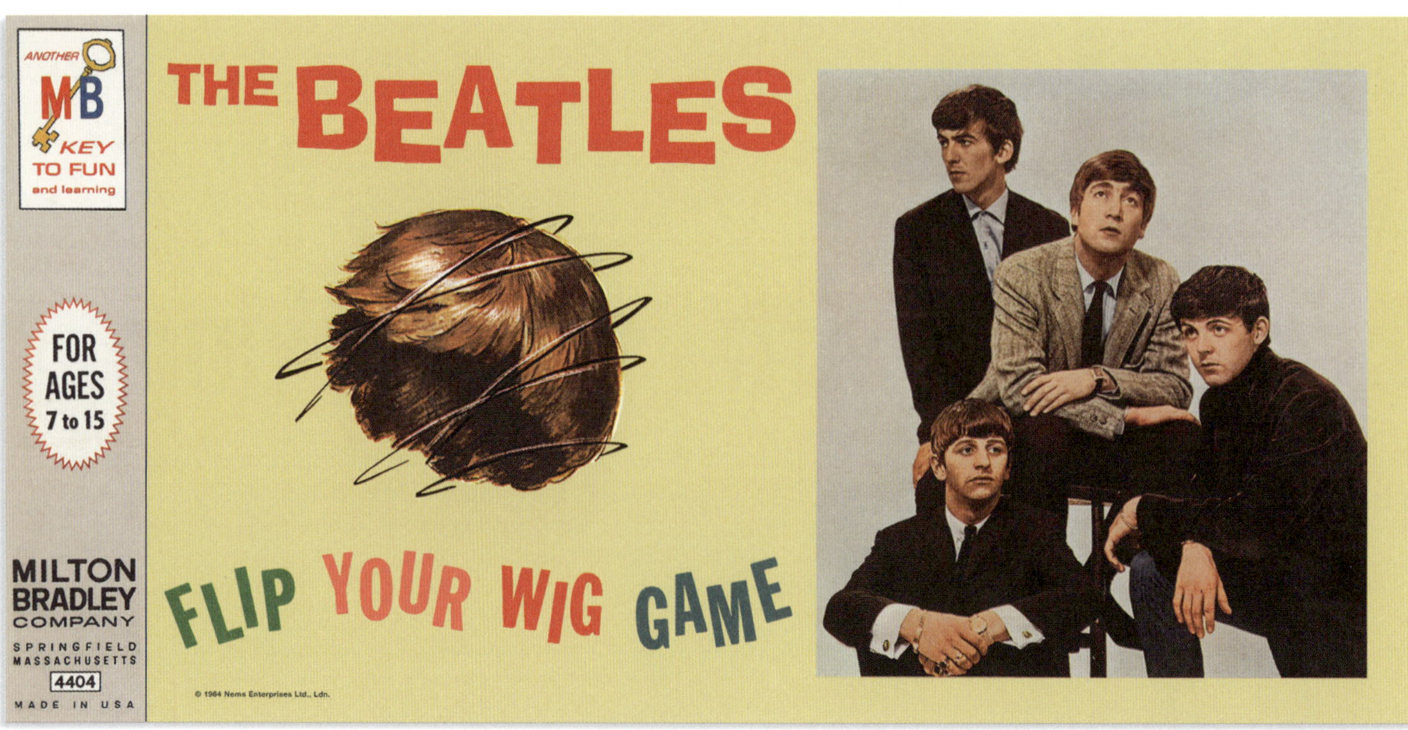

I'm a
PAUL McCARTNEY
RINGO "RINGS" STARR
OFFICIAL BEATLES FAN
GEORGE HARRISON
JOHN LENNON
RINGO
JOHN
GEORGE
PAUL
THE BEATLES
DAVE CLARK FIVE
FAN CLUB
THE ROLLING STONES
I LOVE
HERMAN'S HERMITS
I LOVE the "BEATLES"
I LOVE PAUL
I LOVE RINGO
I'M 4 BEATLES
I LOVE The "DAVE CLARK" "FIVE"

Remco's darling, wiry-haired Beatle dolls from 1964 were hot sellers, but their likenesses ran hot and cold. John and Ringo were spot-on. But George had Prince Charles teeth, and Paul resembled a Zanti Misfit.

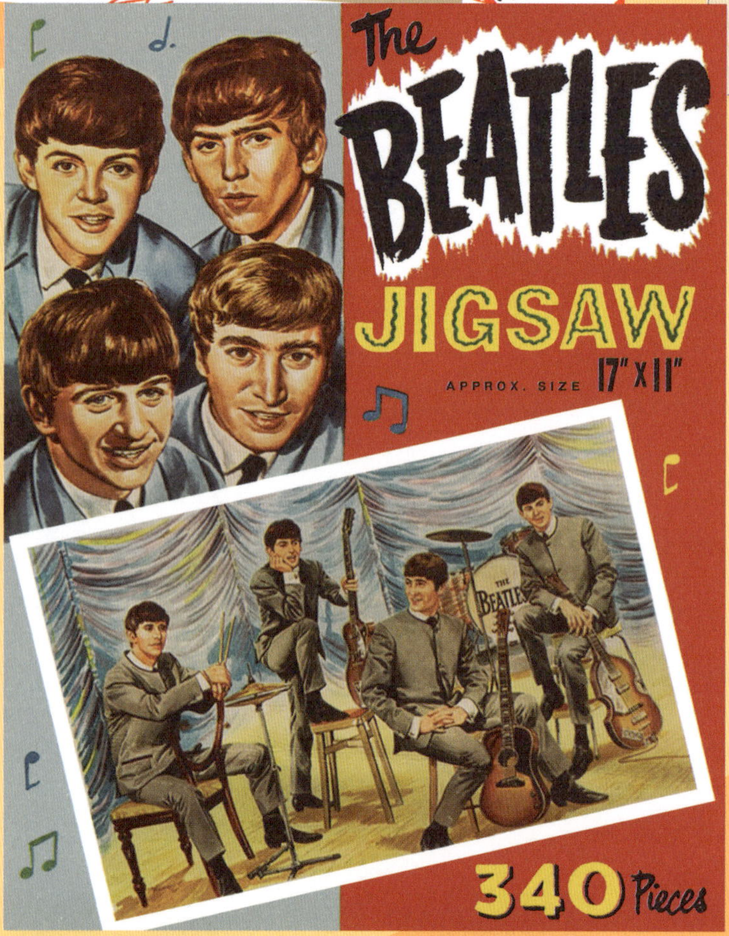

You name it

Brian Epstein was said to have been, shall we say, overly liberal in approving licensing deals on behalf of his young charges. In America, where the dollar is king, manufacturers seemed willing to plaster the Beatles' names and faces on just about anything. From top left: Merit's Beatles magnetic toy; packaging for the "only" Authentic Beatle Wig from Lowell; Bronson's Beatles Shampoo ("for all the family"); a Beatles Jigsaw Puzzle; Bronson's Beatles Hair Spray ("brushes out instantly"); and packaging for (probably unlicensed) Beatle Combs. Also for sale were Beatles stockings, pens, lariat ties, tie pins and (note careful spelling) "Beetle" boots.

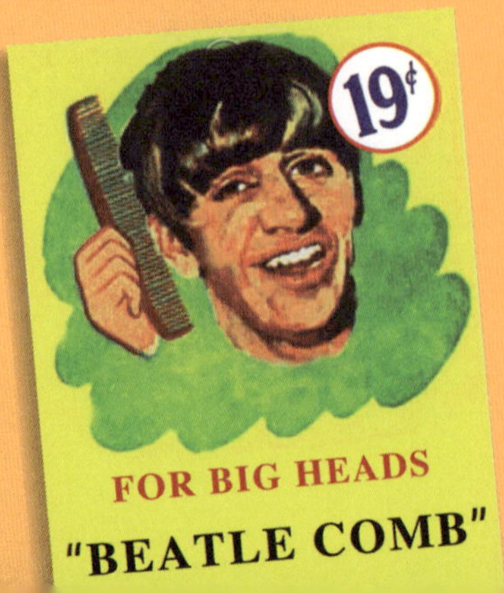

Plastic pals

The Beatles weren't the only rockers immortalized in doll form. From above: Hasbro's Show Biz Babies figure of Peter Noone (1967); Play Pal's figure of, we're guessing, Charlie Watts (1964); Remco's figures of Dave Clark Five members Rick Huxley and Mr. Clark himself (1964).

Schooltastic

Above: Aladdin's Beatles lunch box with fab art by Elmer Lehnhardt (1965). Left: Are those guys supposed to be the Stones? Rolling Stones jigsaw puzzles (not to be confused with the "Beggars Banquet" song).

Selcol of Braintree, Essex, in England made rock-themed toys (not to mention garden ornaments). From left: Rolling Stones Big 6 Guitar; Beatles Big 5 Guitar logo; Rolling Stones Party Pack box art with harmonica; Ringo Starr drum.

No bubble-bath toys or Saturday morning cartoons based on the Rolling Stones were marketed to American children. But these illustrations (redrafted from Selcol's Big 6 Guitar toy box art) provide a glimpse of what kid-friendly Stones might have looked like on this side of the pond.

Frozen four

Is it still a collectible if you can *eat* it? Beatle Bars (left and below left) were "delicious ice cream bars covered with chocolate crunch." The frozen treats were marketed in 1965 by Hood, an imprint of the Country Club Ice Cream Co. in Paterson, NJ. On the side of the box was an offer for a "lucky Beatle coin" redeemable from Alking Enterprises in Los Angeles. The coins — embossed with the boys' faces, of course — could be obtained by mailing in one wrapper (or a facsimile) plus 50 cents. Bottom left: A Beatles Candy box promised a free hand puppet inside. (These were simply color printing on clear plastic.) Below: The Ringo Starr hand puppet. *Yeah ... Yeah ... Yeah ...*

Habit-forming confections

Remember those politically incorrect sweets known as "candy cigarettes"? The tooth-decay-enabling confections that made kids feel like miniature Humphrey Bogarts? Beatles Candy, manufactured by World Candies Inc. of Brooklyn, were called "candy sticks." The caricatures on the box art were based on the King Features Saturday morning cartoon series. We're betting any guitars awarded in the candy's monthly guitar sweepstakes weren't exactly Rickenbackers or Hofners. Yellow Submarine Sweet Cigarettes were also sold. Long Eating Licorice Records — that is, licorice candy made to resemble 45-RPM singles — were manufactured by England's Clevedon Confectionery. Kellogg's Rice Krispies offered a fan club badge. Nestlé's Quik (both chocolate and strawberry flavors) offered inflatable Beatle dolls.

JOHN
"KOOKIEST OF THEM ALL"
Revell
Authentic Kit
BEATLE
PRECISION MOLDED PLASTIC • EASY TO ASSEMBLE

PAUL
"THE GREAT McCARTNEY"
Revell
Authentic Kit
BEATLE
PRECISION MOLDED PLASTIC • EASY TO ASSEMBLE

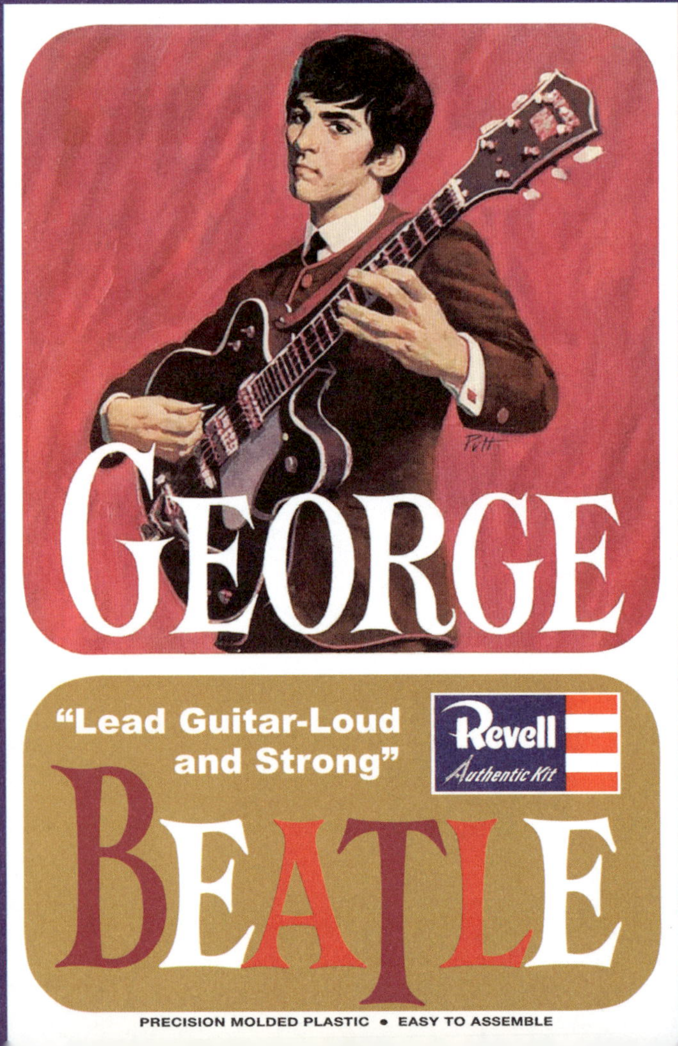
GEORGE
"Lead Guitar-Loud and Strong"
Revell
Authentic Kit
BEATLE
PRECISION MOLDED PLASTIC • EASY TO ASSEMBLE

RINGO
"WILDEST SKINS IN TOWN"
Revell
Authentic Kit
BEATLE
PRECISION MOLDED PLASTIC • EASY TO ASSEMBLE

Kit krazy

Hawk Model Co., home of the Weird-Oh models, put out Brit-inspired kits with its "Frantics" line. Left: "Steel Pluckers" and "Totally Fab" box art by Weird-Oh creator Bill Campbell (1965). Right: Painted-and-glued Pluckers. Opposite: Revell's nicely done Beatles box artwork signed by Putt (1964).

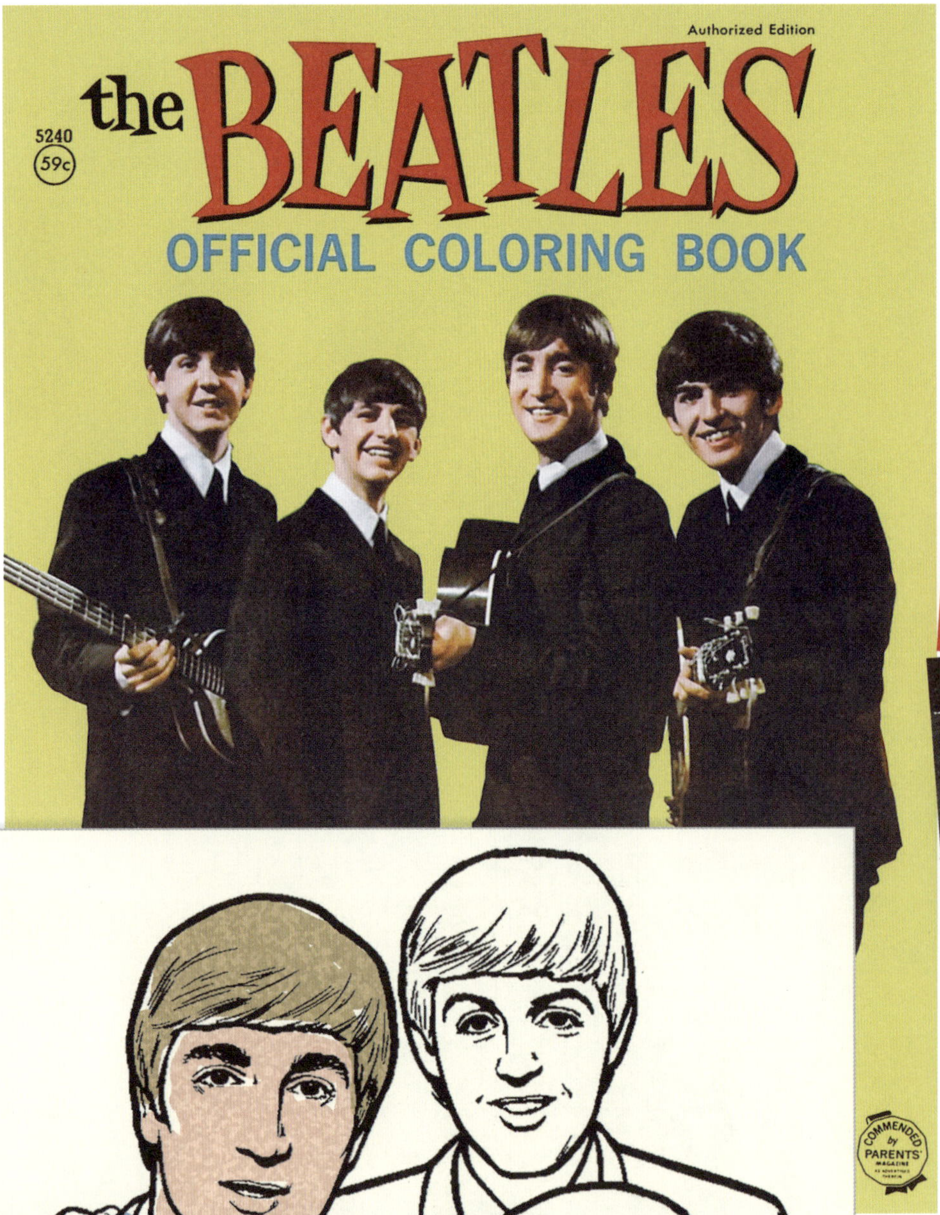

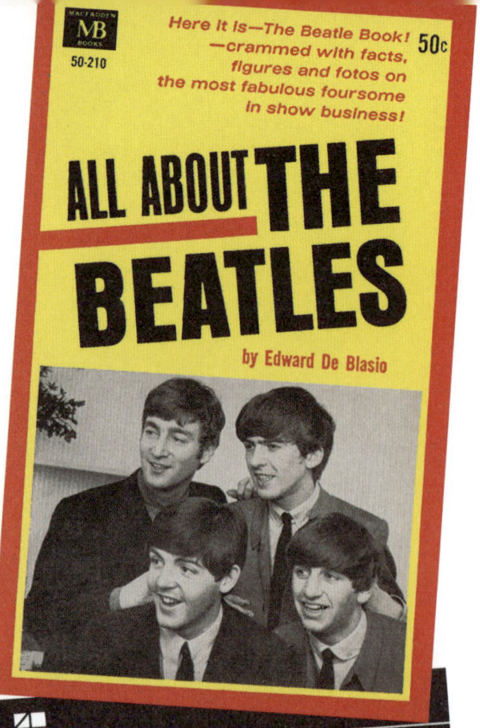

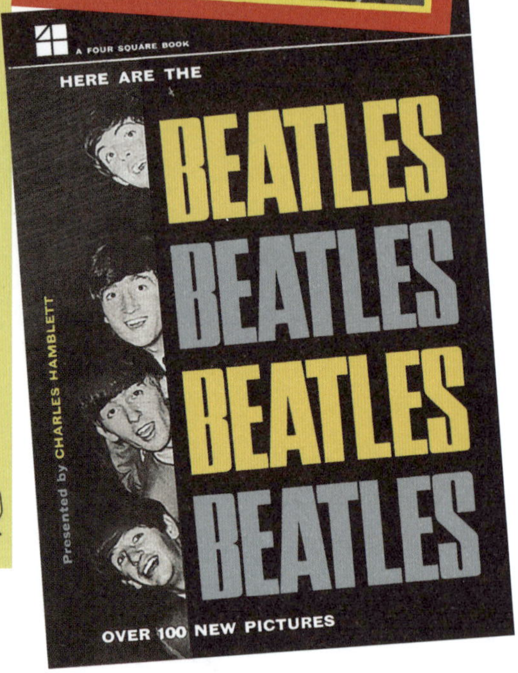

Print mint Top left: "The Beatles Official Coloring Book" and interior page. From top right: The paperbacks "All About the Beatles" and "Here are the Beatles." Below: Topps trading cards. Opposite: A copywriter posing as Ringo Starr explains Beatlemania on the back of card #11 in one of Topps' Beatles series. All are from 1964.

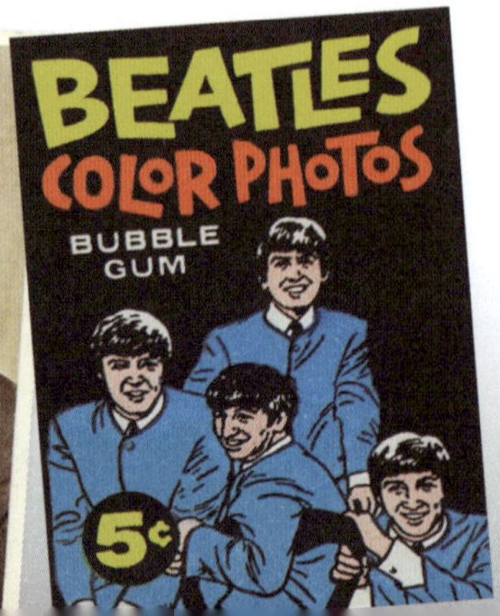

BEATLES

11

COLOR CARDS

Question: What is Beatle-mania?

Ringo Speaking: Tch! Tch! That's a strange new sickness. Lucky for us, there is no cure. Once you get it, you're hooked with it. Its symptoms are screams, fainting spells, and tears whenever The Beatles are performing. And it's very contagious too, you know. I'd recommend lots of rest for the victims of BEATLE-MANIA, so that they'll be strong enough to survive the next attack—the next time The Beatles perform.

PRINTED IN U.S.A.

The Beatles
Starring in their first full-length, hilarious, action-packed film!
"A Hard Day's Night"
6 BRAND NEW SONGS
PLUS YOUR BEATLES FAVORITES!
also starring
WILFRID BRAMBELL
produced by WALTER SHENSON
screenplay by ALUN OWEN
directed by RICHARD LESTER
released thru UNITED ARTISTS
Hear the Beatles on the one, the only, the original sound track album from United Artists Records!

LOOKING FOR A SHOW TO BLOW YOUR COOL?
Well, swing loose, bust out, and HOLD on...you've never heard faster beats or seen wilder fun!
HEAR "A must to avoid," "Hold On" and all the other go-go gone hits on the MGM Records soundtrack recording
METRO-GOLDWYN-MAYER presents
HERMAN'S HERMITS
IN
"HOLD ON!"

HERMAN'S HERMITS
raving up a riot of fun...and a bevy of beautiful birds...from Manchester to London!
"Mrs. Brown, you've got a lovely daughter"
ENJOY THE HIT SONGS
"Mrs. Brown, You've Got A Lovely Daughter"
"The Most Beautiful Thing In My Life"
"The World Is For The Young"
"There's A Kind Of Hush"
"It's Nice To Be Out In The Morning"
"Ooh, She's Done It Again!"
METRO-GOLDWYN-MAYER presents AN ALLEN KLEIN PRODUCTION in PANAVISION and METROCOLOR
WITH STANLEY HOLLOWAY

"HELP! I'm kidnapped!"
"HELP! I'm lost on a tropic island!"
"HELP! I'm surrounded by women!"
"HELP! keep our city clean!"
STOP WORRYING!
HELP!
IS ON THE WAY!
The Colorful Adventures of
THE BEATLES
are more Colorful than ever...in COLOR!
HELP YOURSELF TO SEVEN GREAT NEW BEATLE HITS!

The Dave Clark 5 are "Having a Wild Weekend"
Ready or not, here they come in the year's big dramatic surprise!

Pointing a lens at the phenom

YOU'VE GOTTA HAND IT TO FRANKIE AVALON AND Annette Funicello. "A Hard Day's Night" opened on July 7, 1964. Only 15 days later came "Bikini Beach," a Frankie-and-Annette "beach party" movie that skewered the Beatles. *That's* quick work.

Besides his usual role as Funicello's fella, Avalon dons a wig, glasses and double-neck guitar as British pop star Potato Bug. (Get it? Another insect?) Avalon sometimes plays both characters at once in split-screen. As Potato Bug, he adopts a Terry-Thomas cadence, saying things that the Beatles *never* did ("cheerio," "jolly good").

When Potato Bug's singing makes the beach girls scream, the "real" Avalon grouses: "They've all gone 'Beatle' over a Potato Bug!" He barks at Funicello: "Don't tell me *you've* flipped over that crumpet eater?"

The jokes keep coming. The surf-rocking Pyramids take the stage in Beatle wigs, which are removed to reveal bald heads. When one oldster who spots Potato Bug exclaims "What is that?," another replies, "England's revenge for the Boston Tea Party."

"Bikini Beach" isn't the only beach movie to jump on the bandwagon. Quips an old-timer in "Girls on the Beach" (1965): "The Crickets! The Beatles! The Cockroaches! What'll they think up next?" The plot has three beach bums pretending to know the Beatles in order to impress some sorority girls who want to book the band for a fundraiser.

The guys promise to get Ringo Starr on the phone. Their ringleader, Duke (Martin West), imitates Ringo by saying "Yeah, yeah, yeah," "jolly well" and "pip pip." (This nonsense eats up 8 minutes and 25 seconds!)

Fans saw the Animals and the Dave Clark Five in "Get Yourself a College Girl" (1964); Freddie and the Dreamers in "Every Day's a Holiday" (1964) and "Out of Sight" (1966); the Hollies, the Merseybeats, Lulu and the Animals in "Go-Go Big Beat" (1965); and the Animals in yet another beach flick, "It's a Bikini World" (1967).

And give the Zombies props for appearing in "Bunny Lake is Missing" (1965), a Laurence Olivier drama directed by Otto Preminger. Ooh ... *classy.*

Frankie Avalon as Potato Bug. (Get it?)

© American International Pictures

MUSICIANS TRIED THEIR HANDS AT ACTING: PAUL Jones in "Privilege" (1967), John Lennon in "How I Won the War" (1967), Ringo Starr in "Candy" (1968) and "The Magic Christian" (1969), Mick Jagger in "Performance" (1970). The Yardbirds appeared as an alternate-reality version of themselves in "Blow-Up" (1966), Michelangelo Antonioni's thriller set in London.

"We were pretty much down at the time," former Yardbirds guitarist Jeff Beck told me in 1999. "We'd changed managers at that point. Simon Napier-Bell took over; he pulled a few strings. By hook or by crook, we were asked to do this 'Blow-Up' scene, which was great. Four days of lying around, falling asleep on tables and chairs, waiting to go on and do our number. It was fun. Big movie. Big-bucks movie."

"It was all done over five days," Yardbirds drummer Jim McCarty told me in 2003. "Tell someone from the film business now and they say, 'That's incredible! You spent so long doing that shot!'

"We'd be up in a studio out in Hertfordshire, 30 or 40 miles from London. We'd spend all day doing that bit of music. The set was very odd, because it was an exact copy of a club we used to play in Windsor called the Ricky-Tick. You walked onto the set, and it was like walking into the club."

WHY DID "STROLL ON," THE SONG THE Yardbirds played in "Blow-Up," sound so much like Tiny Bradshaw's "Train Kept A-Rollin' "?

"When we got the gig, we decided to go and write some songs, one of which we'd play in the film," McCarty recalled. "Antonioni didn't like any of those. He said he'd rather hear 'Train Kept A-Rollin'.' But, you know, for the sake of copyright, we changed the lyrics. But basically, it was that song we played in the film."

The Yardbirds' sequence culminated in Beck destroying a guitar onstage, Pete Townshend-style — something that wasn't part of Beck's act in real life.

"Antonioni wanted Jeff to break up the guitar. Obviously, he'd gone to see the Who," McCarty said with a laugh.

"The rumor was that he'd asked the Who to do the film, but they'd turned it down. But he liked that sort of destructive element. He even gave us some acoustic guitars to practice on. It was pretty funny."

From top left: Lennon puzzles; Pattie Boyd and McCartney; "minder" Shake in a rush; Harrison toys with a photographer.

'A Hard Day's Night' (1964)

B-R-R-R-A-N-G!

That iconic opening chord to "A Hard Day's Night," the song, is the opening salvo of "A Hard Day's Night," the movie.

With one resounding strum, we're off to the races with the Beatles — racing against time to get on the train, to get to the TV studio, to get ahead of the sprinting mob of screaming girls.

Richard Lester's film is so much more than a mere showcase for a pop band. In depicting the global entertainment phenomenon that was the Beatles, the movie makes wry commentary on the media machine that cynically enabled their rise.

In two "typical" days in the lives of John, Paul, George and Ringo, we see the boys mock reporters at a press reception; let off steam at a dance club; elude their hapless "minders" Norm (Norman Rossington) and Shake (John Junkin); and perform a set to a sweaty, teary, packed house for a television broadcast.

Commentary on the folly of fame is sharpest during a sequence in which George mistakenly wanders into the wrong office at the TV studio. There, an impresario named Simon (Kenneth Haigh) calls George "ducky," "chickie baby" and "Sonny Jim." Simon assumes George came in to audition as a shill for "trendsetting" TV personality Susan Campy (Edina Ronay, seen in a photo).

"Oh, you mean that posh bird who gets everything wrong?" says George in his most adenoidal Liverpudlian.

"I beg your pardon?" says Simon.

After throwing George out of the office, Simon frets: "You don't think he's a new phenomenon, do you?"

His receptionist (Alison Seebohm) replies: "You mean an early clue to the new direction?" *If they only knew.*

From top left: Paul's granddad takes a gamble; a receptionist grows conspiratorial; the boys at play; the boys at "rest."

THE BEATLES, ESPECIALLY LENNON, WERE FANS of the 1959 comedy short "The Running, Jumping and Standing Still Film" directed by Lester, a Philadelphian emigre in London who previously worked with Peter Sellers on TV spinoffs of "The Goon Show." The boys approved Lester to direct their debut.

Much of the madcap tone of "A Hard Day's Night" can be credited to the director, as well as screenwriter Alun Owen, a Welshman from Liverpool with an ear for the peculiar vocabulary of the Beatles. As research, Owen shadowed the Beatles for several days, jotting down notes the entire time. His script, based on these observations, captured the Beatles' personalities.

Production on "AHDN" was rush-rush-rush, just in the off-chance that the Beatles proved to be only a "one-month wonder."

The schedule was so tight that Lennon, McCartney, Harrison and Starr each joined Equity (the U.K.'s acting union) on the *first day* of shooting — March 2, 1964 — immediately before filming scenes at Paddington Station in London.

A TITLE WAS NEEDED QUICKLY, TOO. SAID LENNON of the movie's title (in a 1980 *Playboy* interview): "I had used it in 'In His Own Write' (Lennon's 1964 book), but it was an off-the-cuff remark by Ringo, one of his malapropisms — a Ringo-ism — said not to be funny, just said. So Dick Lester said, 'We are going to use that title,' and the next morning, I brought in the song."

If there's a fifth Beatle in "A Hard Day's Night," it is Dublin native Wilfrid Brambell as Paul's "very clean" troublemaker of a granddad who calls the boys, in a fiery brogue, "powdered gee-gaws." The character is a masterstroke by Lester and Owen. Paul's granddad fulfills his movie-trope duties as a sounding board for the leads, but his age and guile make him the (very) odd man out.

The Beatles are quite good in the film. By all accounts, they took the job seriously. "They weren't Beatles and I was an actor; we were *all* actors in a scene playing off each other," said Junkin, who played Shake, in a 2001 documentary about "A Hard Day's Night." "They were so brilliant and so non-starry and so generous."

THE BEATLES HAD BEEN WARY, AND RIGHTFULLY so, of previous rock 'n' roll movies, which were often transparent commercials for songs built around thin, forgettable plots. They chose the right guy to remedy this in Lester. "All I did was to try to make sure that they were presented in a way that was respectful and as honest as it could be," Lester said in the 2001 documentary.

"A Hard Day's Night" is a one-of-a-kind comic treasure — not even the Beatles could top it. The movie takes all kinds of liberties, winning every standoff. Its documentary feel lends it immediacy; it employs farce (such as when the Beatles run alongside the moving train, yelling for their "ball"); it breaks the fourth wall (when Paul says "Zap!"); and, for better or worse, it's a powerful harbinger of the music-video format.

Still, there was some hand-wringing by American investors who viewed Lester's finished edit. He recalled that the Americans initially declared the movie OK, but decreed that the four Beatles would have to be "revoiced." (The director won *that* argument, thank goodness.)

Added McCartney (in "Anthology"): "They'd tell us that an American audience wouldn't understand some English phrase. We said, 'Are you kidding? We watch all your cowboy pictures, and you go "Yep," and we know exactly what you're sayin'!' "

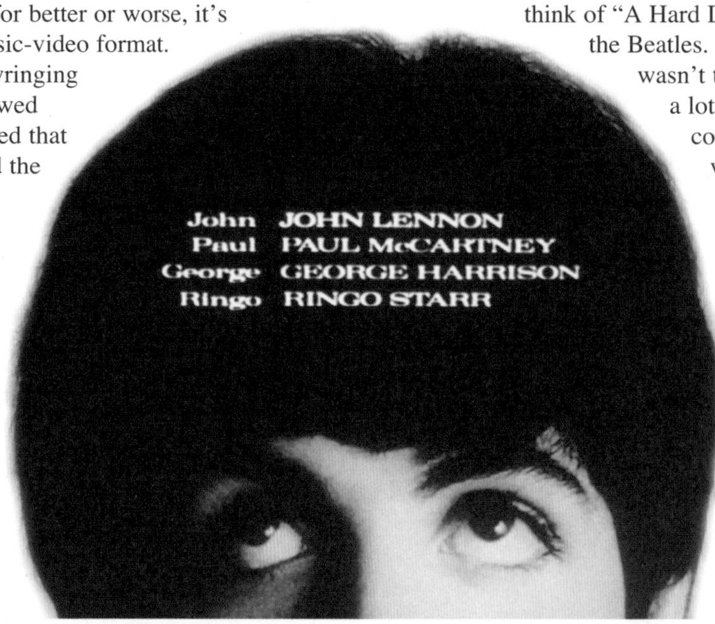

SIGNIFICANTLY, THE FILM REPRESENTED A turning of the tide, a crossroads, regarding criticism of the Beatles in the United States. When the four musicians landed in America in February 1964, they were greeted by a hostile press and an openly disrespectful entertainment establishment. By August, reviews of "A Hard Day's Night" were generally positive. The honeymoon, following a delay, had finally begun.

It's not hyperbole to state that "A Hard Day's Night" is as important to the Beatles' legacy as "Sgt. Pepper's Lonely Hearts Club Band." But leave it to Lennon to provide a reality check.

In 1971, Dick Cavett commented to Lennon that many people think of "A Hard Day's Night" as a true reflection of the Beatles. Lennon was having none of it. "It wasn't that carefree, ever," he said. "It was a lot more pressure. That was a sort of comic-strip version of what actually was goin' on. The pressure was far heavier than that. That was written after the author (Owen) spendin' about three days with us when we played in London, and then in Dublin, and then back in London again. He wrote the whole of the film based on our characters — you know, clod-hopping Ringo, sharp John, whimsical Paul and stern George. All those Beatle character myths were formed from three days watchin' us. Which was a lot of junk, really."

The Beatles didn't want to repeat the rock-movie formula of "just" playing songs. But they still played plenty of songs.

Richard Lester took full advantage of color for the Beatles' sophomore outing. Below: Eleanor Bron takes aim. © Subafilms

'Help!' (1965)

"A HARD DAY'S NIGHT" WAS A BRUTAL ACT to follow. Richard Lester's "Help!" is a choke, but the film has glimmers of comedic brilliance and, of course, a collection of songs that are beyond reproach.

Setup: Ringo has obtained a ring, the "dreaded, sacred, sacrificial ring of the dread Kaili," a religious cult that needs the oversized bauble for its rituals. The Kaili chases the Beatles all over the globe, dooming the film as a glorified travelogue.

But "Help!" coulda been a contender. An early sequence hints at the magic that often surrounded the Beatles. When the boys return home after a performance — not to a remote mansion, but a cookie-cutter block of "terraced housing" (as the Brits call it) — they enter four separate dwellings that are revealed to be one conjoined residence. Once behind closed doors, the boys each retreat into their own private pleasures. Paul emerges from the floor playing an organ; John retreats with a book (of his own authorship) into a pit of pillows; George oversees the grooming of an indoor lawn using novelty clattering "teeth"; Ringo hunts for a snack among the handy vending machines.

The implication is that the boys are so wealthy now, they inhabit a fantasy world of their own creation.

The Beatles perform good old-fashioned slapstick in a restroom sequence. A Scotland Yard superintendent (Patrick Cargill) sniffs at the boys and says haughtily, "So *this* is the famous Beatles," to which John replies with pitch-perfect Liverpool snark: "So *this* is the famous Scotland Yard."

Eleanor Bron wears many fab costumes as Ahme, a glamorous cultist who is secretly on the side of the Beatles. "Help!" sometimes has a James Bond feel. (An almost actionable approximation of Monty Norman's iconic 007 riff is heard.) Watch for two "A Hard Day's Night" returnees: Victor Spinetti (as a mad scientist) and Jeremy Lloyd, the "jumping" dancer from "AHDN" (as a diner).

Ultimately, "Help!" attempts to coast on its far-flung, colorful locations, as if it's enough just to see the Beatles — who were high on pot much of the time — gallivanting on skis (in the Austrian Alps); on the beach (in the Bahamas); on a battlefield (at Salisbury Plain, with a glimpse of Stonehenge); or in a stately mansion (Cliveden). Alas, it ain't.

'Ferry Cross the Mersey' (1964)

ANOTHER BLACK-AND-WHITE MUSICAL COMEDY from 1964 about a band from Liverpool with screaming fans?

"Ferry Cross the Mersey" — a title shared with Gerry and the Pacemakers' #6 hit — was in serious danger of seeming like a "Hard Day's Night" remake. Some behind-the-scenes movers and shakers shepherded both projects: George Martin (musical director), Gilbert Taylor (cinematographer), and Brian Epstein (credited as the "presenter" of the Pacemakers' movie).

But Jeremy Summer's "Ferry Cross the Mersey" is about Liverpool, not West London, and explores how the port city's socioeconomics shaped its musical exports. The movie bids us to enter the scene's epicenter: the Cavern Club (where the Pacemakers play Larry Williams' "Slow Down," also recorded by the Beatles).

The film opens to the strains of "It's Gonna Be Alright," as the Pacemakers land in a BOAC jetliner; are mobbed by fans; and race to a recording studio. Taylor's framing in the studio sequence recalls "A Hard Day's Night," but the movie does something new.

We are transported, via flashback, to a time before hit records and screaming girls. The Pacemakers are not pop stars, but happy-go-lucky art students who tool around Liverpool on Lambretta LI 150 scooters. We see the boys perform the title track *on* the ferry, as it crosses the vast River Mersey.

Julie Samuel plays Dodie, a love interest for Marsden, and they create a breezy chemistry. The boys are in for a shock when she invites them to her family home: It's a butler-equipped mansion.

Dodie convinces well-dressed talent agent Jack Hanson (T.P. McKenna, who seems to be a cypher for Epstein) to represent the Pacemakers as the group gears up for a talent competition.

Cilla Black, another protégé of Epstein, performs, as do the Fourmost and the Black Knights. Radio personality Jimmy Savile plays himself. (Never mind what he was up to off-camera.)

Gerry Marsden and Julie Samuel get cozy. © United Artists

Summer employs a silent-movie motif, recreating the Keystone Cops (1920s-style piano and all) as the Pacemakers search for their mislaid instruments in time for their set at the competition.

The film sometimes struggles to rise above its low-budget production values, but the music is terrific, and "Ferry Cross the Mersey" has a magic, a sweetness, all its own.

Lenny Davidson, Rick Huxley, Mike Smith, Dennis Payton and Dave Clark. Below: Barbara Ferris as Dinah. © Anglo-Amalgamated

'Having a Wild Weekend' (1965)

YES, IT STARS THE DAVE CLARK FIVE. YES, SONGS by the Dave Clark Five are heard throughout. But John Boorman's film (titled "Catch Us If You Can" in England) is not about a British Invasion band. It's a sweet, sometimes sad romantic comedy in a modern setting with modern stresses.

Steve (Clark) and his four buddies (Mike Smith, Lenny Davidson, Dennis Payton and Rick Huxley, collectively the DC5) are "stunt boys" — fit young men who perform stunts and do extra work in films. The boys live in a trampoline-equipped church repurposed as the headquarters of their company, Action Enterprises Limited. The place is kind of like the Beatles' funhouse in "Help!" that same year, or the Monkees' zany group home that soon followed.

Meanwhile, Dinah (Barbara Ferris) is known everywhere as the "butcher girl," a fashion model who has become the face of the glories of meat consumption. ("Meat for Go!!" is the slogan of the ad campaign for which Dinah's face is plastered all over England.)

But Dinah and the boys yearn to get away from the whole phony business. While filming a commercial in which they play burglars (in comical disguise) escaping from crusading butchers, Dinah and Steve continue driving their hired car, a gorgeous white Jaguar convertible, through London rather than circle back to the shoot as planned.

Dinah is openly attracted to Steve, but he keeps his private feelings private. Still, they plot to go AWOL to visit a small island Dinah dreams of owning.

This is distressing news for Leon Zissell (David de Keyser), who heads up the advertising firm that handles the meat account. Leon implies to the newspapers that Dinah has been abducted by Steve, and the narrative takes on a life of its own. Soon police, reporters, and ad-firm lackeys are in hot pursuit of Dinah and Steve as they abscond on their "wild weekend."

DINAH AND STEVE ENCOUNTER BEATNIKS — MORE like proto-hippies — who are squatting in a bombed-out building in Salisbury Plain. An unexpected military exercise, complete with bombing, sends everyone scrambling for cover. (The Jaguar is a tragic casualty of an explosion.)

While hitchhiking, Dinah and Steve are picked up by well-to-do older marrieds Nan (Yootha Joyce) and Guy (Robin Bailey) who, in their awkward ways, hit on the younger couple. Nan and Guy invite Dinah and Steve — plus the re-assembled DC5 — to a raucous costume ball, at which many of the attendees are dressed as "golden age" Hollywood movie stars. Luckily, Dinah is not recognized in her Harpo Marx getup.

"Having a Wild Weekend" cleverly explores the pitfalls of fame without resorting to British Invasion conventions (screaming girls, lip-synched songs). Clark — who was a professional stuntman prior to the rise of the DC5 — knew the territory, and can be seen performing his own stunts.

Marianne Faithfull (unwisely) turned down the role of Dinah.

Shelley Fabares and Peter Noone go on an old-fashioned date. Below: The Hermits go (gasp!) bald. © Metro-Goldwyn Mayer

'Hold On!' (1966)

IN ARTHUR LUBIN'S CUTE BUT BANAL FILM, U.S. astronauts let their children pick a "good luck" name for a new rocket ship. The kiddies name it after their favorite singing group, Herman's Hermits, causing shock waves felt from NASA to Washington. A military wonk sputters: "Do you know what the whole world is going to think if we put an English name on an American nosecone? That we're still a colony in Great Britain! That we lost the Revolutionary War!"

Meanwhile, the Hermits' wily manager (ever handy Bernard Fox) is holding the boys as virtual prisoners in a West Coast hotel, from which Herman (Peter Noone) must escape if he's ever going to romance an American girl he fancies (Shelley Fabares).

Herbert Anderson plays an American assigned to shadow the Hermits. Sue Ane Langdon plays an opportunistic actress posing as a "close friend" of the Hermits, in a ploy to further her career.

"I'D BEEN AN ACTOR, AN ENGLISH CHILD STAR, SO I had started out acting," Noone told me in 2011 of making "Hold On!" "But acting has a learning curve. It's not as easy as it looks.

"We were thrilled to be working with (director) Arthur Lubin. Arthur Lubin, we knew from the Three Stooges. All English people have seen every Three Stooges moment.

"Arthur took us to meet his latest comedy star: Mr. Ed. We got our picture taken with Mr. Ed. It was surrealistic — these teenaged boys from Manchester posing with a horse. I mean, we knew the Beatles, and they'd had all kinds of experiences like that.

"But Arthur Lubin was really talented. He made us better than we actually were, which is what a good director does. I mean, this band was not exactly ready for Stanislavski."

TO NOONE'S SURPRISE, LUBIN AND CREW OFTEN asked for the band's input. "This amazed me," the singer said. "I mean, I was 16, and people were asking me what I thought about this idea or that. All *we* knew was how to play songs."

The Hermits decided to goof on Lubin while preparing a scene.

Recalled Noone: "Arthur Lubin tells us that we're going to do a scene in a spaceship. We're going to be traveling in space. But it's not a *real* spaceship. He's talking to us like we're 7-year-olds.

"So Arthur Lubin asks us if we have a song we could do in the spaceship. I suggested an old song by (1930s-era comic singer) George Formby: 'I'm Leaning on a Lamp Post.' All the Hermits laughed when I said it. Arthur Lubin said, 'I don't get it.' I said, 'Don't worry, our *fans* will understand.' So he goes, 'OK.'

"Well, we hadn't recorded it ever — it wasn't like it was something we had a version of — so we had to record it right there and then. And they put it in the movie!

"But that's what makes for those joyous kind of memories."

Herman (Noone), Tulip (Sheila White) and friend. Below: Judy (Sarah Caldwell) models groovy threads. © Metro-Goldwyn Mayer

'Mrs. Brown, You've Got a Lovely Daughter' (1968)

MANCHESTER MAY LOOK DREARY, BUT ITS colorful denizens are anything but. The Hermits play themselves, more or less, not as a famous singing group, but as five pals who play music to fund their true mission: the care and feeding of Mrs. Brown, a sleek racing dog who has a shot at the big time.

Herman Tulley (Noone) works as a clerk for an advertising agency, but he's worthless at corporate politics. Herman lives with his suffer-no-fools "gran," Gloria (Marjorie Rhodes), who is always ready with straight talk and a bowl of porridge. Herman is pursued by a hopelessly romantic neighborhood "bird," Tulip (Sheila Brown).

He encounters Percy (Lance Percival), a vagrant who speaks in a posh accent despite his grimy rags. Percy, too, has musical inclinations: *He* plays the spoons.

After Mrs. Brown wins a trophy in a qualifying race, the boys meet G.G. Brown, a wealthy "fruits and veg" vendor (played with theatrical flourish by British musical-comedy star Stanley Holloway, then 78). They are introduced to G.G.'s daughter, Judy (Sarah Caldwell), a famous fashion model in London. Herman is immediately smitten.

Herman and company travel to London for Mrs. Brown's next important race. A potential landlady, upon hearing the boys are from Manchester, hisses: "Bloody foreigners!"

The band's clash with a bullying nightclub owner again underscores the London-vs.-Manchester dynamic.

According to Noone, the scenario for Saul Swimmer's film came from actor-writer Trevor Peacock. (The script is credited to Norman Thaddeus Vane.) "Trevor was a friend of ours," Noone told me in 2011. "He was a playwright also. He hung out with the band for a few days, and designed a script around who we really were.

"I lived with my grandmother; I was very young when the band started. He basically created these characters based on who were ourselves. It was really a middle-class-vs.-upper-class kind of story. It needed better actors, but somehow we pulled it off. They let us do our own stunts, which was great. We were a bunch of yobbos, anyway, so we could do our own stunts."

Working with Holloway was a thrill for the band. (Holloway played Alfred P. Doolittle in "My Fair Lady" on West End, Broadway and in the 1964 film version.) Holloway even sang a number with the Hermits, "Lemon and Lime."

"Everyone knew Stanley Holloway," Noone said. "He was a British hero. He was in American movies! He was in 'My Fair Lady.' I mean, this guy was the *man*. We were in shock that he would even do our little movie."

Another memory for Noone regarding "Mrs. Brown," the movie: "You get to see how I become fatter and fatter as the film progresses."

'The Ghost Goes Gear' (1966)

A SPOOKY COMEDY STARRING THE SPENCER Davis Group? You coulda knocked me over with a Hammond B3. Hugh Gladwish's "The Ghost Goes Gear" never had a theatrical release in the United States. Honestly, we didn't miss much.

But it stands as a document of the Spencer Davis Group in its prime. Namesake Davis exudes easy charm. The band's 18-year-old breakout star, singer-keyboardist Stevie Winwood, looks like he's avoiding the camera. But there he is, with his immense talent on full display. His brother, SDG bassist Muff Winwood, and the band's drummer, Pete York, do their best to scare up some laughs (pun intended). York wears a pirate costume for much of the film.

The plot has the SDG staying at a haunted mansion, the moldering family homestead of their manager, Algernon Rowthorpe Plumley (played by Nicholas Parsons, in real life a TV game show host). The band never knew that "Algie" comes from a wealthy family. When he learns that his parents (Joan Ingram and Tony Sympson) are now destitute, Algie cooks up a scheme to host tours and parties on the grounds of the estate.

The mansion has a resident ghost in the form of singer Lorne Gibson, who wears Elizabethan garb and a pompadour. But this ghost is benign, singing sweetly rather than rattling chains.

In her film debut, Sheila White is no shrinking violet, dancing suggestively and mugging shamelessly as Polly, the rock 'n' roll-obsessed maid who plays air guitar with her feather duster.

The SDG all sleep in the same bed, Three Stooges style. Wearing pajamas, they play a smoky "Nobody Knows You When You're Down and Out" (previously recorded by Bessie Smith, later by Derek and the Dominos). SDG's version has Winwood channeling Ray Charles in his soulful singing and piano playing.

"The Ghost Goes Gear" wraps with a sprawling outdoor garden fete played by acts of wildly varying styles that never quite gel.

Stevie Winwood, then 18, belts one out. © Associated British-Pathé

Acker Bilk and his Paramount Jazz Band is an eight-piece playing British-ized swing in matching vests. The Three Bells are wigged blondes performing in two outfits: spangly pink nighties and mustard onesies that terminate in bell-bottoms. Pop star Dave Berry ("Mama") apparently likes to hide behind vegetation while he sings. Two more groups, St. Louis Union and the M.6., play pop-rock more in keeping with the Spencer Davis Group.

The movie has no real payoff, but if you set your Silliness Tolerance Level on 10 and hold your nose, you'll be fine.

Pete York, Spencer Davis and Muff Winwood rock out in "The Ghost Goes Gear." © Associated British-Pathé

Jimmy Page (inset) and Jeff Beck take their movie-star turns.

'Blow-Up' (1966)

BRITISH INVASION FANS RECALL MICHELANGELO Antonio's "Blow-Up" for one reason, chiefly: It presents a performance by the Yardbirds, with two guitar giants of the period, Jeff Beck and Jimmy Page, trading licks. But there are other reasons to put Antonioni's first English-language film on one's watch list.

"Blow-Up" is akin to Alfred Hitchcock in its basic premise: Did a fashion photographer witness a murder, not with his eyes, but with his camera? You could almost picture Cary Grant or James Stewart in such a role. Antonioni's twist is to set "Blow-Up" in "Swinging London," bringing us close to the action — the clubs, the parties, the pretty people, the pot-smoking, the sex.

But this *is* Antonioni, and anything he shows us must be filtered through his metaphorical lens. Take the Yardbirds sequence. The band's audience is joyless, if not catatonic, until Beck smashes a guitar, Who-style, and throws its remnants into their midst. The suddenly animated audience fights over the unsalvageable shards. This has been interpreted as Antonio's statement on disaffected youth. Whatever the symbolism, you'd scarcely have found an audience of such sad zombies at a real-life Yardbirds show.

"Blow-Up" follows an arrogant, unnamed photographer (David Hemmings) for whom life is a game. Hemmings uses affected charm and transactional coercion to get what he wants, both in his work and in his sexual pursuits. Though Hemmings is the film's protagonist, it's hard to love a guy who barks orders into a car phone from his spiffy Silver Cloud III Rolls Royce convertible.

In the film's most famous sequence, Hemmings photographs a sexy, slinky model (real-life model Veruschka). Put bluntly, the photo session is a pantomime coitus. Hemmings commands, cajoles and even kisses his model to manipulate her performance. Still shooting, Hemmings directs Veruschka to lay on her back,

Model Veruschka and photographer David Hemmings at work, and play, in "Blow-Up" (1966).

and then he straddles her. The subtext is screaming out loud here.

The film's Hitchcock moment comes when Hemmings, while absent-mindedly strolling through a park, spots a couple who are, it appears, getting to know each other. She (Vanessa Redgrave) is 30-ish, he (Ronan O'Casey) is 50-ish. From a distance, Hemmings casually photographs them as they frolic, or seem to.

Later, after developing the film, Hemmings sees things in the couple's body language that weren't apparent at first glance.

Don't expect a Hitchcockian resolution. Most of "Blow-Up's" information is doled out, not via exposition, but non-verbally. The movie documents a place in time, and its mysteries grow less opaque, albeit ever so slightly, with each viewing. "Blow-Up" is a "journey" movie, not a "destination" movie, to be sure.

'Yellow Submarine' (1968)

"PEPPERLAND IS A TICKLE OF joy on the blue belly of the universe," says the Chief Blue Meanie. "Let's *scratch* it."

The Beatles' psychedelic animated movie "Yellow Submarine" is like a Peter Max poster come to life. Produced by Al Brodax and directed by George Dunning, the film made it possible for the Beatles to satisfy their three-movie deal with United Artists while taking a break from the Beatle bubble. What emerged is an immersive — albeit, short on story — kaleidoscopic experience with great songs.

Setup: The Meanies silence the usually musical citizens of Pepperland by turning them into gray statues. Pepperland's wrinkly Lord Mayor dispatches Old Fred, newly promoted to Lord Admiral, to seek help in an ornate submarine built for such emergencies. (It's *yellow,* by the way.)

Ringo, meanwhile, seems in need of a little adventure. "Liverpool can be a lonely place on a Saturday night, and this is only Thursday morning," he laments. "I'd jump into the River Mersey, but it looks like rain."

Old Fred follows Ringo to the Beatles' headquarters, where they join forces with John, Paul and George to rescue Pepperland.

There are references for movie buffs. We see the Frankenstein monster (which transforms into John); King Kong clutching a Fay Wray type; and a Marilyn Monroe figure.

The script is sprinkled with Beatle in-jokes. When the submarine takes off, it is accompanied by the chaotic orchestral climb from the climax of "A Day in the Life." When they meet the "Nowhere Man," Jeremy Hillary Boob, John exclaims, "Who the Billy Shears are you?" In the Sea of Holes, John remarks, "This place reminds me of Blackburn, Lancashire." Coming face-to-face with his alter-ego, John says, "I am the ego man, goo goo g'joob."

The Beatles were voiced by John Clive (John), Geoffrey Hughes (Paul), Peter Batten (George) and Paul Angelis (Ringo). Some sleight-of-hand was employed to mask this inconvenient truth; the credits say "Starring Sgt. Pepper's Lonely Hearts Club Band."

The good guys and bad guys of Pepperland.

Jean-Luc Godard intercut footage of the Rolling Stones in the studio with sociopolitically-themed vignettes. © New Line Cinema

'Sympathy For the Devil' (1968)

THERE'S AVANT-GARDE FOR THE SAKE OF AVANT-garde, and there's provocation for the sake of provocation.

And then there's Jean-Luc Godard's "Sympathy For the Devil."

As perfect an example of "throw it against the wall and see what sticks" as any movie *can* be, Godard's quasi-documentary is nonetheless unignorable for Rolling Stones completists. This is because "Sympathy" offers an eyewitness account of the recording of a Stones classic: the 1968 song that gives the film its title.

Godard intercuts footage of the Stones creating the song in a London recording studio with staged vignettes about political revolution and anarchy. The spray-paint budget alone for this film was high; we see people spray-painting on cars, a bridge, a pub, windows and a sidewalk. One of the spray-painted sayings: "FBI + CIA = TWA + PAN AM." (Maybe it made sense back then?)

One particularly provocative vignette depicts Black revolutionaries brandishing machine guns in a riverside Battersea junkyard full of demolished vehicles. Three White women in white robes emerge from a car and are executed off-camera, with bright red paint used as blood. (Godard did the movement no favors here.)

We visit a used book store that is well-stocked with pornographic magazines and superhero comic books, at which customers give the "Heil Hitler" salute after selecting reading material, and the ringleader of the store reads aloud from "Mein Kampf."

GRANTED, IT'S OFTEN LIKE WATCHING PAINT DRY as the Stones incrementally build up their song. (There is boredom and stagnation in that studio, and it's infectious.) But cinematographer Tony Richmond *does* capture some memorable moments.

Twice, we see Brian Jones bum a cigarette from Keith Richards. It becomes apparent that Mick Jagger has the lyrics and his vocal approach down, and it's just a matter of putting the song into final form. When the Stones draft in Ghanaian conga player Rocky Dzidzornu, "Sympathy For the Devil" finally begins to sound like something. Charlie Watts responds to Dzidzornu's rhythms, using the butt end of a drumstick on the rim of his snare drum.

It's a peek into rock history, and the Stones' private world, when we see those iconic "woo-woo" backing vocals being recorded. Circled around a microphone are Jones, Richards, Watts, Bill Wyman, Anita Pallenberg and Marianne Faithfull. (Richards stands between his then-girlfriend, Pallenberg, and her previous boyfriend, Jones. All parties have apparently moved on. It's kinda sweet.)

It's said that "Sympathy For the Devil" chronicles Jones' deterioration, that he was too far gone to contribute. But in this edit, Jones still seems to be in there pitching, if impotently so.

Godard was really taking a chance with his choice for the final words heard in his film. They are: "Yes, it was all a waste of time ... I've gotta get away from this mess."

The bittersweet documentary chronicles the demise of the Beatles. But there are funny little moments, too. © Apple Films

'Let It Be' (1970)

THE PHRASE "PAUL IS GOD" WAS AMONG JOHN Lennon's bitter comments about the final cut of Michael Lindsay-Hogg's documentary "Let It Be." Paul McCartney's heavy hand is indeed felt onscreen and off. Alas, he did himself a disservice.

Originally intended as a fly-on-the-wall look at the live-in-the-studio recording of a Beatles album, "Let It Be" instead bore witness to the band's demise. McCartney comes off as a passive-aggressive martinet whose compositions are favored, and who attempts a divide-and-conquer coup among his compatriots.

At least, that's the narrative that emerges in the way "Let It Be" is edited (by Graham Gilding and Tony Lenny).

There's the oft-recounted and surreptitiously filmed exchange between McCartney and Harrison. "I'm trying to help you," McCartney says after some bickering. Harrison's reply: "I'll play whatever you want me to play. Or I won't play at all, if you don't want me to play. Whatever it is that will please you, I'll do it."

Also telling is a sequence in which McCartney grumbles to Lennon about Harrison. In the edit, Lennon does not speak; he only nods placatingly while smoking. (The fact that Harrison quit the band for five days is not expressly alluded to in the film.)

And yet, there's plenty of joy and many funny little moments to be found herein. The boys grin as they bond on old songs like "Shake, Rattle and Roll" and "You Really Got a Hold On Me."

"Let It Be" also reiterates what a uniquely inventive band the Beatles were. The chemistry between Lennon and McCartney still feels like love and joy, even this late in the game.

Ringo Starr, ever the peacekeeper, sits quietly behind his kit waiting for any drama to play itself out. Yoko Ono is omnipresent. (She and Lennon were a package deal at this point.) Cast and crew relocate from Twickenham Studios to Apple headquarters on Savile Row. When Harrison returns to the fold, he brings along keyboardist Billy Preston, whose presence helps the band get over itself.

WHICH BRINGS US TO THE ROOF. "LET IT BE" ENDS with a magical performance atop the Apple building on a cold January weekday. Below, Londoners crane their necks and listen (with some climbing onto abutting roofs). Police are summoned, but the baby-faced "bobbies" who briefly join the Beatles on the roof seem more like well-placed extras than fearsome enforcers of the law. Lindsay-Hogg and his cinematographer, Tony Richmond, capture it all with seemingly omniscient camera work.

There's a thing in rock 'n' roll about recording vs. performing live. You sit to record; you *stand* to perform live. The roof may not have been the Albert Hall show McCartney pushed for. But plugging in and playing up there in front of strangers — and the world — made the Beatles come alive one final time.

Mick Jagger, Tina Turner, Charlie Watts and Keith Richards onstage and off in "Gimme Shelter."

'Gimme Shelter' (1970)

THE DIRECTORS ALBERT AND DAVID MAYSLES and Charlotte Zwerin employ an ingenious framing device, in laying out the complicated story of how the Rolling Stones' 1969 tour culminated in a seriously botched "free" concert at which an 18-year-old man was killed in view of the stage.

They accomplish this by filming two members of the Stones — singer Mick Jagger and drummer Charlie Watts — as they watch early cuts of footage while the filmmakers patiently explain, almost as if to children, how they plan to edit the film.

Really, they are setting the scene for *us,* the viewing audience.

Even in 1970, when "Gimme Shelter" was released, the audience knew what the directors were building up to: the infamous, ill-conceived Altamont concert, which was mounted with a callous indifference to the basic needs of 300,000 souls in terms of food, water and humane crowd control (unless you consider enlisting Hells Angels as "security" to be a sensible, satisfactory solution).

Along the '69 tour, the instances of ironic foreshadowing captured on camera indicate that the filmmakers were either omniscient or, you should pardon the expression, dead lucky.

Two particular moments illustrate this: when Jagger predicts, during a press conference, that the free concert will be a model of "how one can behave in large gatherings," and when a suited gentleman in the office of San Francisco attorney Melvin Belli refers to crowds that were already migrating West (even though a venue had yet to be locked in) as "lemmings to the sea."

If you're curious to see the violence — including the pool-cue justice meted out by the Hells Angels, the stabbing death of a gun-wielding audience member, and Jagger getting randomly punched in the face earlier in the day — "Gimme Shelter" delivers that. It also serves up many instances in which hippies are no longer seen as saviors of society, but as deluded fools in fringe.

Examples: The Jesus-lookin' guy in the American-flag cape with the forehead star ... the fat naked guy who attempts to dance before being led away ... the fat naked lady who climbs over everyone in her path as she nears the stage ... the guy *on* the stage who appears to be changing into a werewolf, Larry Talbot style ...

But if you dig the Stones, there are standalone songs from the tour — if not from Altamont itself — to cherish. See "Love in Vain" (with heartbreaking slide from Mick Taylor), "Jumpin' Jack Flash" and "Satisfaction," not to mention Tina Turner's suggestive performance of "I've Been Loving You Too Long" which alone should have won "Gimme Shelter" an R rating.

In 2021, Peter Jackson put out a six-hour docuseries derived from countless hours of unused footage from the Beatles' "Let It Be" sessions. One can only imagine what could emerge if "Gimme Shelter" got the same fresh-look forensic treatment.

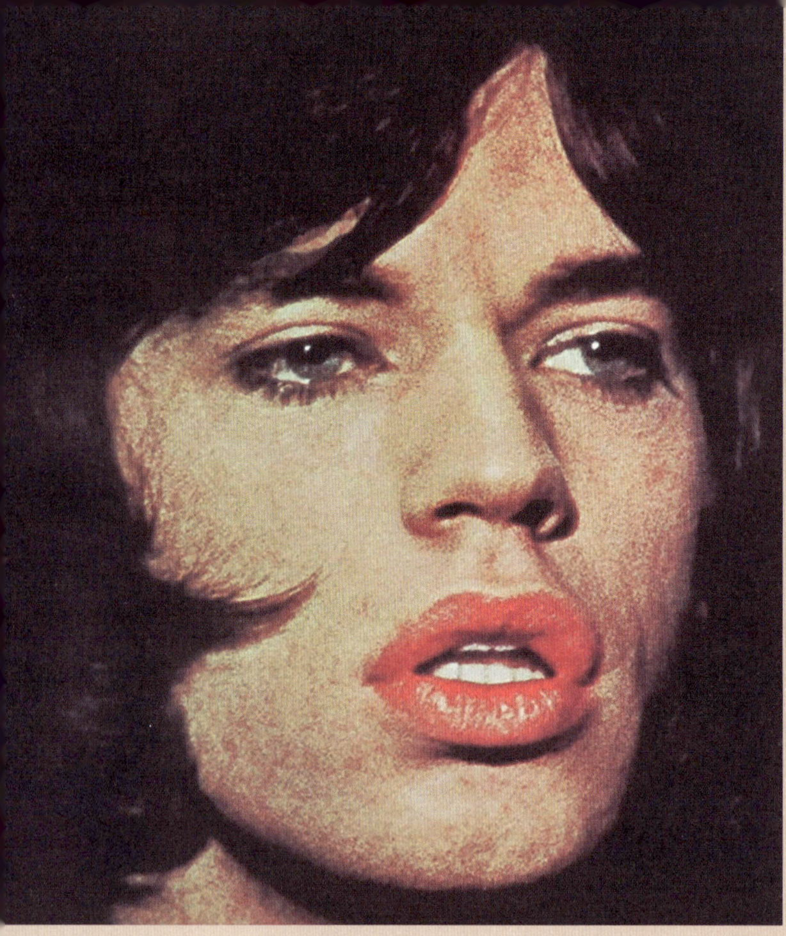

Jean Shrimpton and Paul Jones in "Privilege" (1967). Left: Mick Jagger explores his sexually ambiguous side in "Performance" (1970).

Pop stars played themselves, kind of, in early British Invasion films. Then neo-reality set in, so pop stars played ... fictional *pop stars.*

Peter Watkins' political farce "Privilege" (1967) is set in "Britain in the near future." We first see our reluctant protagonist, pop star Steve Shorter (played by Manfred Mann singer Paul Jones), waving "Heil Hitler"-style to admirers during a ticker-tape parade in his honor. Steve is the most popular entertainer in Great Britain, but he didn't get there via talent and ambition alone. Bankers, the government and the church created this Frankenstein as a way of controlling young members of the proletariat.

The Ministry of Culture hires artist Vanessa Ritchie (played by model Jean Shrimpton) to paint Steve's portrait, but she has a hard time getting near him. Vanessa watches helplessly as Steve grows more sullen and remote, while his handlers push him through concerts, photo shoots, board meetings, a sham award ceremony, and a TV commercial for apples (to correct a freak glut in the crop).

"He does not belong to himself," says one such handler (Mark London) to a documentarian's camera. "He belongs to the world, and therefore, he no longer has any rights to himself."

DONALD CAMMELL AND NICHOLAS ROEG'S "Performance" (1970) is a frequently bizarre treatise on gender fluidity and bisexuality, with Rolling Stones singer Mick Jagger at the peak of his girly-man allure as faded pop star Turner, a recluse adrift in a hazy world of drugs and threesomes.

Turner's polar-opposite would seem to be Chas (James Fox), a dapper underworld fixer who finds himself on the run from the law and his own gangster boss (Johnny Shannon). Chas needs a place to hide out and heal after barely surviving an attempted hit. When he overhears a musician talk about a possible room for rent at a certain address, Chas finds it, bluffs his way in, and encounters Pherber (Anita Pallenberg), a dark-eyed blonde with a German accent who negotiates, and accepts, the first month's rent.

Chas settles in, but then meets Turner, who wears long, dark hair and red lipstick. "There's been a mistake. You can't have the room," Turner informs Chas upon their first meeting.

"I need a Bohemian atmosphere. I'm an artist, Mr. Turner, like yourself," says Chas, who is posing as a stage juggler, and can't help but notice the sexual goings-on among Turner, Pherber and their houseguest of the moment, boyish Lucy (Michèle Breton).

For now, Turner acquiesces. Later, Chas spots an old poster for a Royal Albert Hall show headlined by Turner, and then it clicks.

"He wasn't that big," Chas tells a young girl in the neighborhood (Laraine Wickens). "They come and they go, pop stars."

Pherber later says of Turner: "He had a gift, too, once upon a time. You should have seen him 10 years ago."

After ingesting a hallucinogenic mushroom, Chas begins to adapt to his surroundings, donning a wig, makeup and jewelry, and receiving a kiss in bed from Turner — or was that Lucy? (Cammel and Roeg sometimes play tricks on us.)

This new Chas looks mighty strange to his old gangster buddies, when they finally catch up with him.

"Performance" anticipated the music-video format with the slide-heavy song "Memo From Turner," in which Jagger plays both "butch" (hair slicked back, suit) and, well, *Jagger*.

The singer-turned-actor is magnetic, but this was clearly not the beginning of a long career in the movies. There didn't seem to be many roles suited for Mick Jagger beyond ... faded pop star.

“That’s as bad as listening to the Beatles without earmuffs,” said James Bond (Sean Connery) of drinking warm Dom Perignon ’53.

Commander Bond can be forgiven. He always *did* seem like the kind of guy who would play Miles Davis in the background as he lowered a female acquaintance’s spaghetti straps.

And one who wouldn’t be caught dead in the Cavern Club.

But it speaks volumes that the Beatles’ incredible fame reached even the rarified ears of Agent 007. America’s voracious hunger for All Things British in the wake of Beatlemania spread to mediums beyond the musical, including mainstream movies.

To be clear, Eon Films’s James Bond series preceded Beatlemania in the United States. “Dr. No” was released in 1962 and “From Russia With Love” in ’63. But the series’ breakthrough — the movie that made James Bond 007 irrevocably famous in the U.S. and internationally — happened to be “Goldfinger” (1964), the one in which Bond disparages the Beatles.

The movies that followed through the decade — “Thunderball” (1965), “You Only Live Twice” (1967), “On Her Majesty’s Secret Service” (1969, starring George Lazenby) — enhanced, and were enhanced by, the over-arching phenomenon of Britmania which pervaded 1960s America. Bond and the Beatles were supercool, but even Dracula and Frankenstein possessed that panache, that suavity, which fueled and sustained Britmania.

AS WITH THE 007 MOVIES, HAMMER FILMS’ horror series preceded Beatlemania. “Curse of Frankenstein” came out in 1957, “Horror of Dracula” in ’58. Also like Bond, the movie monsters continued their big-screen adventures through the 1960s.

Hammer stars Peter Cushing and Christopher Lee had suavity to spare in such films as “The Revenge of Frankenstein” (1958), “The Brides of Dracula” (1960), “The Evil of Frankenstein” (1964), “Dracula, Prince of Darkness” (1966), “Frankenstein Created Woman” (1967), “Dracula Has Risen From the Grave” (1968) and “Frankenstein Must Be Destroyed” (1969).

These weren’t low-budget quickies. Hammer’s stylish colour films were well-written, well-staged and well-cast, with excellent visual design. (*Another* thing Bond and Hammer had in common: pretty ladies in revealing outfits. Oh, those saucy Brits.)

Hammer’s Frankenstein series followed the exploits of the bad doctor (Cushing) as he traveled from remote European burg to remote European burg, using fake names to mask his identity and continue with his unholy experiments. (Unholy, indeed. In “Frankenstein Created Woman,” Dr. Frankenstein performs an ultra-rare *soul* transplant.)

Films in the Dracula series always ended with the title fiend (Lee) suffering a wild death (cracked ice, electrocution, thorny bushes). Lee’s final two films as Count Dracula whisked him to the present day. Swinging London, though waning by then, was depicted in “Dracula A.D. 1972” — rock band, crazy fashions, pretty people and all — proof positive of the movement’s effect on even established character series.

SEX-OBSESSED DRAMEDIES flowed like aphrodisiac-spiked cocktails from the other side: “The Wild Affair” (1965), “Georgy Girl” (1966), “For Men Only” (1967), “Prudence and the Pill” (1968), “The Touchables” (1968). Michael Caine starred in “Alfie” (1966) as an aloof Londoner who doesn’t have to work to attract women and the perks they offer — not only sex, but dry cleaning, pedicures, steak-and-kidney pie. But after being thrown over for a younger man, Alfie becomes philosophical. “It ain’t through the eyes that you feel beauty,” Caine says to the camera. “It’s how the heart *hungers* for something that makes it beautiful.”

The Invasion re-energized All Things British, including movie imports starring Christopher Lee (top) and Connery.

After the first flush of Britmania, the British Invasion bands began reinventing themselves — at least, the ones that would endure did.

You could say it started when the Beatles practically invented "Stadium Rock" with their sold-out concert on Aug. 15, 1965, at Shea Stadium in Flushing, Queens. The point was that the demand to see the group was overwhelming, so why slog it in smaller venues when you can play one biggie? (The Beatles' tour the following year was their final. Over the ensuing decade, playing at stadiums became *de rigueur* for rock bands.)

Shea happened when Sid Bernstein — the first American to book the Beatles, and the guy who brought many more Invasion bands over — became frustrated after turning away ticket-seekers when he brought the Beatles to Carnegie Hall. Bernstein initially proposed Madison Square Garden as a followup venue.

"But I changed my mind after I saw how many people we turned away at those two (Carnegie Hall) shows," Bernstein told me in 2001. "I called Brian Epstein and I said, 'Brian, forget my offer on Madison Square Garden. I wanna do Shea Stadium.' He says, 'What? How many seats is that?' I said, '55,000.' He said, 'Do you think we'll fill it?' He kept asking me again and again, 'Will we fill it?' This was on an overseas call.

"Finally, I said, 'I'll give you $10 for every seat we don't sell.' And that's what gave him the confidence — that if the promoter feels they're gonna sell out 55,000, he'd go with it. And then I gave him a figure that had never been heard of before. I gave him a $100,000 guarantee against 60 percent of the gross. It was a big coup to get Brian to accept it.

"And the gross was — well, they walked out with $180,000 for the 28 minutes that, I think, they did. One show at Shea Stadium."

And how was the *sound* at Shea?

"It doesn't matter," Bernstein said.

"Today, I'll occasionally meet somebody who was there, and I'll often ask with humor, 'Did you enjoy the sound?' And invariably they'll say, 'It didn't matter. We were there. It was a moment in history.' Which it was. I still get goose-bumps talking to you about it. It was a moment in history."

Mick Jagger recalled being at the show. This was arranged by talent manager Pete Bennett, who happened to be shepherding the Rolling Stones in New York that day.

"This was in 1965," Bennett told me in 2007. "We were celebrating one of the big new albums of the Stones on the yacht we had, which was called The Princess.

"I told the Stones, I told Mick, I said, 'Listen, the Beatles are at Shea Stadium. Let's go and see them.' It was in the afternoon. He said, 'Really? I didn't realize that.' So we took the boat and docked it in Queens. I called Shea Stadium. They had the police and limousines. We went there. We only stood there about 15 minutes. I met the boys again, the Beatles, in the dugout with the Rolling Stones."

In newsreel footage, from left: Taking the field; McCartney and Harrison harmonize; Lennon basks in the moment.
Photo illustration

Beatles vs. the Stones

It was one of the *questions of the 1960s: Are you a Beatles fan or a Rolling Stones fan?*

Of course, you could be both, but which way you leaned said a lot about your personality. And still does.

The Beatles wore non-threatening smiles; the Stones wore sneers. The Beatles were honored with MBEs; Stones members were prosecuted on drug charges. A Beatles hit was "I Wanna Hold Your Hand"; a Stones hit was "Let's Spend the Night Together."

And, if legends are to be believed, there was a rivalry between the two leading British Invasion bands. I asked Ringo Starr if the Beatles spent much time with the Stones in the old days, when Starr and I spoke in 2001.

"There wasn't a lot of crossover," Starr said.

"I mean, John and Paul did write their first (Top 20) hit ('I Wanna Be Your Man'). You know, we'd bump into each other. We'd end up at some nightclub, we'd be at some party. But it's not like we were hanging out together all the time. I think everybody was too busy, really."

That same year, I asked Rolling Stones bassist Bill Wyman if the Stones felt competitive toward the Beatles.

"We were always the very best of friends," Wyman said. "They came to see us before we made a record, even, and we became friends that night. They came back to our apartment — well, Mick and Keith and Brian's apartment. We stayed up all night, talking music and playing music. We became friends. And we were friends ever since.

"We'd liaise between each other when records were being released, so we wouldn't get in each other's way."

Where did all this talk of a rivalry come from?

"The rivalry was built up by the media," Wyman said with a laugh. "Just, you know, to bounce back and forth, and get sort of comments and things."

One of George Harrison's final recordings was a Beatles/Stones crossover. Harrison played slide on the song "Love Letters" by Wyman's solo band, the Rhythm Kings. The track was released in 2001, the year Harrison died.

"He was very sweet when I asked him to play on the album," Wyman told me in 2004. "He said, 'What are you callin' *me* up for, Bill? You've got two of the best guitarists in the world in your band' — you know, Albert Lee and Martin Taylor. And I said, 'I want your sound, George.' He said, 'But I only play one note.' And I said, 'George, *that's* the one I want!'"

In 2004, the Rhythm Kings covered Harrison's 1966 song "Taxman." Said Wyman: "I just decided to do that as a 'thank you' to George, actually."

Photo illustration

The good old daze: Reality or myth?

FOR THOSE OF US WHO WEREN'T LUCKY ENOUGH to have been part of so-called "Swinging London" in the 1960s, we've romanticized it. We have this image of nightly parties at stately mansions, with John Lennon pulling up in his psychedelic Rolls-Royce; and Marianne Faithfull dancing; and Brian Jones popping pills in the powder room.

But was it *really* like that? Or is that all a myth? I put this wordy, somewhat nutty question to a few people who would know.

Spencer Davis: "Actually, I did go out with Brian Jones, though I wasn't into swallowing handfuls of whatever it was he swallowed. But we did end up in some strange places. I did go to Paul McCartney's house, when they recorded 'Sgt. Pepper.' A publicist by the name of Allan McDougall — a Scotsman, obviously — he called me up. He said, 'Meet me at such-and-such a pub. We're going to have a drink.' I said, 'OK.' So I met him. I picked him up and then we drove off. I said, 'Where are we going?' He said, 'Oh, we're going to St. John's Wood.' 'Oh, OK.' There's plenty of pubs in St. John's Wood.

"And the nice thing was, we went to Cavendish Avenue, rang the doorbell, and a voice came over. 'Who is it?' McDougall says, 'Spencer and McDougall.' The buzzer went. A big black door opened. I was greeted by Paul McCartney. He gave me a bottle of Magnusson Stout in one hand and one of them funny cigarettes in the other. He said, 'Watch the dog crap from Martha.' And he played us the whole of 'Sgt. Pepper's' on a reel-to-reel machine. After listening to that, I was wondering whether I should continue in the music business."

Roger Daltrey: "There was one summer. The summer of '67 was like that, but it was only a blip. You're talking, probably, a maximum of six months, and then it was as if a window had been broken. They're wonderful memories. That's when I met my wife (Heather Taylor), so there's a lot tied up with that year. It was wonderful. And it was just as you described it."

Jim McCarty: "All at once? (Laughs) I can't really remember a party like that. No, the nearest thing would be a nightclub called the Speakeasy in Central London. It was great, because all the bands used to gather after they'd played. You'd go in and there'd be just *anybody* there. You know, John Lennon and Paul McCartney and Keith Moon and the Pretty Things and us lot. We'd all be having a drink together, and then maybe go off to some party. It certainly wasn't a big place, where everybody was doing all that stuff at once. But if anyplace, it would be that club."

Chad Stuart: "I think there was a great deal of just about anything you could imagine — the serious party-givers with lines of coke down the middle of the dining table. Those guys were out there. There were rock stars whose record companies got them diplomatic passports, so they could take their coke across international barriers. All of that happened.

"But it was a lot rarer than you think. People led much quieter lives. The press talked it up. People want to believe that things were really outrageous. But, I mean, how could you keep that up?"

Ringo Starr: "Yeah, I was there for all of that. But it wasn't *all* the '60s. That didn't really start kickin' in until the middle '60s through to 1970. Then it went disco and things fell apart. But it was a beautiful moment. I mean, everyone that I was hangin' out with, a lot of the musicians — it wasn't worldwide. We'd like to think it was. But it was interestin' that the music era we were in at that time, the dress and the attitude, certainly changed from the early '60s. So I thought it was a beautiful time. And I'm still out there recognizing it with peace and love."

Peter Noone: "Well, I saw Brian; I used to hang out with Brian Jones a lot. And John Lennon would pull up in the Rolls-Royce. You see, I was just a kid, so I was as impressed as everybody else. But I was kind of a bit of a pest. I would walk up to John Lennon and talk to him like I was a pal, but I was a kid, you know? Everybody else was 20, and I was 15.

"So I would go, 'Hey, John, how ya doin'?' And he'd go, 'Oh, bloody hell, this kid's leeched onto me again! How do I get rid of him?' And I'd say, 'What do you have goin' next?' and stuff like that, because I was naive. I didn't know they were tryin' to get rid of me. I thought they were just busy. I was like the younger brother who shows up at dates and messes up the romance, you know?"

Dave Davies: "Some of the bits sound about right. There used to be a club called the Scotch of St. James in the West End, where Eric Burdon had a flat upstairs. I was hanging out there at the time. So were Paul McCartney, the Who, and all these rock musicians. There were a lot of places like that in London. There was Annabel's. That's what you did in London."

Eric Burdon: "Brian Jones didn't have to go into the bathroom to pop pills. He was just doing it openly all the time. Marianne Faithfull, she was one of the boys, what can I tell you? She's a great girl. I still have fond memories of her, of being in her presence. She's one of these people who realizes that you get into the performing arts because of longevity. You don't have to pack it in when you're 26. I mean, you only start to be who you *are* when you are halfway through a lifetime."

Justin Hayward: "It was really like that. It was going to people's flats. Nobody watched TV. You listened to music. You got stoned. Or *I* did. You went out with lots of people. Yes, everybody knew everybody. It was a small musical community in London in the '60s, really. You didn't need to be introduced to anybody. Everybody knew who everybody else was. You could go up to anybody and talk to them. It was a big party, as far as I remember. Not always a happy one. In the middle of it, I was struggling to survive and to pay the rent and make the payments on the guitars. But I wouldn't have missed it for the world."

Colin Blunstone: "Well, I think it probably was like that, but I have to say that the Zombies worked all the time. For the three years we were together, we traveled all the time. So I think we missed out on all the wildness going on in London in the '60s. But then, we made up for it in the '70s."

Outside looking in

AT THE START OF THE SWINGING LONDON scene, Mick Fleetwood wasn't a famous rock star — *yet.*

"I had this sort of little, mini, double life," Fleetwood, the drummer for Fleetwood Mac, told me in 2002.

"One was a struggling musician who was living the rough life. And the other was just these incredible possibilities of being with people who are artistic. When I went to London, I dreamt of all the sort of artsy things, the beatnik sort of thing. And then it all started coming true."

Fleetwood was quick to point out that, when it came to inserting himself into the scene, he had two advantages.

"I was so blessed just from living with my sister (Sally Fleetwood), who was an art student in London at a very young age," he said. "She was connected with the fashion business in London, with the early David Hockneys and Vidal Sassoons and Mary Quants and Twiggys. I knew all those people through my sister. I'd be with my sister at all the parties and openings."

Mick Fleetwood

Then there was Fleetwood's ex-wife, model Jenny Boyd, who then had a rather famous brother-in-law.

Said Fleetwood: "The extra dynamic of Jenny's sister, Pattie, marrying George (Harrison) in the Beatles — I really became a fly on the wall. Because I used to hang out and go 'round with them. We would go clubbing in London!

"Everything was so vibrant, that whole 'Austin Powers' thing, where you literally find yourself jumping into cars, jumping out and running into clubs. It actually happened — Portobello Road and Carnaby Street and the Chelsea scene. I used to hang out in Chelsea, which was a sort of high-brow area of London which became very artsy."

Fleetwood marveled at the fact that the music from the era has endured. "That in itself gives you some idea of the power of what was going on in England," he said.

Rod Argent: "I think it did happen, but strangely enough, it was the year we (the Zombies) split up. 'Time of the Season' was an enormous hit in the States in '69, but we actually split up at the end of '67. You know, the early part of the '60s were really quite naive in lots of ways. Drugs were starting to be around, but only just. I was sort of aware of cannabis, if you like, but there wasn't much of it around. There really wasn't. And then the whole psychedelic drug thing really kicked in. That whole sort of area of the '60s really exploded, but by then, we were broken up."

John Entwistle: "Um, well, no. I mean, the car *was* painted psychedelic, so some of that's true (laughs). But, yeah, I remember that sometimes it was like that. A lot more freedom, sexually, back then."

JEFF BECK RECALLED HOW FASHIONS GREW more and more outrageous throughout the Swinging London era.

"It was pretty miserable for somebody who really liked Elvis' look and Gene Vincent, to have to put up with all these stupid clothes," Beck told me in 1999.

"The fashions were pretty ghastly. Everybody was walking around with feather boas and flared trousers. Everybody was trying to outdo each other with the most silly clothes they bought from an old lady's shop! It was the fashion for guys to cut down fur coats — like, your granny's fur coat — to a reasonable length above the waist, and just wear *those*. Eric (Clapton), I think *he* had one on the 'Blues Breakers' (album cover). He had a fur jacket.

"So every day was a fashion change, especially King's Road. Carnaby Street came a bit later, I think. King's Road was where all the art students would hang out, and they would set the trends — going from long black sweaters with the sleeves three feet too long. Stuff like that, you know what I mean? Painting their faces white and all that. And three tons of hair spray.

"I never went out with a girl who had hair that wasn't like fiberglass. It was terrible, like those pads you clean pots with."

OVER THE NEXT FEW YEARS, THE TIMES, THEY were a-changing. The British Invasion bands were growing their hair longer and making music that was more, shall we say, *experimental*. (Drugs may have had something to do with it.)

1967 through 1969 was the golden age for this thing called ... *grooviness*. It spread across many media and many lands.

Meanwhile, the next wave of British bands to "invade" our shores did not play the same game. There were no screaming girls chasing after Cream, Traffic, Joe Cocker or Ten Years After.

The "psychedelic album" came into being during this period, and Invasion bands were at the forefront with the Beatles' "Rubber Soul," "Revolver" and "Sgt. Pepper's Lonely Hearts Club Band"; the Rolling Stones' "Their Satanic Majesty's Request"; the Zombies' "Odessey and Oracle"; and *anything* by Pink Floyd.

Coinciding with the psychedelic album was the "concept album" — a collection of songs that are not random, but part of an over-arching theme or narrative. These include the Moody Blues' "Days of Future Passed"; the Small Faces' "Ogden's Nut Gone Flake"; the Kinks' "Preservation Act I" and "Act II"; and the Who's rock opera "Tommy." (Paul McCartney fancied "Sgt. Pepper" a concept album, in the sense that the Beatles were playing "as" the fictional Lonely Hearts Club Band while recording.)

DURING THE RISE OF MAMMOTH POP FESTIVALS, Invasion artists showed up. The Who and Eric Burdon played the Monterey International Pop Festival in 1967. The Who played Woodstock in 1969. The Rolling Stones headlined the Altamont free concert in 1969 — not that this was something to brag about.

Altamont proved to be the symbolic end of the Aquarian Age. This was not "three days of peace and music," as Woodstock had advertised itself, but one day of acid freakouts and death.

Eighteen-year-old audience member Meredith Hunter, who was brandishing a gun, was stabbed to death by Hell's Angels member Alan Passaro. The incident, which was caught on film by a cameramen who was working on the Stones documentary "Gimme Shelter" (1970), was later ruled an act of self defense.

Altamont happened in the final month of the decade, making the infamous concert the end of the '60s, literally *and* figuratively.

Invasion bands — and the graphic artists who designed their album covers — began feelin' groovy. Photo illustration

'Paul is dead'

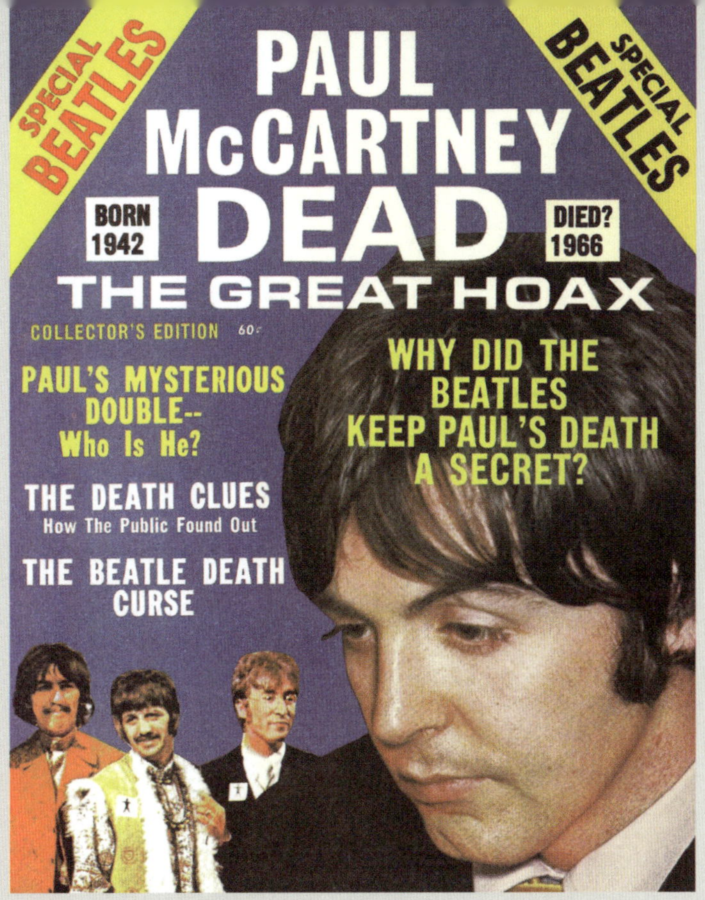

URBAN LEGEND? CONSPIRACY THEORY? RADIO hoax? Mass hypnosis? Plain old stupidity?

It's a "You had to be there" moment from 1967. A rumor that Paul McCartney died in a car accident mushroomed until talk of "clues" about McCartney's death spread over the radio and on college campuses. Such clues were found in Beatles lyrics and album graphics, according to theorists with nothing better to do.

Before you knew it, "Paul is dead" was a thing. Not only that, these theorists theorized, but McCartney's death was covered up, and a faux Paul took his place. (You had to give this impostor credit — he looked and sang exactly like McCartney.)

Yeah, a *lot* of marijuana was smoked in the '60s.

The clues are still there for new generations of Beatles fans to uncover. Everyone's favorite seems to be the "Abbey Road" cover photo. The Beatles are arranged as participants in a funeral procession, with George Harrison as a gravedigger in a workshirt and jeans; McCartney as the barefoot corpse in an outdated suit; Ringo Starr as a mourner in black; and John Lennon as a long-haired, bearded Jesus all in white. Near them is a license plate with the number "28IF." ("If" Paul was alive, he would have been "28.")

More clues: The "Glass Onion" lyric "Here's another clue for you all, the walrus was Paul" (walruses being some symbol of death) … the garbled voice allegedly saying "I buried Paul" in "Strawberry Fields Forever" … the (again, alleged) backward lyric "Turn me on, dead man" in "Revolution 9" … the hand that appears to be floating over McCartney's head on the "Sgt. Pepper" cover (to which theorists attached some mystical significance) … McCartney with his back to the camera (while the others face forward) on the "Sgt. Pepper" back cover … McCartney wearing a black rose in "Magical Mystery Tour" (the others wore red) … the "Day in the Life" lyric "He blew his mind out in a car" ...

Lennon referred to the "Paul is dead" phenom in his bitter rant about McCartney, the 1971 song "How Do You Sleep." Sang Lennon: *"Those freaks was right / when they said you was dead."*

Gravedigger

Corpse

Mourner

Savior

The walrus was ... Paul?

And in the end

The more time keyboardist Billy Preston spent with the Beatles, the more it dawned on the musician that the end was near.

"I used to sit in the Beatles' room where they had their meetings and stuff," Preston told me in 2000. "They were going through problems, finding out what happened to the money and this and that. I kind of felt that it was in decline at that moment."

Preston (1946-2006) was drafted to perform on the band's final album, "Let It Be" (1970), after George Harrison saw him in Ray Charles' backup band. Preston played the giddy electric piano solo on Paul McCartney's rocker, "Get Back."

"Oh, Paul loved it," Preston said of his solo. "I was playing a Fender Rhodes on 'Get Back.' They just told me, 'Take a solo!' I wasn't expecting to *do* a solo. To my surprise, when the record came out, they put my name on the record. That was a real blessing."

The Beatles play the roof. Inset: Billy Preston.
© Apple Films; Preston photo © A&M Records

Talk about being a "fifth Beatle." Preston also played with the Beatles during the group's final public performance, on the roof of Apple Records in London on Jan. 30, 1969. The set, which was visited by police responding to disturbance complaints, was preserved in the film also titled "Let It Be."

"Yeah, that was a thrill up on the roof," Preston said. "It was *cold,* for one thing. It was very cold up there. We kind of knew the police were going to come," he added with a laugh. "That's why they had cameras waiting for them downstairs, when they came knockin' on the door."

Preston's first inkling that there was disharmony in the band came when Mal Evans, the Beatles' longtime personal assistant, paid him a somewhat ominous compliment.

Recalled Preston: "Mal, who was their right-hand man, was telling me what a hard time they were having getting things together. He said that me being there gave them some energy and some pleasure in the sessions. Because before, they were struggling to finish it. But I didn't know they were going to break up."

That realization came later, when Preston was signed to do an album for Apple Records, the Beatles' label. "As we were working on it, we kind of noticed that Paul stopped coming in," said Preston, who attributed this to the hiring of Allen Klein as the Beatles' manager, which famously caused a rift in the band.

"When Allen Klein, in fact, was invited to be their manager, Paul wanted to have Allen checked out," Preston said. "John believed in Allen. So John got him and Paul stopped coming in. So I kind of knew that was the end."

Still, Preston said he would always remember the Beatles as a fun, talented group of musicians. "Just being around the boys was a great time," the keyboardist said. "They all had a great sense of humor. Whenever they were together, there was a glow in the room. They just had such energy."

ANOTHER BAND SIGNED TO APPLE RECORDS WAS Badfinger who, under the Beatles' tutelage, became solid hitmakers in their own right with "Come and Get It" (#6 in 1969), "No Matter What" (#8 in 1970), and "Day After Day"(#4 in 1971). A chance meeting with Harrison at Apple provided a bit of a wakeup call for Badfinger. This occurred when the McCartney-penned "Come and Get It" was riding high in the charts in 1969.

"One day, George Harrison was comin' down the stairs," said Badfinger singer-guitarist Joey Molland, a Liverpool native, when we spoke in 2000. "He was really friendly, really open. I was just really stunned, you know, because he was one of the *Beatles*. But he was really very nice and very natural.

"He said, 'It's great, you know. "Come and Get It" is a big hit all over the world. You guys are on your way. I'll bet you're all really excited about it.' We were all, 'Yeah, we're really excited!'

"Then he said, 'Well, you understand, though, that you'll have to play "Come and Get It" every day for the rest of your life.'"

Molland categorized the vibe at Apple Records as "very rock 'n' roll. It was a very relaxed atmosphere at Apple because the Beatles owned it, and because that was what *they* were like. They were very normal people, not super rock stars or anything. There wasn't a hint of spandex in the place."

Molland recalled when Harrison contributed slide guitar to "Day After Day." Said the musician: "We were working it out, (Badfinger guitarist) Pete Ham and I. Well, George came in and he asked me, 'Would you mind if I played slide on this?' I said, 'No!' So he gets his guitar out. He and Pete did the slide guitar on it. It took a long time — six hours or something — to work those parts out and get 'em perfect, you know?"

As for the backing vocals: "It was all three of us around the mic. It's just a thing that the Beatles had us do, that George had us do, was to always do our 'oohs' and 'aahs' together, so we'd get that vocal blend. Also, it taught us to sing in tune *now*. Because the other guys were depending on you."

But Badfinger's legacy is ultimately one of tragedy. Two members committed suicide: Ham in 1975 and Tom Evans in 1983.

THE FIRST TIME THAT JOHN LENNON CALLED drummer Alan White, the ex-Beatle got hung up on for his trouble. Recalled White (later the drummer for Yes): "When I got the call, he said, 'It's John Lennon. I saw you play in a club last night in town. I want you to play in Toronto tomorrow.' I thought it was a friend of mine just messing around. So I hung up on him!

"Then John called back five minutes later. He said, 'I'll send a limo tomorrow. I want you to get in the limo and meet us at the V.I.P. lounge. We're going to do a gig in Toronto, and I think you'll be good on it.' That was my introduction to John Lennon."

The gig was the Toronto Rock 'n' Roll Revival held Sept. 13, 1969, which boasted some of Lennon's musical heroes such as Chuck Berry, Little Richard, Jerry Lee Lewis and Bo Diddley. For the show, Lennon literally threw together a band. But *what* a band: Eric Clapton on guitar, Klaus Voormann on bass, White on drums.

White was in Lennon's most trusted company. Clapton was the guy Lennon suggested the Beatles could "get in" when Harrison temporarily left the band. Voormann was a friend of the Beatles going back to Hamburg (and happened to be the former boyfriend of Astrid Kirchherr when she first hooked up with Stuart Sutcliffe).

But this "supergroup" had yet to play a single note together.

"It was totally chaotic," laughed White. "We had never played with each other before, but we all knew the songs John wanted to do. He really wanted to do this gig. We rehearsed on the plane, actually. They (Lennon, Clapton and Voormann) just had a couple of acoustic guitars and an electric bass. I took some sticks and played on the back of one of the seats on the plane."

Officially, the Beatles were still a band at the time of the Toronto show, albeit largely in name only. That situation would come to a head, but more because of media overreaction to some vaguely worded publicity than a proper unified statement.

On April 10, 1970, McCartney issued a press release about his solo album "McCartney" (1970) in which he cited "personal differences, business differences, musical differences" as the reason behind his "break with the Beatles," adding, "Temporary or permanent? I don't really know." This may not convince as a breakup announcement, but in the eyes of the world, it stuck, further alienating Lennon and Harrison (who hardly needed further alienating).

Former Rolling Stones guitarist Mick Taylor in 2003.

Photo by Kathy Voglesong

"A GOOD TRIAL BY FIRE FOR MICK TAYLOR" IS what Keith Richards once called the Rolling Stones' Hyde Park concert on July 5, 1969. The performance — dedicated to founding guitarist Brian Jones, who died two days earlier — was Taylor's debut as Jones' replacement in the band. Taylor seemed to pack a lifetime into the remainder of that year: the Stones' 1969 tour, the recording of "Sticky Fingers," the infamous Altamont concert.

"It was a bit like that, yeah," Taylor told me in 2003.

"Well, it was a lifetime in five or six years, my period with the Stones. I mean, we all lived in the studio, basically. When we weren't in the studio, we were on the road. Consequently, you have all those great albums from that period. It was a very intense period of their career, and some people think one of the most creative. Everything revolved around the music. And the madness."

Taylor's extended solo on "Can Ya Hear Me Knocking'" from the 1971 album "Sticky Fingers" is a hallmark of classic rock.

"Yeah, well, and Keith's amazing work, too," Taylor was quick to add. "It was just a spontaneous jam, which we'd often actually do. But on that particular occasion, the producers just let the tape roll, and it sounded so good that it became part of the album."

He was called the "quiet Beatle." But George Harrison made a big noise after the Beatles broke up, with "All Things Must Pass."

"Over the years, I had such a lot of songs mounting up that I really wanted to do, but I only got my quota of one or two tunes per album," Harrison said on "The Dick Cavett Show" in 1971. "That way, I would have had to record about a hundred Beatle albums just to get out the tunes I had in 1965."

Harrison surprised everyone when "All Things Must Pass" (1970) went to #1 in both England and America — not bad for a then-pricey triple album. On it, Harrison and co-producer Phil Spector assembled the cream of rock, with Spector's trademark "Wall of Sound" very much in evidence thanks to armies of backing vocalists, strings, horns, and lots and lots of echo.

Badfinger guitarist Molland was star-struck during the sessions. "Oh, it was a knockout," Molland told me in 2000.

"Eric Clapton was there. Most of Derek and the Dominos — (keyboardist) Bobby Whitlock, (bassist) Carl Radle. Ringo was there, Alan White was there."

Keyboardist Gary Wright ("Dream Weaver," "Love is Alive") was, like Molland, in awe of the assembled talent.

As Wright told me in 2011: "I walked in and there was Ringo and Eric Clapton and Billy Preston and George and all of these other fantastic musicians. I was immediately intimidated. But George came over and was very warm and charming and friendly. He immediately alleviated any kind of anxiety that I had. I wound up playing on the entire album."

Wright said the focus of the triple album shifted as the sessions continued.

"Toward the beginning of the sessions, it was more of a huge Phil Spector production with two drummers, two piano players, eight acoustic guitars," Wright said.

"As the album progressed, it became simpler. It was then Eric, myself; and Klaus Voormann or Carl Radle on bass; and Jim Gordon or Ringo on drums. And, of course, George on guitar. It was totally cool, because George would sit and play the songs to us on acoustic guitar. They were just unbelievable songs. I felt so honored and so privileged to be part of that historical moment, when that album was made."

George Harrison in gardening boots on "All Things Must Pass." © Apple Records

Peter Frampton — later to win stardom with "Frampton Comes Alive" (1976) — was in Humble Pie when Harrison enlisted him.

"When he started doing the more country ones, like 'If Not For You,' I was added to the bevy of acoustic guitars," Frampton told me in 1999. "And then there was Badfinger and me and George. We were all in a semi-circle, playing acoustics. I overdubbed on just about every track on the album — I would say at least 80 percent of them, apart from the flat-out electric ones."

As for the atmosphere at the sessions: "Phil Spector would be in the booth complaining about his ulcer," Frampton laughed, "and saying, 'OK, we need more echo! More echo!'"

BEFORE NO NUKES, ARMS, LIVE AID, AND FARM AID, there was the Concert for Bangladesh, a star-studded relief effort spearheaded by Harrison. In a long beard and white suit that matched his white Fender Stratocaster, Harrison hosted two shows on Aug. 1, 1971, at Madison Square Garden in New York City. On the bill were Bob Dylan, Eric Clapton, Ringo Starr, Leon Russell, Billy Preston, Badfinger, Jim Keltner and Ravi Shankar.

Molland recalled that Harrison had been producing Badfinger's album "Straight Up" when the ex-Beatle suddenly became aware of the genocide in the wake of the Bangladesh Liberation War.

"We actually were recording with George in London; he was producing our 'Straight Up' album," Molland told me in 2000. "But then the Bangladesh tragedy happened. Ravi Shankar got in touch with George and asked if maybe they could get something together, try and arrange a little money to help these people. George came to us, and he was apologetic and everything. He was real nice, but he said he felt that he had to try and do something.

"About a month or so later, George calls up and asks us if we wanna go to New York and play guitars at the Bangladesh concert. And of course we said, 'Yeah!' He said, 'There won't be any money in it. All you'll get is your air fare and some food.' Well, of course, that's fine, you know? We were all just excited to be part of it."

According to Molland, Harrison was planning to perform his "All Things Must Pass" album live. That changed as more artists began to materialize.

"All through the week, the different musicians rolled up," Molland recalled.

"Leon Russell came in and all the backup singers came in, and the band kept gettin' bigger and bigger. By that Saturday, we went to Madison Square Garden and did the dress rehearsals. It was during those dress rehearsals that Eric Clapton showed up and Bob Dylan showed up.

"Bob Dylan came on stage by himself and played a bunch of songs. It was great. It was just us sittin' in Madison Square Garden — just the band and the production crew — and there's Dylan on stage singin' 'Blowin' in the Wind' and all the rest of 'em. And George, of course, jumped up on stage with him. So did Leon Russell and so did Ringo. They kind of put a bit of an impromptu set together for the show, you know?"

From the way Molland told it, it's too bad the cameras weren't rolling at the after-party. "Oh, they partied that night," the musician said with a laugh. "All the band and 'Moonie' (Keith Moon) and (John) Entwistle from the Who came. It was crazy. Phil Spector got up and was singin' 'Da Doo Ron Ron' and all that."

Jimmy McCulloch, Denny Laine, Joe English, and Paul and Linda McCartney in "Wings Over America" album art (1976).

It was an English band that began in Scotland with a handshake, and ended in Japan with a pot bust: Paul McCartney and Wings.

Wings was the post-Beatles band formed by McCartney in 1971 with his wife, Linda (1941-98), and his fellow Invasion-era musician, guitarist Denny Laine, formerly of the Moody Blues.

"The year before, I'd played at the Jimi Hendrix show at the Saville Theater, which was owned by Brian Epstein," Laine told me in 2007. "John and Paul were in the audience. I know that it was a really successful night for me, because I was doing something different. Jimi Hendrix gave me his seal of approval.

"So Paul — really with that in mind, I think — called me one day, just out of the blue. He said, 'Look, do you fancy puttin' a band together?' Because he knew I was still out there doing something inventive. So the next day, I was on a plane to Scotland."

The founding lineup also included drummer Denny Seiwell (who played on McCartney's previous album, 1971's "Ram") and guitarist Henry McCullough (from Joe Cocker's Grease Band).

Seiwell defended Linda, who was then maligned for singing and playing on her husband's albums. "She wasn't a great piano player or singer, but she had a great attitude," Seiwell told me in 2001. "She gave it her best shot. I think she did a helluva job."

As for recording Wings' debut album "Wild Life" (1971): "Five of the eight songs were first takes in the studio. Paul wanted to give the world just an honest, true album, so people wouldn't have a chance to really compare it with the Beatles."

Wings embarked on a European tour in 1972. In Sweden, McCartney was busted for possession of marijuana. "Some fan sent us a little marijuana in the mail, and the police caught it," said Seiwell. (McCartney used virtually the same excuse the following year, when police found pot plants on his farm in Scotland.)

"We paid a ($2,000) fine and the police let us go. But at the time, the United States was trying to kick John Lennon out of the country because of drugs. So it (the Sweden bust) really kept Paul from touring America until 1976. For four years, he couldn't get over here to tour one of the largest markets in the world."

BEING A MEMBER OF WINGS PRESENTED OTHER dangers. In 1973, McCartney released "Live and Let Die" (#2), his theme song for the James Bond film of the same title starring Roger Moore. Accompanied by an orchestra, Wings performed the song on the prime-time TV special "James Paul McCartney." In keeping with the 007 theme, McCartney's piano was rigged to "explode" — a planned special effect for the TV cameras.

Recalled Seiwell: "The lid from the piano was made of balsa wood. But when this (explosive) went off, it was much bigger than anybody anticipated. And this piano lid just went into a ball of flames, and went flying up over these old violin players! They were clutching their Stradivariuses and shouting, *'Oh my God! What is that?'* I thought they were going to have heart attacks."

SEIWELL AND McCULLOUGH QUIT WINGS AT AN inopportune time: prior to the band leaving for Nigeria to record "Band on the Run" (1973). "We ended up having just the three of us there," said Laine. "The studio was all old EMI equipment. Half of it didn't work. Flies were hangin' out the walls and that. But we had our little team again, so we knew we could pull it off."

Guitarist Laurence Juber was a member of Wings from 1978 until the group disbanded in 1981. He said Paul and Linda McCartney relished being able to combine work and family life.

"When we were out on the road, the kids were present," Juber told me in 2006. "So it wasn't, like, a wild and crazy, destroying-hotel-rooms kind of situation. It was still very much a family affair. It was not like being on a Rolling Stones tour.

"Even though (the McCartneys' son) James was less than a year old when I joined the band, Linda was very much a part of the process. She was really a very important part of the band. I don't think it would have been the same without her."

But *is* the road a safe space for little ones? Alas, McCartney's fondness for weed would one day put an end to the family fun.

Recorded amid chaos, "Exile on Main St." explores R&B, country, gospel and nihilistic lyrical themes.

Cut off from civilization. An absentee singer. A guitarist so strung out, everyone must wait as he sleeps off his latest buzz.

Is this any way to record the greatest album of your career? Somehow, it worked for the Rolling Stones.

"Exile on Main St." — the 1972 masterpiece which explores R&B, country, gospel and nihilistic lyrical themes — was never presented as the group's "best." And certainly, critics and fans didn't declare "Exile" as such, when the double album's freaky cover collage (showing an array of black-and-white photos of vintage novelty acts) first graced record-store racks.

But over the decades, the legacy of "Exile" has grown, and the album (produced by Jimmy Miller) has consistently landed on Top-100 lists, sometimes topping the lists — a case of delayed acclaim that surprised the Stones themselves.

THE BAND HAD RECENTLY FLED TO THE SOUTH of France to avoid exorbitant British taxes. Isolated from music-business influences — and with no nearby studios that struck their fancy — the band decided to record at Keith Richards' fabled house, *Nellcôte* in *Villefranche-sur-Mer*. Two former Stones, guitarist Mick Taylor and bassist Bill Wyman, agreed that recording "Exile on Main St." was anything but an organized process.

"Well, it was done in Keith Richards' house, so that in itself meant that there was a lack of structure," Taylor told me in 2003.

"It was complete mayhem!" bassist Wyman told me in 1999.

The initial challenge was daunting enough, according to Wyman: getting the band in the same place at the same time.

"We all lived in different houses, and we all tried to get to Keith's house to record," Wyman said. "Some days, it'd be me, Mick Taylor and Charlie (Watts) there. Keith'd be asleep, so he wouldn't even come downstairs. We'd mess about all day, and go home. The next night, it'd be Mick (Jagger), Keith and me, and Charlie wouldn't be there. The day after that, it'd be Charlie, Mick and me, and there wouldn't be any Mick Taylor or Keith. It went on like that. It was almost like a joke, in a way. Obviously, there were times when we were *all* there, but it was very bitchy and messy.

"And then Mick went off. He married (first wife) Bianca and went off to Paris and left us — didn't he? — when Bianca was having the baby (their daughter Jade) and all that. And we were working it out, even, for long periods of time. It was a crazy situation. We had people flying in and out all the time."

Taylor corroborated Wyman's account that Richards would be unconscious while the rest of the band waited, sometimes in vain.

"Whenever he woke up, we'd start recording," Taylor said with a laugh. "Then when he decided to go to sleep, we'd finish recording. And it went on like that, day after day, month after month, all summer long. But it was great fun making it.

"It has a very rough sort of quality to it that people really like. But it wasn't intended. It was just because the studio conditions were quite primitive. It was done in a basement, and we kept having constant power failures. There was a leaky roof. Sometimes when the power would go, we'd all sit by candlelight, strumming acoustic guitars. But I remember it with great affection."

"You had the involvement of drugs, and all that came into it," Wyman said. "It was a kind of a nightmare in a nice way, though it wasn't a frightening or horrendous nightmare like Altamont was. But it was a 'God, are we ever going to finish this' thing."

"It was a very stoned, very hazy period," Taylor agreed.

"But things got done, amazingly," Wyman added. "It wasn't in any way what you'd think of as creative. We did things, but we did them because that's what we do. And we did some very nice things, but it was a year of doing it, you know, backwards and forwards."

The 18 songs (some of which were enhanced leftovers from earlier sessions) were finished in Los Angeles. The band was taken aback over the enduring popularity of "Exile on Main St."

"None of the Stones, you know — not just me — but none of the band actually liked the album when it came out," said Taylor.

"People say it's probably the best album we've ever done," Wyman said. "But it wasn't glamorous in any way, was it ever. It was probably the most mixed-up time."

‘Our life together / is so precious together’ — John Lennon

The closest thing to a Beatles reunion while the Fab Four were living was Ringo Starr’s album “Ringo” (1973), on which all four ex-Beatles played. It opens with the Lennon-penned “I Am the Greatest,” on which three ex-Beatles — Starr, Lennon and George Harrison — perform. Paul McCartney wrote the lovely “Six O’Clock” and put the kazoo-ish solo on “You’re Sixteen.” The album gave Starr two #1 hits: “Photograph” and “You’re Sixteen.”

But as the ’70s dragged on, it became painfully clear that the party wasn’t over, and it was still claiming casualties. On Sept. 7, 1978, Keith Moon, 32, was found dead by girlfriend Annette Walter-Lax after overdosing on medication to treat his alcoholism.

It’s sad to say, but everyone kind of expected Moonie to die young. After all, the guy pushed his luck. But no one anticipated that an ex-Beatle would be shot down in the street.

LENNON’S COMEBACK SONG “STARTING OVER” had been climbing the charts by Dec. 8, 1980 — the day the musician was shot dead at 40 by an obsessed fan outside of the Dakota, the apartment building in New York City where he lived.

Lennon had recently re-emerged from a five-year hiatus and was busy promoting “Double Fantasy,” his album with wife Yoko Ono. In another of his new songs, “Watching the Wheels,” Lennon slyly referred to the hiatus: *“Don’t you miss the big time, boy? / You’re no longer on the ball.”*

One of Lennon’s final engagements prior to going on hiatus was his appearance on a 1975 charity radio marathon over WFIL in Philadelphia alongside disc jockey “Banana Joe” Montione.

“At the time, Yoko was pregnant with Sean, and right after that, she delivered,” recalled Montione when we spoke in 2000.

“I remember John was at my house during that weekend, and he was on the phone with her for three hours. He really did love her. It was an incredible thing. And then he retired. So it was really his last public appearance before he went underground.”

Said Montione of working with Lennon: “He told me, ‘Don’t interview me. Teach me how to be a DJ.’ He introduced records, read the news, the weather. He said, ‘Here’s the news. The Queen is still alive. That’s the news.’ He was truly an incredible guy.”

Lennon had such a ball, he hooked Montione up with a McCartney interview. Said the DJ: “When Paul came to Philly (for a 1976 Wings show), he called me on the WFIL ‘hotline.’ He says, ‘Hello, Banana? This is Paul McCartney.’ I said, ‘Right. And I’m the queen of England.’ He goes, ‘No, that’s Elton.’ ”

Guitarist Earl Slick played on “Double Fantasy.” I asked Slick about Lennon’s demeanor while recording this, his final album, when we spoke in 1981. “Very easygoing,” Slick said. “The atmosphere in the studio with Lennon was like if you were in a band that got along. John’s sense of humor prevailed at all times. Very lively and sort of nice and loose. No pressure.”

Slick recalled being coached by Lennon for the track “Kiss Kiss Kiss”: “John said, ‘Do whatever you want to do.’ I said, ‘What do you mean?’ So I just went out there and just went nuts. John was jumping up and down, and Yoko was smiling, so I thought I must be doing it right, so I kept doing it.”

Lennon was planning to tour behind “Double Fantasy.” Slick recalled that the last time he saw Lennon was “about two weeks before (the shooting). John was going to come out to L.A. a couple of weeks after the record was all finished for business or whatever. And then I was going to see him, and we were going to talk about getting everything straightened out to do the tour.”

The headline that nobody ever expected to see.

Montione, too, recalled Lennon’s planned trip to Los Angeles.

“When ‘Double Fantasy’ was coming out, I was at KHJ in Los Angeles,” he said. “John sent me a note that said, ‘I’m coming there.’ He wanted to preview the album at the Roxy on Sunset (Boulevard). But he wanted to come in as an unknown. So he said, ‘Would you bring me onstage? I want to kind of do this stealth.’ I said, ‘Of course. I’ll be there.’ Three weeks later, he was dead.”

Others I spoke to who knew or worked with Lennon commented on his outspokenness, his sensitivity and, of course, his humor.

Recalled newsman Larry Kane: “Yes, he was acerbic, but he said in public what a lot of people felt in private about issues. John and I shared a passion for issues that surrounded the world at the time — war and assassination and the Civil Rights movement in America and the world. I admired him for his willingness to use the platform in a positive way. John was one of the first celebrities to utilize a public platform like that.”

Recalled keyboardist Billy Preston: “John was amazing, man. He’d say anything that came into his mind. He would just do whatever he felt. It was a lot of fun just being around him.”

Recalled Peter Noone: "Herman's Hermits were going to the Philippines, and I asked John about it. He told me, 'Just say yes to everything.' I thought, What a great line. 'Say yes to everything. You'll love it.' Otherwise, you'll do the completely wrong thing."

Recalled Pete Best: "You were attracted to him. He had something which stood out. There was something about John — his character, his banter, his humor, his very presence.

"When we were playin' in Hamburg, I got very close to John. We spent a lot of time together. Even when we came back to Liverpool, he was always at my house, I was at his house. I saw another side of John. It wasn't the aggressive, sardonic, sometimes acidic humor that the audience saw. With John, that was as close as the audience was gonna get to him. They weren't gettin' any closer. In a way, it was a defense mechanism.

"I found there was a very loving and a very tender side of John which the public never saw. But I was very fortunate to see it. Those are the memories of the person, along with his creative talent, that the public didn't see. It was like I had an inside story into what John Lennon's personality was all about. I treasure it."

The ARMS band poses for the cover of the Rolling Stone.

NOT LONG AFTER HIS onetime songwriting partner's death, Paul McCartney would pull the plug on his solo band, Wings. The seeds of his decision were sewn on Jan. 16, 1980, when McCartney was busted yet again for marijuana possession, this time at Narita International Airport in Tokyo.

"It was certainly an intense situation, but more than anything else, we were concerned for Paul's welfare," said Wings guitarist Lawrence Juber, who was standing next to McCartney at the time of the bust. "All of a sudden, he was off being put in jail! He was kept there for 10 days. That was a great concern.

"We'd just traveled halfway across the world. All of a sudden, you're at the airport, and everything changes in the blink of an eye. I think they singled him out for special treatment.

"I believe that was the beginning of the end for Wings. Because at that point, Paul and Linda realized that they didn't want to be dragging the kids around on the road. They wanted to keep them in school and have a fairly normal upbringing."

According to Wings guitarist Denny Laine, the Tokyo bust was one in a series of events that led to the dissolution of he band.

"It wasn't just the Japan thing," he said. "Things had come to a head. It (the bust) meant that we would be going back into the studio and not touring. I was really missing going on the road and touring and playing to people. I did a solo album, 'Japanese Tears' (1980). And then Paul and I just kind of drifted apart, really.

"Things that were reported in the press were totally exaggerated and out of context. Me 'n' Paul did fall out a bit over it, but we've had a lot of good things happen since, communication-wise."

FORMER YARDBIRDS GUITARISTS ERIC CLAPTON, Jimmy Page and Jeff Beck were never in that band at the same time. This made 1983's ARMS tour — which benefitted Action Research into Multiple Sclerosis — all the more special.

The ARMS tour was spearheaded by Ronnie Lane, the ex-Small Faces bassist and MS sufferer who called to arms his heavyweight friends such as Kenney Jones, Bill Wyman, Charlie Watts, Joe Cocker, Paul Rodgers, Andy Fairweather Low and Ray Cooper. (Steve Winwood played with ARMS in London.)

As Jones told me in 2005: "The whole tour was very emotional. The makeup of the band was sensational, anyway. That's only because Ronnie had touched everybody's lives. He'd worked with everybody in that lineup. When Ronnie asked to raise money for multiple sclerosis, nobody batted an eyelid.

"In fact, that was the first time Jimmy Page had gone out (since Led Zeppelin broke up following John Bonham's 1980 death). You know, he was paranoid that he couldn't play any more. But he was wonderful. We were helping each other on that tour."

Wyman said he and Watts had to unlearn some bad habits they had picked up courtesy of the Rolling Stones.

"Trouble was, me and Charlie had been in the Stones so long," Wyman told me in 1999. "Eric says to us the first morning — in Dallas, it was — he said, 'OK, soundcheck, 11 o'clock. We meet in the lobby at 11.' So we said, 'OK.'

"So me and Charlie are very conscientious. We're the two most conscientious Stones," Wyman added with a laugh. "If someone says 11 o'clock to the Stones, you know that Keith ain't gonna get there 'til half past 2. Mick might make it by 2. Woody might be 4 o'clock; you don't know. Me and Charlie, we'd always get there about half past 11, just in good faith. But we'd *still* be the first ones, and have to wait around for everyone. So we thought, 'We'd better be a bit more conscientious than this.' So we went down at five past.

"Everybody had gone! Five past 11, they'd all gone! So we had to get private transport. When we got there, Eric gave us a bollocking for being late. From then on, everything went like clockwork. Everybody was exactly on time for everything. It was like a revelation to me and Charlie, because we had never worked like that."

Beck recalled with a devilish chuckle that he dodged a panicky request for support from his fellow ex-Yardbird, Page.

As Beck told me in 1999: "The guy went on stage to play (an instrumental version of) 'Stairway to Heaven' without Robert Plant, without John Bonham, without anybody. And I had to let him down, because I actually was supposed to play the melody. And because I had my own set with my band, I felt that I would be encroaching on Jim's set, you see.

"Although, I got a note sent down from his room to my room saying, 'Please play this with me tonight.' I just freaked. I didn't even know the tune! I suddenly had to face this dilemma — the choice between letting my best friend down, my longtime buddy, or just saving my own bacon," Beck added, laughing again.

"Because, I thought people would not take too kindly to me playing Robert Plant's vocal part, you see. But I didn't have a chance to communicate with Jim at that time. He was up in his room, not coming out, and I was in my room, not coming out. But I knew he was in trouble.

"But it (the ARMS show) still went down, in my memory, as one of the memorable things, having the three of us — me and Eric and Jim. It was the greatest excuse for being on the same stage, for a good cause. What the hell."

Rodgers recalled a heart-stopping moment during the tour capper on Dec. 9, 1983, at Madison Square Garden. Lane surprised everyone by walking onstage, with no small effort, while hanging onto the shoulders of his onetime Faces bandmates Jones and Ron Wood. Lane then sang "Good Night Irene" and toasted the crowd. There wasn't a dry eye in the house.

"He was in a wheelchair, was Ronnie, throughout the tour," Rodgers said when we spoke shortly after Lane's death in 1997. "And on the very last day of the tour, right in the middle of a song, this figure walks out across the stage. Ronnie made the effort, somewhat like a miracle. He walked out across the stage and started to sing a song. Everybody held their breath. It was miraculous."

Two years after ARMS came the Live Aid concerts organized by Bob Geldolf to benefit Ethiopian famine victims, held simultaneously in London and Philadelphia. Invasion artists were well represented on the bill: McCartney, the Who, Clapton, Page (with Led Zeppelin), Mick Jagger, Keith Richards and Wood.

BY 1988, RICHARDS WAS SICK AND TIRED OF Jagger's refusal to tour with the Rolling Stones. (They hadn't toured in six years, the longest off-the-road period for the group.)

Richards wanted to tour behind the Stones album "Dirty Work" (1986), but Jagger opted to record a solo album, "Primitive Cool" (1987). Jagger even toured behind his lackluster album, further stoking Richards' resentment. In the Stones' video for "One Hit (to the Body)," a seething Richards appears to threaten a worried-looking Jagger several times with his wildly swinging guitar neck, during a bizarre, loosely choreographed "fight" between the two. It was either a psychodrama playing itself out in front of the cameras, or the Best Acting Ever by rock stars in a video.

In frustration, Richards recorded his first solo album, the title of which clearly alluded to the situation: "Talk is Cheap" (1988).

The album made Richards rock 'n' roll's man of the hour. His video for "Take It So Hard" was in heavy rotation on MTV; he played the season opener of "Saturday Night Live"; and he toured behind the album with his solo band, the X-Pensive Winos. And guess what? The Rolling Stones announced a tour for 1989.

On Nov. 4, 1988, Richards and wife Patti Hansen made an unannounced appearance at U.S. Blues, a bar in Greenwich Village, for an event celebrating *Beggars Banquet,* writer Bill German's Stones newsletter which won the band's endorsement.

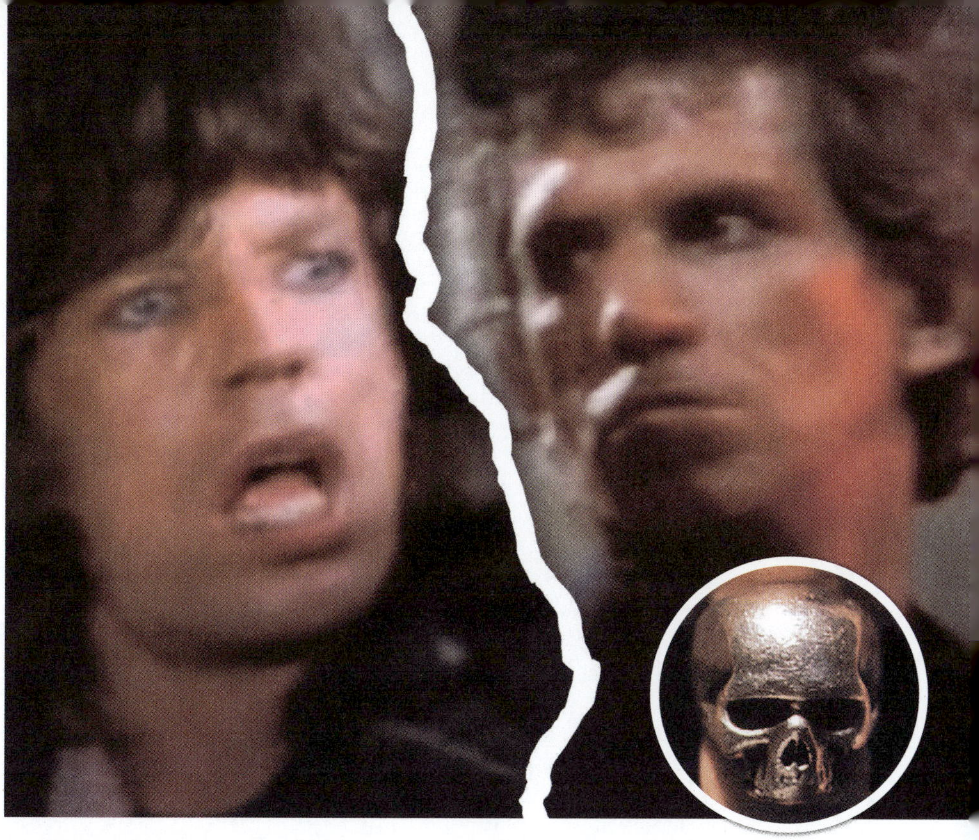

Jagger-Richards psychodrama in a 1986 video. Inset: Richards' skull ring.

In the packed house, I managed to shout two questions over the din to Richards, and bless him, he shouted back two replies.

On why Richards changed his ever-present skull ring from his middle finger to the third finger of his right hand: "Because it was gettin' in the way of playin' guitar. It's silver; it keeps gettin' flattened out. I hit it too hard on that other finger. So I had to shift it, you know. It's just a matter of, like, convenience."

On the response of the Richards' daughters, Theodora (then 3) and Alexandra (then 2), to seeing their dad perform on "Saturday Night Live": "They wanted to know how to get him out of the TV," said Hansen. "They thought they'd lost me forever. 'Now he's stuck in the box!' " said Richards.

A barmaid then asked for the guitarist's drink order, and the moment passed. But I've committed Richards' (likewise shouted) drink order to memory: "Bourbon and ginger! Jack Daniels!"

JUST BECAUSE THE SURVIVING BEATLES TOLD US they had sanctioned a new, "official" Beatles reunion song, didn't mean we had to believe in it. But believe, we did.

In 1995, the four-part docuseries "The Beatles Anthology" yielded "Free as a Bird," a veritable miracle which blended the ghostly voice of John Lennon (from a 1977 mono cassette demo) accompanying himself on piano with fresh performances by McCartney, Harrison and Starr. (Those harmonies! That slide!)

McCartney originally wanted George Martin to produce the track. Alas, by then, Martin was having trouble with his hearing. Production duties were awarded to Jeff Lynne, a frequent collaborator of Harrison's who prevailed upon McCartney to sing beneath Lennon's vocal, to give it more body. "Free as a Bird" was followed by a second Lennon-demo-turned-reunion, "Real Love."

The deep-diving "Beatles Anthology" specials became the highest-rated TV event of 1995. Some of the surviving Beatles' recollections could be self-serving — hey, it's human nature — but ultimately, a lot of important history was preserved.

From the safety of a plane departing New York, Paul McCartney witnessed the Sept. 11, 2001, attacks on the World Trade Center.

He soon returned, and made it his mission to organize the Concert for New York City, a multi-act event held at Madison Square Garden on Oct. 20, 2001, in tribute to emergency responders. McCartney was joined by fellow British Invasion-era artists Mick Jagger, Keith Richards, the Who and Eric Clapton, among many performers. McCartney whipped up a song for the finale with lyrics very different from those on, say, "Red Rose Speedway": *"I will fight / for the right / to live in freedom."*

"IT'S NOT ALWAYS GONNA BE THIS GRAY," SANG George Harrison in his 1971 song "All Things Must Pass."

After learning of Harrison's death from cancer at age 58 on Nov. 29, 2001, fans contemplated the ex-Beatle's life and career. Harrison accomplished much in a span abruptly shortened.

Shortly after 9/11, Paul McCartney organized the Concert for New York City (2001). © Maysles Films Inc.

Besides being a member of the Beatles — only the group that changed music and, in some ways, the world — Harrison created the rock benefit format with his 1971 Concert for Bangladesh, and maintained his devotion to the Hare Krishna faith while navigating the secular, often jaded world of celebrity and privilege.

The morning after his death, I contacted some of Harrison's collaborators and contemporaries, who recalled him not just for his talent but for his spiritualism and humor.

"He was a great songwriter and a very deeply spiritual guy," said Beach Boys singer Mike Love. "George and I celebrated our birthdays — we're both Pisces — in India at Maharishi (Mahesh Yogi)'s place in the spring of 1968. We exchanged gifts. I still have a painting of Maharishi's teacher that he gave me on March 15, 1968. It's hanging in my house, so I see it about every day.

"I identified with George quite strongly, because he was deeply involved in meditation, in spiritual pursuits. His attitude and his whole philosophy was very evolved. Wherever he is now, he's in a great space. I'm sure it's really hard for his wife and his son (Olivia and Dhani) and people who are really close to him. But I feel sorry for them more than George. Because George, I know, is in a good place."

Coming from a trailblazer in sound-on-sound recording and the electric guitar, it's no small compliment when guitar legend Les Paul said of the Beatles: "They were the pioneers."

Recalled Paul: "I met George several times. We've actually played together on the stage. George and I, we just shook hands on the stage and played and just talked for a little bit. I loved his work. I sure love what the Beatles did. To me, that was probably the height of the whole rock era. It's just scary to see 'em disappear. We just go on and put a mark on the wall. George was one of the greats. Put another mark on the wall — we lost a great one."

Harrison worked with former Cream bassist Jack Bruce on the Cream song "Badge," and on Bruce's first solo album. (For both projects, Harrison used the pseudonym L'Angelo Misterioso.)

"He was a very spiritual person," Bruce recalled. "Very kind, very private — similar to myself in that he loved the music but didn't like the music business or the celebrity side of it. I'd see him occasionally at Ravi Shankar concerts. I remember going to his house, along with a lot of people, listening to Ravi play there."

Bruce lauded Harrison for incorporating Indian sounds into rock music. "He was, of course, the first one to get it across to a mass market, absolutely," Bruce said. "And I think he changed the face of the Western music, the rock music, probably forever."

"I always remember George as the quiet man," said Pete Best. "That was my title for him. A lot of the media adopted that title as well. He was very much into his music. He'd spend hours practicin', rehearsin' his guitar techniques. People realize that now, you know, with the stuff which came out with the Beatles and with his Eastern influences and the sitar playin' and all the rest of it. He was the youngest member in the band. I suppose you could say he was the baby of the band."

Said Dave Mason, the guitarist for Traffic and a solo artist: "George gave me my first sitar. The occasion was that I was at his house in the South of London to listen to 'Sgt. Pepper.' They (the Beatles) had just finished it. They'd put the whole album together. So I got a preview of 'Sgt. Pepper' *and* a sitar. Not bad."

Said newsman Larry Kane: "George Harrison was absolutely no-nonsense. He kept to himself more than the others. But this guy was much more textured and deep than anybody gave him credit for. Later on in his career, people found out that he was truly a very deep thinker. He just, unfortunately, had this pre-puberty face. He was very young-looking."

Said former Deep Purple guitarist Ritchie Blackmore: "He was very serious, very deep. It's a terrible tragedy that this has happened to now two of them. It's a shame this has happened again to obviously the world's biggest band. But George was a very deep, sensitive person and a good guitar player."

Said former Alice Cooper drummer Neal A. Smith: "There was a mystique around George. John and Paul were pretty much in your face; what you saw was what you got. Ringo was kind of goofy but a great drummer. But George was the one; you never really knew what was going on with him, which was kinda cool."

Said former Renaissance singer Annie Haslam: "I loved his music and his spirit. It was: Love is very important in life. He did a lot of good, especially with (the Concert for) Bangladesh.

"He left a strong legacy. I think one of his messages was: Don't be afraid of dying, because that's not the end. *He* wasn't."

Harrison's parting gift to the world was his posthumously released album "Brainwashed" (2002). When his deteriorating health disrupted recording, Harrison wrote detailed notes to his son, Dhani (who was also a guitarist), on how each track should be finished. "Brainwashed" was completed with reverence and loving care by Dhani and Jeff Lynne, Harrison's erstwhile producer.

Some who died before their time. From top left: Stuart Sutcliffe, Keith Relf, Syd Barrett, Brian Jones, Ronnie Lane, Chas Chandler, John Entwistle, George Harrison, Paul Atkinson, John Lennon, Steve Marriott, Brian Epstein, Rory Storm, Derek Leckenby, Keith Moon, Dusty Springfield, Ronnie Bond and Brian O'Hara. Photo illustration

Throughout the project, Dhani and Lynne strove to guess: What would George do? The title track is undistilled Harrison, a rant against the material world and a plea for "God, God, God" to "lead us through this mess." The album closes with a stunner: Harrison chanting *"Namah Parvarti"* (doubled with the voice of his son). It's an uplifting message from another realm.

THE NEXT YEAR WE LOST ANOTHER GREAT, WHO bassist John Enwistle, who was found dead at age 57 in his Nevada hotel room on June 27, 2002, on the eve (literally) of a Who tour. Cocaine was found in Entwistle's system, and he had been intimate with a self-described groupie. You *could* say that Entwistle died of misadventure. Or better yet: He died with his boots off.

Former Led Zeppelin singer Robert Plant was on tour with the Who that year. "I know that it's brought Roger (Daltrey) and Pete (Townshend) very, very close together," Plant then told me.

"I mean, that's no substitute, and it offers no solace at all for what's happened. I think they were really beside themselves with absolute and total grief at the idea of losing their partner who, you know, had not enjoyed the best of health for quite a long time.

"It was the night before the tour was to begin. That's kind of weird, really, because with 'Bonzo' (Zeppelin drummer John Bonham), it was almost the night before *we* were due to leave for America when he passed away (in 1980). But they obviously sat down and did some soul-searching and decided that everybody was ready to go, and they'd better get going. I think if they hadn't have done that, they probably would never have performed again.

"My manager manages the Who; he manages myself and Jimmy Page. And he said that with the 'Ox' (Entwistle), they (Daltrey and Townshend) kind of looked up into the sky — I know I sound a bit corny — and the Ox would be saying, 'Don't be so stupid. Get on with the bloody show.' And in a way, though it might sound very trite, it's probably right."

Radio hosts Keith Roth and Aimee Kristi interviewed Entwistle over WRAT-FM in New Jersey. (Entwistle even made drinks. His recipe: Pour a bottle of cognac into a pot of hot coffee, liberally adding cream and sugar. Roth called it "the drink of death.")

"For a guy who was in one of the four greatest bands in rock history, he was very down to earth," said Roth. "A total sweetheart. Rock's greatest bassist. I'd argue with anyone about that."

"I no longer think of him as a larger-than-life rock star; I think of him as an English gentleman," said Kristi. "His sense of humor was dry, like the cognac he loved so much."

Said Steve Luongo, the drummer for Entwistle's solo band, on how the bassist died: "I wasn't there, so it's not my place to comment. Was it one too many cigarettes? Was it one too many Remy Martins? Was it one too many anything? I think it was one too many *everything*. I think he simply died of being John Entwistle."

THE IRISH HAVE A SAYING: "AT LEAST HE MADE his three score and 10." Translation: If you make it to 70 when you die, you're OK. But if you die *one day* shy of your 70th birthday, you've died tragically young. (Aren't we funny, though?)

So here's to the lights of the era who, as the saying goes, died before their time: Stuart Sutcliffe, Brian Epstein, Brian Jones, Rory Storm, Keith Relf, Keith Moon, John Lennon, Steve Marriott, Ronnie Bond (of the Troggs), Derek Leckenby, Chas Chandler, Ronnie Lane, Brian O'Hara (of the Fourmost), Dusty Springfield, George Harrison, John Entwistle, Paul Atkinson and Syd Barrett. It was Ritchie Blackmore, commenting on Harrison's death, who said, "I'd like to have seen them go onto old-age pensions, all of them."

Alas, they all *can't*. If only we could all go out like Charlie Watts, the Rolling Stones drummer from 1963 until his death at 80 in 2021. Watts was soft-spoken and elegant. (No one in rock could dress like this guy.) He nonchalantly sidestepped the drama that would have engulfed a lesser man. And could he crack a snare!

Of all the tributes that rolled in after Watts' death, one from Black Sabbath drummer Bill Ward really hit the mark. Ward called Watts "a solid fixture in a band that always seemed like it was falling off the edge of the world."

A long road (literally) for British Invasion artists

AS THE 1970s EVOLVED, GROWN-UP CHILDREN OF the British Invasion era saw many artists of the period reign as rock gods during the rise of so-called Stadium Rock. The Rolling Stones, the Who, Paul McCartney and Wings, Jimmy Page (in Led Zeppelin), Eric Clapton, Jeff Beck, Pink Floyd, Graham Nash (in Crosby, Stills, Nash and sometimes Young), the Kinks and Manfred Mann's Earth Band toured as headliners, and continued to create vital music heard on FM radio and sold in these things called "record shops." (They're hard to find now.)

Then came the '80s, which found our heroes ill-advisedly wearing mullets, perms, "trendy" clothes, and becoming overly infatuated with advances in recording technology. (Who thought synth-drums were a *good* thing?) Not to mention the pervasive influence of the dreaded "M" word: MTV.

But as the decades flew by, it dawned on these artists that their fortunes lay in their catalogs, not their "new album" of the moment.

Baby Boomers with deep pockets shelled out to see their childhood heroes recreate the old magic onstage. Thus, the Stones, the Who, McCartney, Starr (with his ever-rotating All-Starr Band), Clapton, Page, Beck and other Invasion-era artists toured well into the age of atherosclerosis and onset dementia. The musicians still looked good, moved well and sounded great — no small feat.

Musicians from the Invasion era toured constantly. In collage, from opposite top left: Terry Sylvester (in 2005), Pete Townshend (2000), John Entwistle (2001), Ringo Starr (2003), Jimmy Page (2000), Roger Waters (1999), Peter Noone (1998), Dave Davies (1998), Roger Daltrey (1998), Jeff Beck (2003) and Graham Nash (2001). Photos by Kathy Voglesong

A LENGTHY-BUT-IMPORTANT DIGRESSION: By the late 1960s, British bands in a *later* wave — many of whom were influenced by the Beatles, the Stones, et al., and only slightly younger than same — were coming up, and would rule the '70s in the Stadium Rock era. They include (but are not limited to) Jethro Tull, Deep Purple, Black Sabbath and, of course, Led Zeppelin.

These bands' British Invasion influences and connections?

■ **Jethro Tull** were guests on the (albeit, shelved) TV special "Rock and Roll Circus," and so rubbed elbows with the Stones, Marianne Faithfull, the Who, John Lennon and Clapton.

■ **Deep Purple** covered the Beatles' "Help" and "We Can Work It Out." George Harrison was friendly with Purple, and jumped onstage with the group in Australia in 1984 on "Lucille," introduced as "Arnold from Liverpool." Purple drummer Ian Paice played on McCartney's album "Run Devil Run" (1999).

■ **Black Sabbath** were inveterate Beatles fans. Ozzy Osbourne told *Rolling Stone*: "I feel so privileged to have been on this planet when the Beatles were born." Sabbath drummer Bill Ward told Brian Voger: "When I listen to the first Sabbath album, I hear the Beatles." (Many pundits credit that album, 1970's "Black Sabbath," as the birth of heavy metal. Could it sound *less* like the Beatles?)

■ **Led Zeppelin** was led by Yardbirds guitarist Jimmy Page, fer cryin' out loud, and once called itself the "New Yardbirds."

End of lengthy-but-important digression.

As Harrison observed, all things must pass. Clearly, he was projecting hope, but the sentiment cuts both ways.

One sad day, the last of the British Invasion artists will take his or her final bow. The city of Liverpool, and the Reeperbahn, and that rooftop on Savile Row, are all still with us. Though the artists who put them on the map won't be, their music always *will*.

Epilogue

In 1964, I was 5 going on 6. Instead of wanting to see the Beatles at Steel Pier in Atlantic City, I wanted to see Mr. Peanut waving at passers-by at the Planters Peanuts store directly across *from the pier.*

But as grammar school gave way to high school — a period when a lad takes up the often painful search for identity — British Invasion bands were still a huge part of the culture and my life. Our fledgling little amateur rock bands played Beatles songs (badly), and we devoured all of their then-current solo albums.

The first Beatle I ever laid eyes on was George Harrison. His 1974 tour touched down at the late, lamented Philadelphia Spectrum for three shows in December of that year, when I was 14. I made it my mission to attend. The reason: Harrison's triple album "All Things Must Pass" was my *religion.*

I remember first spotting it at Franklin Music in the Echelon Mall when I was a gawky seventh grader trying to figure stuff out. I was like, What's *this?* Harrison was on the cover wearing a "Grapes of Wrath" hat and a ZZ Top beard, lookin' all contemplative in a forest flanked by … lawn gnomes? I *had* to fork over for this pricey album, and divine its secrets. The rewards were great: "What is Life." "I Dig Love." "Apple Scruffs." "Let It Roll." "Behind That Locked Door." "Beware of Darkness."

(At the time, me and my gang were concurrently discovering the albums we'd missed as children. The Beatles' final album, "Let It Be," was my first. The "White Album" came out in '68; I first heard it in '73. The Who's 1969 double-album rock opera "Tommy" entered my bloodstream.)

So by 1974, I considered Harrison less an ex-Beatle than a solo artist. The '74 tour was the first by any Beatle since 1966 — by then, ancient history.

The tour supported Harrison's fifth album, "Dark Horse." Billy Preston, Willie Weeks, Andy Newmark, Jim Keltner, and a horn section were in Harrison's band. It was a very full sound.

But there was one problem. Reviews of earlier shows on the tour reported — accurately, it turned out — that Harrison's voice was giving out. One reviewer called him a "hoarse dork." (Ooh!)

Reviewers also complained that Harrison only played four Beatles songs. I'm guessing these were older writers who didn't own "All Things Must Pass," and were therefore more prone to think of him strictly as an ex-Beatle.

RAVI SHANKAR AND A GROUP of fellow Indian masters were on the tour to give a mid-show recital each evening. Except in Philly. Shankar was ill, Harrison told the audience. However, he assured us, Shankar's sister-in-law was a very fine, very respected musician who would ably lead the ensemble in Shankar's stead.

So, rather than seeing the great Ravi Shankar — who mesmerized the throngs at the Monterey Pop Festival and the Concert for Bangladesh — I saw his sister-in-law, *Mildred* Shankar. *

Harrison was said to have been irked by the negative reviews, and he never again toured the States. His only other tour happened 17 years later, a 12-show stint with Eric Clapton in Japan in 1991.

** OK, her name was Lakshmi Shankar. But when I tell the story, I call her Mildred. It's funnier.*

LAYING EYES ON JOHN LENNON WAS ANOTHER rare occurrence that transpired via another small window of opportunity. Lennon, you see, never toured. He did one-offs. If the rare Lennon gig didn't happen in your neck of the woods, or you were unable to travel to same, you were out of luck. Fortunately for me, Lennon had a Philly moment. He didn't play or sing, mind you. But there he was — as Beatles posters used to say — "in person."

Here's what happened: On a balmy evening one weekend in May of 1975, two buddies and I took a bus to Philadelphia to visit a fourth buddy in the hospital. We were all high-school juniors on the track team at Cherry Hill High School East in South Jersey.

On this weekend, John Lennon was in Philly for the Helping Hand Marathon, 54 hours benefiting local charities sponsored by WFIL, a Top 40 station at 56 on the AM dial. (This was just prior to Lennon's hiatus, often referred to as his "house husband" period.)

But for Lennon, this was no quickie appearance. He was on the air constantly, reading pledges and introducing songs. (I monitored the broadcast and recorded it whenever Lennon came on.)

Introducing both the Beatles' and Elton John's recordings of "Lucy in the Sky With Diamonds," Lennon quipped: "I was on both versions, and regret neither one." Introducing a Chuck Berry song, he preached, "Don't forget, without Chuck Berry, there would be no Beatles, no Rolling Stones, no Led Zeppelin, no Bad Company." (Yes, he name-checked Bad Company. It was 1975.) He introduced an Elvis Presley song of his own choosing by saying, "This is the one that started it all: 'Hound Dog.' "

WFIL'S DISC JOCKEYS WERE TELLING LISTENERS that once every hour, Lennon would appear in the WFIL parking lot to sign autographs for cash donations to Helping Hand. After the hospital visit, me and my buddies decided to take a bus to WFIL on City Line Avenue, north of Center City, to check it out.

We arrived to a surprisingly manageable crowd. (Lotsa people, sure, but this was no Woodstock.) Huge speakers blasted Beatles songs. Lennon was expected to materialize at any moment. Wooden saw-horses separated us from WFIL staffers.

Out Lennon came, without fanfare or introduction. He wore a "newsboy"-style cap, long hair, and small, round, dark glasses. I recall him nodding to the music with his fingertips in his hip pockets. He smiled and waved to the crowd. He seemed like a normal guy. No "rock star" airs. It was so cool to see him up close.

There were young ladies wearing matching outfits with WFIL identification who collected donations for Lennon's autograph. Anyone could get one — it was easy! If you brought something you wanted autographed (like an album cover), you passed it with a donation to one of the girls. They'd have Lennon sign it and pass it back. (No customized autographs, just his name.) Otherwise, Lennon signed blank white sheets of paper from a pad, which the girls traded for dollar bills. That's right, *dollar bills*.

Yes, I got an autograph. No, I no longer have it. Why didn't I put it under lock and key? Because I'm a frickin' idiot!

MY GANG OF NE'ER-DO-WELLS SPENT OUR TEENS and 20s going to concerts by British Invasion bands who were, at the time, still young adults themselves, come to think of it.

Seeing the Rolling Stones at the Spectrum in 1975 was a rite of passage. As the band kicked off with "Honky Tonk Women," the stage floor opened up like the petals of a flower. Mick Jagger straddled a giant inflated phallus while singing "Star Star." Billy Preston wore a huge Afro. (Um, I don't remember much else.)

John Lennon as he appeared in 1975, when he took part in a charity fundraiser at WFIL in Philadelphia. © WFIL

Seeing the Who with Moonie in '75 gave me bragging rights for life. We had "obstructed view" tickets that my dad got from a buddy at the refinery, but it worked out. The seats were directly behind the Who. So when the band played "See Me, Feel Me" and the house lights came on — bathing the entire audience in super bright light — our point-of-view was of the Who in their prime playing the rock anthem to tens of thousands who were on their feet and pumping their fists. *Imprinted* on the brain, yo.

FLASH-FORWARD: SOMETHING UNEXPECTED AND wonderful later occurred regarding Invasion artists. Youngsters discovered them. It happens again and again, decade after decade. With no parental prodding, kids keep falling in love with the Beatles, the Stones, the Who, et al. (When we were kids, we'd *never* have listened to Glenn Miller or Benny Goodman.)

It goes to show that the chemistry, the spark, of this music defies the era in which it was created. It's timeless. It's universal.

"I Want to Hold Your Hand" still sounds damned good. So does "Satisfaction" and "My Generation" and "You Really Got Me" and "It's My Life" and "She's Not There" and "Bus Stop" and "For Your Love" and "Catch Us If You Can" and "Ferry Cross the Mersey" and "There's a Kind of Hush" and ...

Acknowledgments

My heartfelt gratitude to those who provided materials and support, especially Brian Voger (a rock memoir expert), Howard Bender (a comic book expert), Ian Voglesong (a genius filmmaker), and Eric Krause (proprietor of Groovy Graveyard in Asbury Park, NJ).

Thanks to John and Pamela Morrow, Eric Nolen-Weathington, Scott Peters and everyone at TwoMorrows Publishing.

Thanks to the musicians, artists, actors, writers, broadcasters and others who graciously submitted to my interrogation: Rod Argent, Peter Asher, Jeff Beck, Pete Bennett, Sid Bernstein, Pete Best, Jay Black, Ritchie Blackmore, Colin Blunstone, Jack Bruce, Eric Burdon, Petula Clark, Alice Cooper, Roger Daltrey, Dave Davies, Ray Davies, Spencer Davis, Bonnie Delaney, John Entwistle, Mick Fleetwood, Peter Frampton, Annie Haslam, Justin Hayward, Kenney Jones, Lawrence Juber, Larry Kane, Aimee Kristi, Denny Laine, Mike Love, Steve Luongo, Dave Mason, Nick Mason, John Mayall, David McCallum, Jim McCarty, Ian McLagan, Joey Molland, "Banana" Joe Montione, "Cousin" Brucie Morrow, Graham Nash, Peter Noone, Les Paul, Robert Plant, Billy Preston, Shirley Alston Reeves, Keith Richards (a two-question interview shouted in a bar, but I'll take it), Paul Rodgers, Keith Roth, Denny Seiwell, Tony Sheridan, Joe Sinnott, Earl Slick, Neal A. Smith, Ringo Starr, Chad Stuart, Terry Sylvester, Mick Taylor, Roy Thomas, Kenny Vance, Alan White, Allan Williams, Gary Wright and Bill Wyman.

A tip of the visor to journalistic colleagues for editorial favors great and small. "Britmania" got the once-over from Wallace Stroby (nine novels strong) and Vanesa Johnson (she of the eagle eyes). Thanks to fellow alums of my almae matres *The Star-Ledger* and *The Asbury Park Press:* Kathy Dzielak, Kelly-Jane Cotter, Harris Siegel and Jay Lustig (who once interviewed Paul McCartney, the lucky bastidge); and to onetime *Faces Rocks* editor Lorena Alexander and authors Bill German and Roag Best.

"Britmania" presents 26 photographs by my late wife, Kathy Voglesong, who the world lost in 2005. Kathy photographed Who bassist John Entwistle on six occasions. "The Ox" could be an imposing figure, but he always seemed to put his trust in her. Page 51 is one happy result.

Thanks to "Fast Eddie" Zupkus (who has a Beatles-themed washroom at his headquarters), Bob Cahill, Michael DiMaria, Cam MacMillan, Chris Wolfson, and Joe Stewart (my high-school buddy who obsessed over British rock with me).

The endpapers mostly celebrate typography trends of the '60s, not to mention the sometimes shameless hype speak of the time. But one artist deserves a shout-out: Dudley S. Cowes (1895-1946), whose Blitz-themed poster for Great Britain's Ministry of Health is both propaganda and Rockwellian illustration.

In 1995, graphic artist Rob Britt created images of balloons, streamers and confetti for a story of mine published on New Year's Eve. I faithfully used them every year through 2018, when newspapers finally got rid of me. Here they are again on page 172, in my Swinging London photo illustration. (Rob is now better known as novelist Robert Roy Britt.) In 2001, illustrator-photographer Elaine Melko created a broken-record motif to accompany my article about the so-called Beatles-Stones "rivalry." I recycled her motif (with my freshly superimposed images) on page 171.

Every effort has been made to verify the ownership or source of all illustrated material. We regret any errors of attribution, and will make the appropriate corrections in future editions.

To that point: The delightful cartoons on page 119 first came to my attention via Raechel Leigh Carter's blog, Hero Culte. Who was the artist? I'm guessing an editorial cartoonist at a daily paper who was moonlighting. The giveaways are the caricature style; the hand-lettered type; the buttons worn by characters as identifiers; and the use of a special art board that produced a "dot pattern" when a chemical solution was applied with brush. These were popular tools among (now deceased) cartoonists.

I kept the comics section in the 1960s, but I need to recommend the graphic novel "Baby's In Black: Astrid Kirchherr, Stuart Sutcliffe, and The Beatles" (2012), in which Arne Bellstorf tells a bittersweet story in haunting black and white.

The memorabilia collages include composite images created from various sources, which I've altered digitally to correct distortion, wear (when clarity was compromised), inconsistent lighting and disruptive cropping.

Speaking of sleight-of-hand: The Selcol Rolling Stones toy guitar on page 144, it shouldn't be hard to tell, is not a photograph, but a digital illustration based on a tattered old catalog image. In the real world, the Topps trading card on page 151 has the Beatles caricatures on the left and the type on the right. But I wanted the caricatures on the right for maximum impact. Just so you know this is *not* a Topps variant from Canada.

Notes

Page 16: Sutcliffe didn't face the audience: Paul McCartney interview, "The Beatles Anthology" (book), 2000

Page 41: "He did not die a natural death": Anna Wohlin interview by Rachael Bletchly, The Mirror, July 9, 2013

Page 45: (Brian Epstein) was planning a Pacemakers movie: "BBC One Show" TV interview with Gerry Marsden, 2014

age 54: "Bad luck and bad behavior": Ray Davies to Bill Turnbull and Louis Minchin on "BBC Breakfast," Oct. 2015

Page 61: Beck brought along a homemade guitar: "In Conversation With Jimmy Page," Fender, 2019

Page 70: "Their manager sent me a photograph": Mickie Most obituary, The Independent, June 2, 2003

Page 80: "They just didn't do the right songs that day": Brian Poole interview, Mid Sussex Times, Nov. 27, 2014

Pages 88-99: Series broadcast histories: "The Complete Directory to Prime Time Network TV Shows 1946-Present" by Tim Brooks and Earle Marsh, 1988

Page 90: TV watcher John Lennon later called the shows "a blast": "This Bird Has Flown" by John Kruth, 2015

Page 155: Each joined Equity: "John, Paul, George & Ringo: The Definitive Illustrated Chronicle of The Beatles, 1960-1970" by Tim Hill, 2008

Page 155: "I had used it": 1980 interview with John Lennon and Yoko Ono by David Sheff in Playboy, Jan. 1981

Page 155: "We were *all* actors": John Junkin interview, "A Hard Day's Night: Collector's Series," Miramax, 2001

Page 156: "A way that was respectful": Richard Lester interview, "A Hard Day's Night: Collector's Series," Miramax, 2001

Page 156: "We watch all your cowboy pictures": Paul McCartney interview, "The Beatles Anthology" (book), 2000

Page 156: "It wasn't that carefree, ever": John Lennon interview, "The Dick Cavett Show," Sept. 11, 1971

Page 164: Beatles were voiced by: "The Fake Four," The Guardian, Aug. 23, 1999

Page 174: Talk of "clues" about McCartney's death: radio special on WPLJ in New York, 1979

Page 178: "A lot of songs mounting up": George Harrison interview, "The Dick Cavett Show," Nov. 23, 1971

Throughout: Record charting histories: "The Billboard Book of Top 40 Hits" by Joel Whitburn, Billboard Books, 2010

Bibliography

Beatles, the; "The Beatles Anthology" (2000); Chronicle Books, San Francisco

Best, Roag, with Best, Pete and Rory; "The Beatles: The True Beginnings" (2003); St. Martin's Griffin, New York City

Carr, Roy, and Tyler, Tony; "The Beatles: An Illustrated Record" (1975); Harmony Books, New York City

Carr, Roy; "The Rolling Stones: An Illustrated Record" (1976); Harmony Books, New York City

Dalton, David; "The Rolling Stones: The First Twenty Years" (1981); Alfred A. Knopf, New York City

Davies, Ray: "X-Ray: The Unauthorized Autobiography" (1994); Abrams Press, New York City

Epstein, Brian; "A Cellarfull of Noise" (1964); Souvenir Press, London

German, Bill; "Under Their Thumb: How a Nice Boy From Brooklyn Got Mixed Up With the Rolling Stones (and Lived to Tell About It)" (2009); Villard Books, New York City

Hill, Tim; "John, Paul, George & Ringo: The Definitive Illustrated Chronicle of The Beatles, 1960-1970" (2008); Fall River Press, New York City

Kane, Larry; "Ticket to Ride: Inside the Beatles' 1964 and 1965 Tours That Changed the World" (2004); Penguin Books, London

Miles, Barry; "The British Invasion: The Music, the Times, the Era" (2009); Sterling Publishing, New York City

Overstreet, Robert M.; "The Overstreet Comic Book Price Guide" (various editions); Avon Books, New York City

Palmer, Robert; "The Rolling Stones" (1983); Doubleday & Company, Inc., Garden City, New York City

Rawlings, Terry; "Then, Now and Rare: British Beat 1960-1969" (2002); Omnibus Press, London

Richards, Keith, with Fox, James; "Life" (2010); Back Bay Books / Little, Brown & Co., New York City

Rolling Stones, the; "According to the Rolling Stones" (2003); Chronicle Books, San Francisco

Schaffner, Nicholas; "The Beatles Forever" (1978); McGraw-Hill, London

Spitz, Bob; "The Beatles: The Biography" (2005); Little, Brown & Co., New York City

Whiticker, Alan J.; "British Pop Invasion: How British Music Conquered the Sixties" (2015); New Holland Publishers, Wahroonga, Australia

Index

Photo by Kathy Voglesong

About

Shown with Keith Richards in New York City in 1988 — and rocking King Louis XIV hair that was neither wig nor perm — Mark Voger is a 1972 graduate of Holy Rosary School in the Diocese of Camden in New Jersey. He designs pages for *At Home New Jersey,* and lives at the Jersey Shore. Also by Voger from TwoMorrows Publishing:

- "Holly Jolly: Celebrating Christmas Past in Pop Culture" (2020)
- "Groovy: When Flower Power Bloomed in Pop Culture" (2017)
- "Monster Mash: The Creepy, Kooky Monster Craze in America 1957-1972" (2015)
- "The Dark Age: Grim, Great & Gimmicky Post-Modern Comics" (2006)
- "Hero Gets Girl! The Life and Art of Kurt Schaffenberger" (2003)

When in cyberspace, please visit MarkVoger.com

What happened next?

If you dug BRITMANIA, get the rest of the story with TwoMorrows' GROOVY, written and designed by MARK VOGER!

From **Woodstock** to the **Banana Splits**, from **Altamont** to the **Partridge Family**, from **Sgt. Pepper** to **H.R. Pufnstuf**, **GROOVY** features interviews with **Peter Max**, **Brian Wilson**, **Peter Fonda**, **Melanie**, **Donovan**, **David Cassidy**, members of the **Jefferson Airplane**, **Cream**, the **Doors**, the **Cowsills**, the **Shondells** and **Vanilla Fudge**; and cast members of **'The Monkees,' 'Laugh-In'** and **'The Brady Bunch.'** Revisit the era's rock festivals, movies, art — even comics and cartoons. **GROOVY** is one trip that doesn't require dangerous chemicals!

(192-page **FULL-COLOR HARDCOVER**) **$39.95**
(Digital Edition) **$13.99**
ISBN: 978-1-60549-080-9

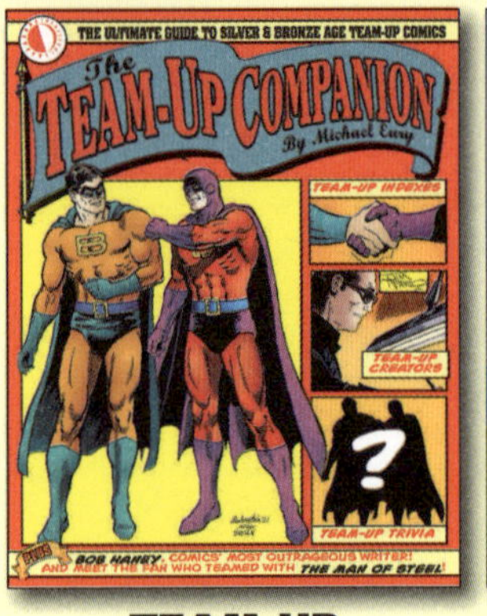

TEAM-UP COMPANION

Surveys Silver/Bronze Age team-up comics (**BRAVE & BOLD, DC COMICS PRESENTS, MARVEL TEAM-UP, MARVEL TWO-IN-ONE**), plus other titles, treasures, & treats!

(272-page paperback) **$36.95**
(Digital Edition) **$15.99**
ISBN: 978-1-60549-112-7

OLD GODS & NEW

Documents the genesis of **JACK KIRBY'S FOURTH WORLD** series, his gods in **THOR** and other strips, how those influenced his DC epic, and affected later series like **ETERNALS** and **CAPTAIN VICTORY**!

(160-page **COLOR** paperback) **$26.95**
(Digital Edition) **$12.99**
ISBN: 978-1-60549-098-4

JACK KIRBY'S DINGBAT LOVE

The final complete, unpublished Jack Kirby stories in existence: Two unused 1970s DC **DINGBATS OF DANGER STREET** tales, plus **TRUE-LIFE DIVORCE** & **SOUL LOVE** mags!

(176-page **COLOR HARDCOVER**) **$43.95**
(Digital Edition) **$14.99**
ISBN: 978-1-60549-091-5

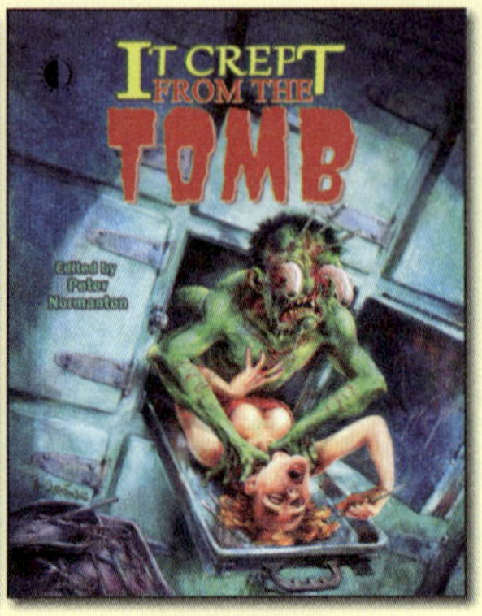

IT CREPT FROM THE TOMB

Digs up the best of **FROM THE TOMB** (the UK's preeminent horror comics history magazine), with early **RICHARD CORBEN** art, **HP LOVECRAFT**, and more!

(192-page paperback with **COLOR**) **$29.95**
(Digital Edition) **$10.99**
ISBN: 978-1-60549-081-6

CHARLTON COMPANION

Definitive history of the all-in-one comics company from the 1940s to the '70s, with work by **DICK GIORDANO, STEVE DITKO, JOHN BYRNE, JOE STATON** and more!

(256-page **COLOR** paperback) **$39.95**
(Digital Edition) **$15.99**
ISBN: 978-1-60549-111-0

HERO-A-GO-GO!

Looks at comics' 1960s **CAMP AGE**, when spies liked their wars cold and their women warm, and TV's Batman shook a mean cape!

(272-page **COLOR** paperback) **$36.95**
(Digital Edition) **$13.99**
ISBN: 978-1-60549-073-1

THE LIFE & ART OF DAVE COCKRUM

Follows his rise from fandom to pro, where he revived the Legion of Super-Heroes, the X-Men, and more!

(160-page **COLOR SOFTCOVER**) **$27.95**
(**LIMITED EDITION HARDCOVER**) **$27.95**
(Digital Edition) **$14.99**
ISBN: 978-1-60549-113-4

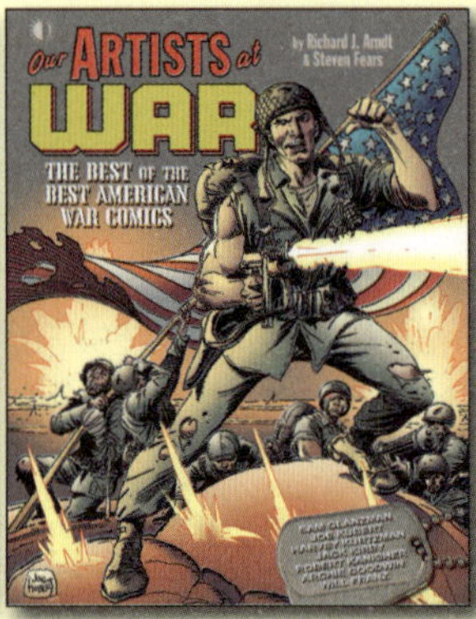

OUR ARTISTS AT WAR

Examines US War comics from **EC, DC COMICS, WARREN PUBLISHING, CHARLTON**, and more! Featuring **KURTZMAN, SEVERIN, DAVIS, WOOD, KUBERT, GLANZMAN, KIRBY**, and others!

(160-page **COLOR SOFTCOVER**) **$27.95**
(Digital Edition) **$14.99**
ISBN: 978-1-60549-108-0

AMERICAN TV COMICS (1940s-1980s)

History of over 300 TV shows and 2000+ comic book adaptations, from well-known series (**STAR TREK, PARTRIDGE FAMILY, THE MUNSTERS**) to lesser-known shows.

(192-page **COLOR SOFTCOVER**) **$29.95**
(Digital Edition) **$15.99**
ISBN: 978-1-60549-107-3

KIRBY & LEE: STUF' SAID

Presents **JACK KIRBY** and **STAN LEE**'s own words to examine the complicated relationship of the creators of the Marvel Universe!

(176-page **COLOR** paperback) **$26.95**
(Digital Edition) **$12.99**
ISBN: 978-1-60549-094-6

AMERICAN COMIC BOOK CHRONICLES
FULL-COLOR HARDCOVER SERIES documents each decade of comics history!
8 Volumes covering the 1940s-1990s

TwoMorrows.
The Future of Pop History.

Phone: **919-449-0344**
E-mail: **store@twomorrows.com**
Web: **www.twomorrows.com**

TwoMorrows Publishing • 10407 Bedfordtown Drive • Raleigh, NC 27614

DAVE'S 'GLAD ALL OVER'
Why?..because the DAVE CLARK FIVE chose

THE BIG VOX SOUND

Britains foremost Radio, T.V. and Recording Stars feature VOX sound equipment

---

WILD!

ROLLING STONES AS YOU NEVER KNEW THEM

DUSTY speaks out
PETER & GORDON - U.S. disclosures

PLUS TOP POP NEWS SCOOPS

Registered in the G.P.O. as a Newspaper

New Musical Express - February 12, 1964

fontana STOP, LOOK and LISTEN... WAYNE FONTANA AND THE MINDBENDERS

new MUSICAL EXPRESS

WORLD'S LARGEST CIRCULATION OF ANY MUSIC PAPER – WEEKLY SALES EXCEED 375,000 – (MEMBERS OF ABC)

As Tears Go By
Marianne Faithful
DECCA

Introducing
THE STARS

● **The Stones**, who are chasing The Beatles in every world chart are having a serious problem. After such a quick rise to No. 2 they are on the way down!

CLICK!

★ THE BEATLES ★

Here is the BRAND NEW Talk Album with THE BEATLES! ED RUDY, the American newsman announcer who is called THE FIFTH BEATLE by The Gear BEATLES, themselves, narrates and asks the questions that you have always wanted answered!!! JOHN, PAUL, GEORGE, and RINGO give you the REAL INSIDE INFORMATION...IN THEIR OWN VOICES!!!THIS ALBUM IS BRAND NEW...THE GREATEST BEATLE-TALK ALBUM EVER!!! O N L Y $2.98 Complete!!!

★ROLLING STONES★

THE ROLLING STONES are undoubtedly the most controversial...and the most unpopular with adults...with an ever growing popularity among teenagers...of any of THE TOP BRITISH GROUPS!!!
Here is the true INSIDE STORY AS TOLD TO ED RUDY, by MICK JAGGER, BRIAN JONES, CHARLIE WATTS, KEITH RICHARD, and BILL WYMAN!!! Many of the things that the R.S. say may surprise you, but you will agree that THE ROLLING STONES DOCUMENTARY TALK ALBUM IS REALLY FAB!!! ONLY $2.98 Complete!!!

★ DAVE CLARK 5 ★

THE DAVE CLARK 5 are frequently considered to be THE BEST LOOKING of all the TOP BRITISH GROUPS...but never before have they revealed the REAL INSIDE STORY of the D.C.5...IN THEIR OWN VOICES! DAVE CLARK, MIKE SMITH, LENNIE DAVIDSON, DENIS PAYTON, and RICK HUXLEY tell ED RUDY about their backgrounds, their likes, their dislikes, and their ambitions... ALL OF THE INSIDE INFO... AND YOU ARE THERE!!! ONLY $2.98 Complete!!!

THE STONES who are currently coming back from the States, as usual in ones and twos, have their new single out *The Last Time*. Again written by Mick Jagger and Keith Richard, it's another certain chart-topper. The 'B' side was written by Naker Pledge, which in case you don't know is the boys again. Their current album, "The Rolling Stones Vol. II" is still top of the LP lists and is certainly likely to become their strongest selling album ever. They are shortly to commence their British tour and it seems certain that the USA will be beckoning again as well. Stones fans will be delighted to know that The Stones' film is currently moving into gear with scripts being thrown all over the place.

RUSH your order NOW!

BEATLEMANIA

!!!EXCLUSIVE!!!
Here is YOUR TICKET to the GREATEST "IN PERSON" PERFORMANCE OF THE FAB !!!BEATLES!!!
Yes, for the first time you can experience the phenomenon of actual attendance at a "LIVE" Beatles' Concert...right in YOUR OWN HOME!!! THE LIVERPOOL LADS re-create the fantastic excitement of the AMERICAN TOUR Concerts...with all of the background sounds and fan interviews RECORDED AT ACTUAL CONCERTS in the U. S. !!! IT'S A GREAT TRIBUTE TO THE BEATLES...And you'll LUV it!!!
O N L Y $2.98 Complete
★★★★★★
Send only $2.98 to:
E D R U D Y
TRIBUTE ALBUM

we predict...

■ that Manfred Mann will end up a big band and start a new trend.

■ that Dusty Springfield will become a best-selling album artist and will cut an LP of Burt Bacharach songs.

OVER QUARTER MILLION COPIES ALREADY SOLD!

PARLOPHONE RECORDS

URMSTON SHOW · ABBOTSFIELD PARK
MONDAY, AUGUST 5th at 7.30
KENNEDY STREET ENTERPRISES Ltd. in association with URMSTON URBAN DISTRICT COUNCIL
proudly present
A FESTIVAL OF POP MUSIC
★ STARRING ★
THE BEATLES
BRIAN POOLE AND THE TREMELOES
THE DENNISONS AND *Full Supporting Bill*
TICKETS 10/- *plus* 2/6 Admission to URMSTON SHOW

the small face
now #1 in Englar
with
SHA-LA-LA-LA-LI
9826
PRESS records LONDO RECORDINGS

TOP NEWS TWENTY

1● **The Beatles** still showing whatever the talk about slipping. still don't believe it as they hold d No. 1 again.
2● **Petula Clark**, who must make s of the best discs in the world, has c up with a real beaut in *Downtown*.

It's Fab!

Say 'fair'- not 'great'

You WON'T hear a Rolli Stone describe somethi as "great". He'll use t word "fair", instead. A "it's a gas" is strictly o In is "knockout".
Anything gear is garded as "the guv'no Mick's favourite word "diabolical". He uses it describe almost anythi he doesn't like!

MOVIE BUYS Dept.

Please rush the movies and/or slid have checked below:

- ☐ 100' **ROLLING STONES** Riot in Fresno.........
- ☐ 50' **ROLLING STONES** Riot in Fresno.............
- ☐ 100' **ROLLING STONES** Cool it by the Pool....
- ☐ 50' **ROLLING STONES** Cool it by the Pool......
- ☐ 100' **ROLLING STONES** Lacerate Long Beach..
- ☐ 50' **ROLLING STONES** Lacerate Long Beach....
- ☐ 100' **ROLLING STONES** Swing in San Diego..
- ☐ 50' **ROLLING STONES** Swing in San Diego....
- ☐ 50' Fabulous **COLOR — ROLLING STONES** ....
- ☐ 100' The **BEATLES** at the Hollywood Bowl....
- ☐ 50' The **BEATLES** at the Hollywood Bowl......
- ☐ 100' Exclusive **BEATLES** News Conference....
- ☐ 50' Exclusive **BEATLES** News Conference......
- ☐ 100' **BEATLES** Best Scene 'Hard Days Night'
- ☐ 50' **BEATLES** Best Scene 'Hard Days Night' ....

ALL 3 GROUPS IN ONE FILM
☐ 100' film of THE ROLLING STONES, THE BEATLES, & THE BYRDS
$5